Tiny Blunders / Big Disasters

Thirty-Nine Tiny Mistakes

That Changed the World Forever

Jared Knott

.

Jared Knott

Jefferson Central Publishing

6600 Sugarloaf Parkway, Ste. 400

Duluth, GA 30097

Visit the website and view the book trailer at
tinyblundersbigdisasters.com

Second printing: October 2020
ISBN: 978-1-7359729-0-9 (paperback)
ISBN: 978-1-7359729-1-6 (ebook)

This book may be purchased in bulk for promotional, educational, or business use. Please contact Jefferson Central Publishing at the address listed above.

Cover by Tekla Benson

This book is dedicated to the men and women I served with in Vietnam who did not come home. Except by the grace of God there goest I.

All men dream, but not equally. Those who dream by night in the dusty recesses of their minds, wake in the morning to find that their dreams were nothing but vanity: but the dreamers of the daytime are dangerous men, for they may act upon their dreams with open eyes, to make them come true.

- T. E. Lawrence (Lawrence of Arabia)

_____

History does not forgive those who were right but who failed to persuade.

        - Barbara Tuchman, *The Guns of August*

_____

Tiny Blunders / Big Disasters

Thirty-Nine Tiny Mistakes
That Changed the World Forever
Jared Knott

TABLE OF CONTENTS

MISTAKES OF FIRE AND BRIMSTONE

WARS AND RUMORS OF WAR

◆◆ SIDEBAR: SIBILING RIVALRY ◆◆

CAPTAINS, KINGS, AND PRESIDENTS
RUNNING OFF THE RAILS

SIDEBAR:
◆◆ONE MAN'S CHALLENGE TO GROUPTHINK ◆◆

FOREWORD

---◆---

BY WIN BLEVINS

Remember history as it was taught in high school? American history, for instance, was a parade of presidents, generals, heroes, and wars won. (According to the textbooks, at least when I went to high school, Americans never lost a war. Unfortunately, that included those fought against Native Americans.) Everyone we studied was a hero, and every deed was noble. And the teachers, the teachers! Were you so bored that you wanted to tear your hair out? Or maybe tear your teacher's out? Energetically?

The reason that history class was so dull is that it was all about the dates, the figures, and the changing of governments. What the teachers forgot or never realized is that human beings care very much about other real human beings more than anything else. That is why Hollywood, People magazine, and soap operas are so popular. They tell stories about challenging, difficult situations that bring forth strong, emotional reactions from interesting people we have come to care about.

Alfred Hitchcock, the famous director, had something in his movies he called the "McGuffin." The McGuffin was the object of the plot for which the characters were striving (the stolen jewels, the money embezzled from the bank, the secret formula, etc.). The audience cared nothing about the McGuffin itself, but they cared very much about the stress, conflict, and emotional need of the characters in the drama.

History classes gave us all McGuffin but left out the human element. It was like an empty bottle with a label on it but with no Coca-Cola on the inside. History is full of colorful, dynamic leaders involved in situations calling for internal strength.

It is peopled with corrupt, vicious, and sometimes noble individuals in positions of power leaving their mark on history. When well told, it is as interesting as any drama coming out of Hollywood.

In this book, Jared Knott tells the stories of many people at their very worst and in some cases their very best, but always in a situation of great crisis. Sometimes the individuals did not realize they are actually at a critical crossroads until it was too late. Knott has especially sought out stories where the slightest mistakes had enormous consequences, stories comic and tragic, which prove that Robert Burns spoke truly when he wrote:

> The best-laid plans of mice and men
> Gang aft agley.

These are the epic and pivotal situations that determine the fate of the people and the nations of the earth. Some noteworthy examples are as follows:

A soldier accidentally kicks a helmet off a fortress wall and causes an empire to collapse.

A glamorous young man has an indiscreet affair with a European beauty queen during World War II. This sets off a chain of events that determines who is to be elected president of the United States in 1960.

The pilot of a single warplane gets lost at night and drops his bombs in the wrong place. This creates a domino effect involving a temperamental dictator that may very well have changed the outcome of World War II.

It is difficult to explain to the Western mind, but the decision by world leaders to leave out one simple diplomatic paragraph in a peace agreement had massive repercussions. The consequences of this decision led to a number of wars that plague the world even to this day.

So small events can have devastating consequences, just like a snowball being thrown off the top of a mountain that causes an avalanche that destroys the civilization down below. Since these multifaceted events are well in the past, there has been a softening of the pain in these sad experiences, therefore making them fun to read about.

You are at the beginning of a great adventure. In the chapters ahead, you will come to know people and events that are fascinating, enthralling, and a great deal of fun. So, you are hereby forewarned: strap yourself in tight and hang on for a bumpy ride.

- Win Blevins, *New York Times* best-selling
author of forty books

AUTHOR'S INTRODUCTION

———○———

THE BUTTERFLY EFFECT
IN HUMAN HISTORY

———○———

One of the most conspicuous examples of the butterfly effect in human history lies at the bottom of the Atlantic Ocean; 450 nautical miles east/southeast of Halifax, Nova Scotia, under two miles of ocean seawater, lies the wreck of the Titanic, crown jewel of the White Star Line. It is also the final resting place of 1,522 passengers and crew.

Somewhere in the wreck of the ship, in a badly deteriorated condition, is a pair of binoculars. These "glasses," as they were called, were sorely needed on the night of April 12, 1912, by the lookouts in the ship's crow's nest. Properly used by trained professionals, these binoculars would have saved the Titanic from its massive disaster. The story, star-crossed and tragic, unfolds as follows:

A man named David Blair was scheduled to be the second officer for the maiden voyage of the Titanic. However, at the last minute, the White Star Line decided that a more experienced officer named Charles Lightoller should be given the assignment instead. In his haste to turn over the job to his replacement, Mr. Blair forgot to give Mr. Lightoller the key to the crow's nest locker. The locker contained the glasses, which therefore became inaccessible.

Without the binoculars, the crew had to search for icebergs and other dangers on the nighttime, open sea with the naked eye. This was a challenging task. They did not see the black iceberg until it was too close to miss.

One of the lookouts in the crow's nest was a man named Fred Fleet, who survived the disaster. When asked by a US senator at the official inquiry if having the binoculars would have made a difference, Mr. Fleet answered that they would have enabled the crew to see the iceberg in enough time to have "gotten out of the way."

According to the inquiry records, Mr. Fleet recalled seeing Mr. Blair with binoculars during an earlier trip from Belfast to Southampton. When asked where Mr. Blair's glasses went, Mr. Fleet replied, "We do not know. We only know we never got a pair." Senator Smith, the chairman of the inquiry, said, "Suppose you had glasses. . . . Could you have seen this black object [at] a greater distance?"

Fleet: "We could have seen it a bit sooner."

Smith: "How much sooner?"

Fleet: "Well, enough time to have gotten out of

the way."

Smith: "Were you disappointed that you had no

glasses?"

Fleet: "Yes, sir."

Mr. Blair was later awarded the King's Gallantry Medal for saving a fellow crew member after he had fallen into the ocean. He passed the key on to his daughter after his death. The key, along with a postcard in which he expresses regret for not being able to make the maiden voyage of the Titanic, brought £90,000 at auction.

There were other minor mishaps which created an environment that led to the sinking of the great ship. These are further outlined in Chapter 19, "The Forgotten Fire That Sank a Ship." They include a fire on board, an attempt to hide the damage, and a captain under pressure and overeager to make it to New York in a hurry. It was a case of several small mistakes interlocking one against the other to trigger a great tragedy.

The phenomenon of having a single tiny mistake early on in a process cascade into an enormous catastrophe at the end of that process has a specific name: the butterfly effect. It was born in the mind of a well-recognized scholar and mathematician.

Edward Norton Lorenz (1917–2008) was an American scientist and a major contributor to what is known today as chaos theory. He coined the term butterfly effect, which refers to the concept of a tiny action (such as a butterfly flapping its wings on one side of the world) producing an enormous effect (a hurricane on the opposite side of the world). Is such a connection between something as infinitesimal as a butterfly and something as big as a hurricane truly possible? Is it real? In this book we show that the butterfly effect is indeed real. The stories in *Tiny Blunders/Big Disasters*, taken straight from history, demonstrate that a little mistake or blunder can indeed set in motion a huge and terrible disaster.

In two journal articles published in 1969, Lorenz laid the foundation for what he later termed the butterfly effect. His insights were the culmination of his research in the 1950s and '60s into what became known as chaos theory. In simple terms, the butterfly effect states that a very small difference in the initial state of a dynamic physical system (such as the atmosphere) can make a big difference in the state of that system at a later point in time.

In a 1972 address to the American Association for the Advancement of Science, Lorenz laid his cards on the table. The title of his talk says it all: "Predictability: Does the Flap of a Butterfly's Wings in Brazil Set a Tornado in Texas?" While Lorenz went on to explain that a "yes" answer to his question was not quite literally true, the basic premise, that a tiny event can go on to produce something much larger, was a real phenomenon. And today the scientific community is in virtually unanimous agreement with him.

Since 1972 the butterfly effect has moved beyond the study of atmospheric and weather conditions to encompass events in other areas, including history. And so we come to the stories found in this book.

Again and again throughout history we find tiny mistakes—blunders, as I call them here—leading to big disasters. Battles and campaigns sometimes turn on a small mistake or oversight, which then produces disaster for one side or the other. Even the fate of nations has sometimes been decided in this way, as this book will demonstrate.

Let us begin our narrative with an example from American politics.

In 1968 Michigan governor George Romney was a candidate for the Republican nomination for president. He fought a losing battle against the eventual nominee, Richard Nixon. Any chance Romney might have had to beat Nixon was lost when, even before his formal campaign began, he committed the tiny blunder of telling a reporter that he had been "brainwashed" by American military authorities during a visit to Vietnam (this was in 1967, when the war in Vietnam was at its height and almost half a million US troops were deployed there). Romney did not mean to convey that he had literally been brainwashed; he instead wanted to make the point that US authorities were trying to paint a false picture of the war. But reporters and the public took his words literally.

Naturally, voters were not keen to advance the cause of a man who had been or could be brainwashed. Romney's little slip of the tongue torpedoed his presidential campaign with an embarrassing controversy.[1]

The story of George Romney's verbal mistake is not one of the chapters in this book; I provide it here in a brief retelling as an example of a tiny blunder that had disastrous consequences. In this case the disaster was personal, affecting George Romney and the Romney family. Of course, had Romney rather than Nixon been elected president in 1968, the Watergate scandal would not have occurred. But whether Romney would have been a good president or a bad one, no one knows. The chapters in this book deal with tiny blunders that definitely changed the course of history. Here are just a few of the astonishing stories you'll read in these pages:

- How an unopened letter saved the American cause in the Revolutionary War.
- How a badly designed paper ballot changed the outcome of a presidential election and led directly to a major war, a war that most now agree should never have been fought in the first place.
- How a German pilot's small mistake saved Britain and changed the course of WWII.
- How an officer who liked cigars accidentally dropped an envelope on the ground and changed the outcome of the Civil War.
- How a lone hunter in the African bush precipitated the AIDS pandemic.
- How a chauffeur's wrong turn sparked two world wars.

And there's much more besides. In a slightly different vein, we also have a chapter called "Murphy's Law Run Amok," which contains a collection of stories about industrial accidents and technological catastrophes caused by small but perhaps inevitable human errors—a phenomenon described in daily parlance as "anything that can go wrong eventually will go wrong." This is the principle of Murphy's Law which has haunted mankind since Adam and Eve.

An ongoing argument among scholars and non-scholars alike, originating decades or perhaps centuries ago, concerns whether great individuals shape history or are themselves shaped by blind forces beyond their control.

I would assert that both notions are partly true and that, taken together, they form a plausible explanation for most historical events. However, it is certainly true, on the evidence of history, that oftentimes the presence or absence of a great leader decides the course of a war or even the fate of a nation. In the chapter "Falling Stars: The Deaths of Generals, Admirals, and Presidents," I discuss prominent examples of the effect a single individual can have on history. In this chapter, I also consider the remarkable story of a man who refused to act, and by his inaction changed the course of history.

But in putting this book together, I also had another purpose in mind beyond my desire to entertain and enlighten the reader. It is my hope that readers of this book, and particularly young people, will draw an important lesson from these stories. Let us return for a moment to George Romney's failed quest for the presidency. At the 1968 Republican National Convention in Miami, Romney, his hopes of gaining the nomination completely dashed, delivered a speech to the assembled delegates. Perhaps reflecting on his own tiny blunder, he wanted to impress upon them the importance of not overlooking details critical to achieving success. He made his point by quoting an old adage:

> For want of a nail the shoe was lost.
>
> For want of a shoe the horse was lost.
>
> For want of a horse the rider was lost.
>
> The rider the battle, the battle the empire.
>
> The empire was lost, all for the want of a nail.

I might sum up Romney's message by quoting the Boy Scout motto: "Be prepared." To put this in stark, real-life terms, I would like to quote from *Never Call Me a Hero: A Legendary American Dive-Bomber Pilot Remembers the Battle of Midway*,[2] the autobiography of Jack "Dusty" Kleiss (1916–2016). Captain Kleiss was a Navy aviator, a winner of the Distinguished Flying Cross, and a hero (whether he wanted to be called one or not) of the Battle of Midway. Midway, of course, was one of the most crucial battles in American history. Our victory there turned the tide of war in the Pacific and gave America sweet revenge for the attack on Pearl Harbor. Naval aviators, including Dusty Kleiss, sank all four of the Japanese carriers that had carried out the notorious sneak attack of December 7, 1941.

In *Never Call Me a Hero*, Kleiss tells us how he prepared for the battle:

> Recognizing the importance of this moment, I double checked everything. My upper left arm pocket contained an assortment of soft pencils to plot information on my clear plastic covered chart board. My chest pockets contained a pencil-sized flashlight and two lipstick-sized containers that held ephedrine [a stimulant] and Vaseline. My leg pockets included a spare

flashlight, new batteries, and two wool cloths, one to clean unwanted items off the chart board and another to wipe my windshield. My life preserver, parachute, and helmet completed the ensemble. I was completely adorned, an aerial warrior ready for action.

The main message of this book, then, is that details left unattended or seemingly small items that are overlooked can snowball into disaster in the long or even the short term. The devil is indeed in the details. If the captain of the Costa Concordia, or Ted Kennedy, or Theresa LePore, or any of the other people whom I write about had been as conscientious as Dusty Kleiss, this book wouldn't exist. The historical record would be bare of tiny blunders leading to big disasters.

Of course, in human affairs, perfection is unattainable. But the reader should reflect on the innumerable avoidable disasters that have occurred as a result of tiny blunders and oversights. It is my hope that the cautionary tales told in this book will encourage future generations to emulate Dusty Kleiss. If even one big disaster is avoided as a result, the time and effort I spent in writing the book will have been well justified.

Jared Knott

SALIENT EXAMPLES

1

THE UNOPENED LETTER THAT SAVED AMERICA

The calculus of warfare is subtle and complex, depending as it does on human ingenuity and audacity, on pure luck, and on a thousand unknowns.

\- Jack Kelly, *The History Reader*

As the year 1776 came to an end, the cause of American independence appeared lost. American morale was at its lowest ebb. The victories at Lexington and Concord and at Bunker Hill in 1775 were but a distant memory. After evacuating Boston in March 1776, the British had regrouped and proceeded to New York, landing first on Staten Island. The ensuing New York campaign had been a disaster for George Washington's army, which was outnumbered and outmaneuvered by the British professional soldiers commanded by General Howe.

It's impossible to exaggerate the desperate state of the patriot cause at the end of 1776. By December not one in ten men of the Continental Army who had fought in the battles on Long Island and Manhattan the previous summer and fall was still serving in the ranks. Desertions were an everyday occurrence. Even Washington's rock-solid determination and faith in victory seemed at times to falter. In a private letter to a cousin written at this time, he seemed to despair of success.

The drastic decline in American fortunes was causing some dissension in the patriot ranks, dissension that was to come to a head the following winter at Valley Forge when the Conway Cabal was formed in an attempt to remove Washington from his position as commander in chief of the army. In December 1776, Washington's chief antagonist was his subordinate, General Charles Lee, an exact contemporary (both men were born in February 1732) and a man with more military experience than Washington, including service in Europe.

At this time Lee began urging Congress to dismiss Washington and place the army under his own command. Fortunately for the cause of American independence, Lee was captured while retreating with his troops across northern New Jersey. (He was later paroled and was to cause Washington further trouble, particularly at the Battle of Monmouth Court House.)

In early December the beaten Continental Army, now numbering only about 6,000 men, retreated across New Jersey to Pennsylvania. The British took up winter quarters in New York City, for in those days winter campaigns were frowned upon by the British Army. It was well for the Americans that this was so, for a determined pursuit by the British and their Hessian auxiliaries could have led to the final destruction of the American forces. This would have put an end to the rebellion, and the colonies would have returned to British rule only six months after they had declared their independence. July 4th would be just another day on the calendar.

The British were overconfident and merely placed weak garrisons in some New Jersey towns, among them Trenton and Princeton. Washington had a spy in place among the British, probably a man named John Honeyman, though the spy's identity has never been established with absolute certainty. Honeyman, posing as a Tory, was able to settle in Trenton and gather information about the garrison there, which consisted entirely of Hessian mercenaries. These German troops had been hired by the British to participate in the American war and were fairly effective professional soldiers.

Honeyman arranged to have himself captured by the Americans, allowing him to give Washington a full briefing about the Hessians at Trenton. He then "escaped" from captivity and returned to Trenton, where he informed the Hessian commander, Colonel Johann Rall, that the Americans were in no state to carry out an attack. Rall believed Honeyman's story.

Washington conceived the bold plan of carrying out a surprise attack on Trenton. The army would cross the Delaware and execute a night march of about ten miles, arriving before dawn and, hopefully, surprising the Hessians in their beds. The night of December 25–26 was chosen for the attack in the belief that the Hessians would be even less alert because of the holiday. The password to be used that night, chosen by Washington himself, was "victory or death."

The crossing of the Delaware (later immortalized in the painting by Emanuel Gottlieb Leutze) and the march were performed with difficulty, for the night was stormy and bitterly cold. Two detachments failed to get across the river, reducing Washington's attacking force to little more than 2,000 men (still larger than the Hessian garrison, however).

The difficulties of the march meant that the Continentals arrived at Trenton after daybreak rather than before, but no matter. The Hessians were taken by surprise, and after a brief engagement most of them surrendered. Only a few of the Hessians were killed, though among the dead was their commander, Colonel Rall, who was wounded by a musket ball and died later that day. The Americans suffered no battle deaths, though some men died later from frostbite. Five

Americans were wounded at Trenton, including future president James Monroe.

The story is often told that the Hessians were taken by surprise because they were sleeping off an alcohol-laden Christmas celebration, but there's no truth to the tale. In fact, a small blunder on Colonel Rall's part cost him both the battle and his life while it gave new life to the American cause, which before the battle had seemed all but lost.

Colonel Rall was a capable professional soldier, the son of an officer. He was fifty years old at the time the battle was fought. He had asked for reinforcements, but these had been denied him. He had ignored recommendations to fortify Trenton, though it's unlikely his forces could have done so in time because they arrived in the town less than two weeks before the battle was fought. Rall had received warnings about a possible American attack, but no definite information about the American plan reached him—until the day before the battle, that is.[3]

On Christmas Eve, Rall was visiting the home of a loyalist in Trenton, a merchant named Abraham Hunt. A letter for Rall arrived at the house and was given to him. Unbeknownst to Rall, it contained information from a British spy about the upcoming American attack. The Hessian commander, distracted by a game of cards (or possibly chess) he was playing, absently put the letter in his pocket. Had he opened it then or after returning to his quarters, Rall could have prepared his troops to defend Trenton—and most likely inflicted a sharp defeat on the attacking Americans. But the letter remained in his coat pocket unopened and was found on his body after the battle.

Such a tiny blunder, mere forgetfulness—but what a disaster for the British cause! The American victory at Trenton, followed days later by another at Princeton, revived American hopes and morale. Above all, it secured the position of the one indispensable man on the American side—George Washington. It's generally agreed by historians that Washington was vital to keeping the army, the Congress, and indeed the country together during the difficult years that preceded final victory. Had Washington been defeated at Trenton, both he and the cause of American independence might have been lost.

The position of the Americans in late 1776 was truly dire. It's sometimes said that Valley Forge marked the low point of the patriots' fortunes. But Valley Forge had been preceded by the Battle of Saratoga, generally regarded as the turning point of the Revolutionary War. And Saratoga was in turn followed by the alliance with France.

In late 1776, on the other hand, we had neither a major victory nor a major ally to bolster our cause. American fortunes were never lower than in those last days before Christmas 1776. It was truly a "time that tries men's souls," as Thomas Paine wrote in *The American Crisis* just days before the Battle of Trenton was fought (his words were read to the troops on December 23).

Britain, which had come so close to suppressing the rebellion that year, ultimately suffered the twin disasters of losing the war and the colonies. And all because a German colonel forgot to open a letter. Had Colonel Rall remembered to read that message, we Americans might still be singing "God Save the Queen" today!

2

THE KENNEDYS: AMERICA'S ROYAL FAMILY AND HITLER'S VENGEANCE

The PT 109 Incident

Like the first domino being toppled in a chain of important events, John Kennedy's PT 109 misadventure in the South Pacific had far-reaching consequences. The reverberations of his actions are still being felt today well into the twenty-first century. In the end, it is a story of great opportunity missed and young lives lost to no purpose.

At the age of twenty-three, John F. (Jack) Kennedy graduated from Harvard and shortly thereafter was commissioned as an ensign in the United States Navy. He was assigned to Naval Intelligence in Washington, DC. While serving in Washington, he was introduced to a newly arrived and very well-connected Scandinavian journalist. Her name was Inga Arvad.

Inga was a strikingly attractive and talented young woman who had been selected as Miss Denmark of 1931. In 1935 she had been granted an interview with Adolf Hitler, one of the very few Scandinavian reporters to be allowed this privilege. In her article about him, she said, "You immediately like him. He seems lonely. The eyes, showing a kind heart, stare right at you. They sparkle with force."

For his part, the dictator was duly impressed with Inga. He described her as "the perfect example of Nordic beauty." She accompanied him to the 1936 Olympics in Berlin.

She sat in his private box, and a picture exists of the two of them laughing together. This association with one of the history's most notorious villains would tarnish her reputation for the rest of her life.

The details are unclear, but Inga apparently also had a personal relationship of some kind with Hermann Goering and Joseph Goebbels during this same period. Soon after, she moved to the United States to pursue her career in journalism. But her hobnobbing with the German High Command put her under a shadow of suspicion with J. Edgar Hoover's FBI, US Naval Intelligence, and even the White House itself.

John Kennedy's involvement with the beauty queen was regarded as a dangerous and misguided romance by many in high places. This was especially true for an officer assigned to Naval Intelligence in Washington, DC. The couple dated for approximately one year. Inga regarded young John Kennedy as a force of nature. "He had the kind of charm that makes the birds come out of the trees." Jack, who liked to give people nicknames, called her "Inga-Binga".

The FBI followed their movements and even recorded their lovemaking in a Charleston hotel room in 1942. In the recorded conversations, JFK revealed some of his insecurities: his older brother, Joe, was smarter than he was, Jack had flunked an Army physical, and he had serious health issues. The young ensign was able to eat only bland foods, which Inga would prepare for him.

Through the intervention of Jack's father, the admirals of the Navy, and even FDR, it was decided that the young officer should be stationed far away from Inga in the South

Pacific. He would be in harm's way but far away from the entanglement of the embarrassing relationship.

Jack reported first to a training facility in Melville, Rhode Island, for longboat navigation and leadership instruction. He distinguished himself in the coursework and was therefore recommended for command of a patrol boat in the Solomon Islands. He arrived in March of 1943, and after serving under another skipper for several weeks, he was given command of his own patrol boat: PT109. The logbook of the PT109 for April 25, 1943, shows the following entries:

> 08:30 Underway for Sespi
>
> 11:00 LT (j.g) J. F. Kennedy assumed command of the boat
>
> 11:45 Moored at usual berth in bushes

The PT boats in John Kennedy's squadron were based at Tulagi, an island in the southern part of the Solomons. In the early days following his arrival, PT109 made routine nighttime security patrols. These patrols were moving pickets that were intended to attack Japanese vessels that might slip through to threaten the Russells-Guadalcanal-Tulagi area. Contact with the enemy was rare, and the patrols were used primarily for training.[4]

The United States had successfully invaded Guadalcanal in 1942 and was now planning to invade New Georgia. On May 30, 1943, PT109 was transferred from Tulagi to the Russell Islands in anticipation of the upcoming invasion.

The Japanese were attempting to reinforce and resupply their forces on New Georgia and Kolombangara by means of nighttime convoys through the Blackett Strait. In the jargon of American GIs, these critical convoys were called the "Tokyo Express."

Admiral William "Bull" Halsey, the US commander for the South Pacific, had already sent large surface ships, cruisers, and destroyers into the strait to intercept the Tokyo Express on a number of occasions. US Navy code breakers were able to identify the arrival and departure times of the Japanese convoys. This resulted in two major engagements: the Battle of Kula Gulf on the night of July 5–6 and the Battle of Kolombangara on the night of July 12–13.

In these battles, the Japanese used their superior "Long Lance" torpedo to good advantage, but the losses on each side were the same: one cruiser and two destroyers lost. The battles amounted to a tactical draw, but more importantly, the reinforcement and resupply mission of the Express was being successfully interdicted.

At the time of Kennedy's arrival in the summer of 1943, the clashes with the Japanese in the Brackett Strait had become heavy and frequent. On July 10, PT109 was ordered to move to Lumbari Island, placing it along the enemy's main supply route. For the green skipper and his new crew, it was now time for direct combat with the Japanese in the open waters of the South Pacific.[5]

August 2–3 marked John Kennedy's first night of actual combat aboard his patrol boat. It was also the first night of action for every member of his crew. PT109, along with a number of patrol boats, was assigned to intercept four large surface ships that made up the Tokyo Express on that particular night.

When the Japanese ships came south on the night in question, Kennedy and his crew somehow missed the initial engagement. One account states that it failed to follow the lead boat into combat and "bugged out," heading away from the conflict toward the Gaza Strait.[6]

When that same convoy was returning north several hours later, somehow and against all odds the Japanese destroyer Amagiri ran over PT109 from its starboard side, cutting through the bow at an angle. A large explosion followed. Two crew members were lost, and one man was badly burned. This was the only time in naval history that a PT boat was ever rammed and sunk by an enemy vessel.

The crew at first stayed with the one-half of the vessel that was still floating. But then the skipper, Lt. (j.g) Kennedy, decided they should swim to a nearby island. Kennedy towed one wounded man, who was too badly burned to swim on his own, with the strap of the victim's life jacket in his teeth.[7] The young skipper also swam out into the ocean at night with a lantern for hours at a time to try and signal friendly ships in the area but to no avail.

After swimming to yet another island, the crew came in contact with friendly natives, and they were eventually rescued. They had been listed as missing in action for one week. It was a harrowing tale with a miraculous ending.

In analyzing John Kennedy's performance under the stress of combat in the Solomons on that night, several items become clear. Whether out of shame over losing his boat, sibling rivalry, or the nature of the man himself, it is undeniable that he showed great courage in attempting to save his crew. This was self-sacrificing bravery—perhaps even bravery to a fault.

However, it is also clear that Kennedy's competence as a captain, green though he was, would not receive high marks from any objective review of the record. The serious flaws in his judgment and his misguided performance as a commander led directly to the deaths of two men and the severe wounding of another. The critical points in this series of events as they relate to his command and judgment can be summarized as follows:

Lost radio contact. Apparently, the radioman, a sailor named Maguire, was not in the chart room (where the radio was located) in the moments leading up to the collision. He was in the cockpit with Lieutenant Kennedy. No one, therefore, was present to hear the last-minute warning that a Japanese destroyer was bearing down on their position and that PT109 was about to be rammed.

Eye contact. The phosphorescent wakes made by the bows of the Japanese destroyers could have been seen from as far as two miles away with excellent night vision and one mile away with normal vision. However, PT109 did not see the Amagiri until just a few seconds before impact. It was the new man, Harold Marney, who saw her first: "Ship at 10:00 o'clock." Clearly, there was a lack of alertness and visual acuity among the crew of PT109. Of the thirteen men on board, several should have seen the large ship coming in ample time to avoid the collision. As mentioned above, this was the only time in the history of the US Navy that a highly maneuverable PT boat was ever rammed by an enemy ship.

Abandoning the wreck. Naval personnel are trained to stay with a wreck as long as possible because this provides the best opportunity to be seen and rescued. Kennedy made the decision to leave the floating wreck and swim to a nearby island. When rescue planes flew over the floating wreckage the next day, no survivors were seen. A rescue might have been achieved had the men remained with the wreck.

Failure to use the Very Pistol. A Very Pistol is a signal gun that fires a flare hundreds of feet into the sky, allowing for communication between vessels. It can easily be seen at night at a distance of several miles. This lifesaving device wasn't used by the crew of PT109. If it had been fired minutes or even as much as an hour after the collision with the Japanese ship, an early rescue might have been possible.

Poor seamanship. One theory of what happened blames PT109's finicky Packard engines. The engines, if accelerated too quickly, would stall. According to this theory, when warned of the oncoming Japanese ship, Kennedy pushed the throttle too hard, causing the engines to choke and falter.

Another possibility regarding the patrol boat's slow response is that Kennedy was running with only one engine engaged. When he attempted to accelerate, the boat did not respond. He might have also turned in a way that put PT 109 more in the path of the oncoming ship rather than avoiding it.

A very experienced and highly decorated fellow commander, William F. Liebenow, spoke with John Kennedy shortly after he was rescued. Liebenow is quoted as saying, "I was kidding him and I said, 'Jack, how in the world could a Jap destroyer run you down?' Jack told me, 'Lieb, I actually do not know. It all happened so quickly." In the official report, John Kennedy himself said that he was running with only one engine engaged.

Douglas MacArthur was later quoted as saying that Kennedy should have been court-martialed for allowing his boat to be sunk. But he subsequently denied having said it. If Kennedy had not been the son of an ambassador—if he had been just a typical junior officer—the official action taken by the Navy might have been very different. However, he was not court- martialed as General MacArthur had supposedly suggested. He was instead awarded the Navy and Marine Corps Medal and the Purple Heart.

The PT109 incident was later of great value in John Kennedy's run for Congress, for the Senate, and for the presidency. It was also the source of jealous resentment on the part of his older brother. This competitive relationship and its consequences are discussed below.

John and Joseph Kennedy

Summary

To understand correctly what happened during John Kennedy's tour of duty in the South Pacific, it is important to see the events in a larger context. Miscalculation and bad luck in combat on the ocean at night are common and sometimes led to the loss of young life. The phrase most often used to describe this chaotic situation and others like it is the "fog of war."

The word fog was first used in this context by renowned military analyst Carl von Clausewitz in his book *On War*. In it he said:

War is the realm of uncertainty; three quarters of the factors on which action is based are wrapped in a fog of greater or lesser uncertainty. A sensitive and discriminating judgment is called for; a skilled intelligence to scent out the truth.

The confusion referred to in this famous phrase was not at all uncommon in naval combat in the Pacific. Only a few weeks before the PT109 incident, an admiral's flagship had been mistakenly sunk by an overeager PT boat crew. In the "fog of war," the crew had mistaken the flagship for a Japanese cruiser.

JFK in His PT 109 Boat

In separate incidents, a number of PT boats had run aground during nighttime operations. Some could not be retrieved and had to be destroyed so as not to fall into Japanese hands. This led to the relief of one experienced commander. On another occasion PT boats had patrolled out of their zone and were too far north. They were attacked by US B-25s. The boats returned fire and shot down one of the bombers, killing three of the crewmen, while a fourth man lost an arm.

When mistakes are made in civilian life, there can be a loss of money, inconvenience, delays in shipping, etc. Mistakes in combat take a heavier toll. When all is said and done, it should be remembered that this was Jack Kennedy's first night in combat. He and his crew were all green. It would be a rare thing if an inexperienced crew and captain did not make serious mistakes during their first encounter with the enemy. Kennedy acted with great courage. With more experience, he would have acted with competence as well.

The Older Brother's Reaction

Joseph Kennedy Jr. learned of his brother's missing-in-action status only a few hours before reading in the press about his spectacular rescue. To his father's consternation, Joe Jr. did not call home to learn any of the details of the event or to express his concern. Instead he wrote a sharply sardonic letter to his parents containing "a few words about his own activities." He seemed strangely bitter at his brother's newfound celebrity.

Joe Jr. was a Navy pilot who was being trained in the United States to fly B-24 Liberator bombers. He was soon to be stationed in Europe. He was the apple of his father's eye and a young man of many achievements, including being an outstanding athlete who had graduated cum laude from Harvard University. He was enrolled in Harvard Law School when the war began but dropped out to accept an officer's commission in the Navy.

A psychoanalytical study of Navy pilots would later conclude that such competitive young men are more defensive than the average person. Merriam-Webster defines the word defensive as it applies to psychological makeup as follows: "Excessive concern with guarding against the real or imagined threat of criticism, injury to one's ego, or exposure of one's shortcomings." In spite of his impressive résumé, this psychological profile seems to well define the Kennedy family's high-achieving, eldest son.

Younger brother John "Jack" Kennedy was awarded the Navy and Marine Corps Medal before Joe even had the chance to fly in combat. To make matters worse, the younger son was receiving huge amounts of national publicity. The Boston Globe ran a story about the PT 109 with the headline "Kennedy's Son Is Hero in the Pacific." Other publications including the widely read Reader's Digest ran feature articles as well.

In her autobiography, their mother, Rose Kennedy, said it was the first time Jack had had an advantage over Joe, and "it must have rankled him."[8]

In September 1943, Joe Jr. was granted leave to return to Boston for his father's birthday. He attended a celebratory dinner in his father's honor. The handsome young man must have been a striking figure in his dress white Navy uniform. At the dinner a family friend proposed a toast: "To Ambassador Joseph Kennedy, father of our hero Lieutenant John F. Kennedy of the US Navy."[9]

Later that evening, Joe Jr. was heard to say, "By God, I'll show them. I'll show them." According to one witness, Joe Jr. went to bed that night crying and repeating the words, "I'll show them; I'll show them." He was opening and closing his fist as he spoke. The seed of self-destruction had been firmly planted.

Joe was assigned to England as a submarine chaser and flew over twenty-five missions. He saw some serious action but nothing to make newspaper headlines. He remarked, "Looks like I will be lucky to return home with the European campaign medal . . . if I'm lucky." The campaign medal was awarded to even the lowliest of service personnel.

In the frustration and anger of being outdone by his younger brother, Joe Jr. made an overreaching decision. He volunteered for a dangerous, even deadly mission that would bring him either glory in battle or an early demise. Joe Jr. himself said that he had only a fifty/fifty chance of coming home alive.

The star-crossed mission over the skies of Europe was in response to Hitler's terror campaign against the people of London. The hate-filled man was raining down his anger upon the civilian population. Women and children were being killed in large numbers. At all costs, this warfare against innocent people had to be stopped.

Hitler's Vengeance Weapons

In 1943 the OSS (Office of Strategic Services) requested a psychological analysis of Adolph Hitler to be prepared by Harvard psychologist Henry A. Murray. The purpose of the report was to access and understand the personality of their chief adversary. What kind of decisions would he be making? How would he behave in the months ahead? The secret report made some surprisingly accurate predictions:

As the war turns against him, his emotions will intensify and will have outbursts more frequently.[10] His public appearances will become much rarer, because he's unable to face a critical audience.

There might be an assassination attempt on him by the German aristocracy, the Wehrmacht officers or Oberkommando der Wehrmacht, because of his superhuman self-confidence in his military judgment.

There will be no surrender, capitulation, or peace negotiations. The course he will follow will almost certainly be the road to ideological immortality, resulting in the greatest vengeance on a world he despises.

From what we know of his psychology, the most likely possibility is that he will commit suicide in the event of defeat. It's probably true he has an inordinate fear of death, but possibly being a psychopath he would undoubtedly weigh his options and perform the deed.

One of the more prescient items in the report was Hitler's need to wreck the "greatest vengeance on a world he despises." This internal drive led to the creation of the *Fürher's Vergeltungswaffe*—weapons of retribution. There were three weapons systems that composed the terror campaign: V-1, V-2, and V-3. They are as follows:

The V-1, also called the Buzz Bomb or Doodlebug, was an early cruise missile. It was essentially a flying bomb that was powered by a pulsejet and flew at a speed of approximately 400 miles per hour. One week after the D-Day invasion (June 6, 1944), the missiles began falling on London. It was the first step in the part of the terror campaign that Hitler hoped would break the morale of the British people. Approximately 9,521 V-1s were directed at London. At its peak, one hundred per day were falling on the city. The missile flew at a speed slow enough that it could be shot down by Allied fighter planes and by antiaircraft ground fire. However, just when it looked like the situation was beginning to come under control, another weapon appeared on the horizon.

The V-2 was the world's first supersonic long-range missile. It was also the first man-made object to enter space because it crossed the Karman line (at sixty-two miles above the earth, is acknowledged internationally as the threshold to space). The V-2 project was headed by Werner von Braun, who was later to head the Marshall Space Center in the United States. Three thousand V-2s were launched by the German Wehrmacht against Allied targets. The attacks resulted in nine thousand deaths. In addition, twelve thousand forced laborers and concentration camp prisoners died as a result of their forced participation in the production of the weapon.

The V-3. Unlike the V-1 or the V-2, the V-3 was a high-pressure propulsion cannon in the process of being built at an underground fortress in Mimoyecques in western France. [11]It was designed to rain explosive shells on London at the rate of one projectile every two minutes. Like the other two vengeance weapons, it was designed to strike fear into the people of London. Churchill said that if this weapon system had become operational, it would have been the deadliest and most damaging of the three.

After the war, Eisenhower said that if the vengeance weapons had been directed at the D-Day embarkation ports, the invasion would have to have been postponed. There was a huge concentration of men, weapons, and equipment in the staging areas around Portsmouth, Port Harbor, Weymouth, and the other points of departure. If thousands of V-1s and V-2s had landed in the midst of this great military congregation, the invasion would likely have failed or been aborted altogether. The outcome for the Allies would have been disastrous.

Sending the missiles against the people of London instead of the invading army was a major mistake on the part of the German High Command. Hitler's need for vengeance was a valuable asset in the Allied cause.

The purpose of the critical mission for which Joe Kennedy Jr. volunteered was to destroy the V-3 site before it became operational. The Allies were not sure exactly what was happening at the fortress of Mimoyecques, but they knew it was very big and had something to do with missiles being fired at the city of London.

The mission was planned as follows: B-17 and B-24 bombers that were no longer fit for duty were stripped of all their equipment and loaded with several tons of Torpex explosives. (Torpex is 50% more powerful than TNT.) The cockpit was fitted with a radio control system and a pair of cameras, one showing the gauges and one showing the ground ahead. The planes would be painted yellow or white and would be flying at an altitude of 2,000 feet. They would be operated by remote control from planes flying overhead at an altitude of approximately 20,000 feet.

Joseph P. Kennedy Jr., Joseph P. Kennedy Sr., John Kennedy

However, the planes could not take off by remote control. They had to be manned by two pilots, who would then bail out over England as the remote-control pilots overhead took over. This operation was attempted a number of times during the war and was successful only once, almost by accident. A number of pilots had been killed in the ill-fated missions.

It was hoped that this massive flying bomb could crack the heavily reinforced launch sites the Germans had built at their underground fortress at Mimoyecques. However, once the plane was in the air, some unknown cause sparked an explosion that destroyed the aircraft in a split instant. Lieutenant Joseph Kennedy Jr. and his copilot, Lieutenant Wilford John Willey, were vaporized. No remains were ever found. Joseph Kennedy Jr. ceased to exist.

No burial took place. However, the names of the two men are listed on the Tablets of the Missing at the Cambridge American Cemetery and Memorial between the villages of Coton and Madingley in Cambridgeshire, England.

An informal board of inquiry was assembled, which reviewed a number of questions regarding the cause of the disaster. The possibility of the crew having made a mistake was discounted as was a jamming or stray signal that could have armed and detonated the explosives.

Now we come the final tiny mistake in this tragic chain of events. An electronics officer, Earl Olsen, believed that the wiring harness had a design defect and had warned Kennedy of this possibility the day before the mission. His warnings were ignored. Perhaps if Kennedy had listened to the officer, the outcome would have been very different. A tiny blunder that had a major impact on history? No one will ever know.

Summary

A series of seemingly small mistakes and quirky circumstances tumbled one against another and involved the members of a powerful American family. The results of this chain of events determined who would become president of the United States in 1960. It was Joseph Kennedy Jr. who was to run for president that year. Jack was brought forward to run for Congress, then the Senate, and then the presidency only with the demise of his "smarter" older brother.

If Inga had never met Jack, if a man had been posted in the chart room to hear the warning of the approaching Japanese cruiser, and if Joe Jr. had listened to the electronics officer, this story would have had a different and much happier ending.

3

HITLER THE UNKILLABLE

Hitler had the Devil's own luck, but luck runs out in the end – it's just a pity it took so long in his case.

- David Lawlor

It is almost certain that we will fail. But how will future history judge the German people if not even a handful of men had the courage to put an end to that criminal?

- Gen. Henning von Tresckow

The fact that Hitler escaped death until he took his own life in his Berlin bunker on April 30, 1945, is quite remarkable. By all rights he should have been killed even before he became a political rabble-rouser in the 1920s. He escaped death again in the 1923 Beer Hall Putsch and went on to become the Führer of the German Reich ten years later. Right after the outbreak of World War II, he survived an assassination attempt that killed several of his fellow Nazis.

Had he died then, Europe would have been saved from immense suffering and destruction. During the later war years, several attempts were made on Hitler's life; all of them failed, often purely by chance. Looking back on his life, one is hard pressed not to conclude that some demonic power, perhaps the Devil himself, protected Hitler again and again, allowing the Nazi dictator to wreak havoc upon the world.

Hitler served at the front throughout World War I. He enlisted in the 16th Bavarian Reserve Regiment and was assigned to its 1st company. He fought at the first battle of Ypres in the autumn of 1914, in which his company suffered 80 percent casualties.

Hitler then became a runner carrying messages from regimental headquarters to other units in the field, a duty he continued to perform until the end of the war. Hitler, though twice wounded, survived the maelstrom and, after being discharged from the army, went on to become a right-wing party leader and revolutionary.

The revolutionary Hitler, leader of the newly formed Nazi Party, attempted to seize power in Bavaria on November 8 and 9, 1923. The plan was to gain control of Bavaria and then march on Berlin, imitating Mussolini's march on Rome of the previous year.

On November 9, 1923, Nazis, led by Hitler and the World War I hero General Ludendorff, attempted to seize power in Munich. As they were marching on the Bavarian Ministry of Defense, they encountered a group of soldiers, who opened fired on the revolutionaries. Sixteen Nazis fell dead. Hitler was not among them, although he did dislocate his shoulder in the melee. The Nazi leader and his followers fled the scene, ending their attempt to seize power. Hitler was later captured, tried, and imprisoned for ten months.

After leaving prison, Hitler made the decision to gain power through legal means. He reached his goal on January 30, 1933, when he was appointed chancellor. After the death of President von Hindenburg in 1934, Hitler declared himself Führer of the German Reich, a position he held until his suicide in 1945.

Hitler was not under any serious physical threat between the aftermath of the failed Munich putsch and the beginning of World War II in 1939. Shortly after the outbreak of the war, however, he narrowly escaped assassination. Ironically, the attempt on his life occurred during a commemoration of the 1923 putsch. Every year on November 8th, the Führer and his old party comrades assembled in the Munich beer hall from which Hitler had launched his attempted revolution. Each year he regaled them with a speech commemorating those who had fallen in 1923 and extolling the Nazi movement's achievements and goals.

Although the war had by no means been welcomed by the German people, Hitler himself was still hugely popular. What opposition to him existed in Germany was unorganized and restricted mainly to a relative handful of traditional conservatives—aristocrats and a few officers in the German Army. The leftist opposition had been suppressed soon after the Nazi takeover of power in 1933. However, one left-wing individual, a lone carpenter, was at liberty and determined to kill the Führer. And he would have succeeded, too, but for mere chance.

Georg Elser was a carpenter with left-wing views, but he was not a dyed-in-the-wool communist. He was simply disenchanted with the cruelty and barbarism of the regime. He was also opposed to Germany becoming involved in another war. He taught himself enough about explosives to build a working bomb.

Over a period of weeks prior to November 8, 1939, Elser made nightly visits to the beer hall at which Hitler would speak. He would hide himself until the hall closed for the night, then go to work. Using his carpentry skills, he was able to hide a powerful time bomb in a pillar near the podium at which Hitler would deliver his speech.

On the evening of November 8, Hitler gave his speech as scheduled. The bomb, its timing mechanism set three days earlier by Elser, was ticking away as the Führer spoke. Sitting close to Hitler and certain to be killed along with him in the explosion were Himmler, Heydrich, Goebbels, and other leading Nazis (Hermann Goering, however, Hitler's designated successor, was absent). But then chance intervened. Fog that night had made it impossible for Hitler to return to Berlin by plane; instead he would have to go by train. As a result, he cut his speech short and left the hall earlier than expected, accompanied by the other Nazi bigwigs already mentioned. Thirteen minutes after Hitler's departure, the bomb exploded, killing eight people.

Elser had done everything right, but mere chance—the foggy weather that night—had foiled his attempt to kill the Führer. Had he succeeded, World War II and the Holocaust would almost certainly have been avoided. With Hitler, Himmler, and Goebbels dead, Goering would undoubtedly have become Germany's leader, and Goering in 1939 was not particularly interested in waging a second world war. He had, in the last days of peace, sought ways to reach an accommodation with Britain and France. He quite likely would have come to terms with the Western powers. What would have followed we can only guess at, but the devastation of Europe and the deaths of sixty million people would most likely not have occurred.

Elser was caught trying to escape over the Swiss border. He was interrogated extensively by the Gestapo and eventually executed in the Dachau concentration camp only a few days before Germany's capitulation in 1945. It is believed that he acted entirely alone. How close this lone carpenter came to changing history!

During 1940 and early 1941, there were no attempts on Hitler's life. This period was a triumphal one for Nazi Germany, as Europe from the English Channel to the Russian border and from the North Cape to Crete fell under its sway. But the invasion of Russia in June 1941, accompanied by the murderous activities of the Einsatzgruppen (death squads charged with shooting Jews and others in occupied Russian territory), caused a few brave individuals in the German Army to begin plotting against Hitler and the Nazi regime.

This handful of officers, most of them aristocrats, was concentrated in Army Group Centre in Russia. The conspirators' original plans were inchoate and impractical—they considered arresting Hitler during one of his visits to Army Group headquarters and then putting him on trial. But as the tide of war turned against Germany, plans to assassinate Hitler took definite shape.

In March 1943, immediately after the catastrophe at Stalingrad, the conspirators took action. On March 13, 1943, Hitler visited Army Group Centre headquarters at Smolensk. The conspirators, led by General Henning von Tresckow, managed to smuggle a time bomb (disguised as a package containing a gift for an officer at Hitler's headquarters in East

Prussia) aboard the Führer's plane. It was timed to go off while the plane was still airborne. But to the conspirator's significant surprise and dismay, Hitler landed safely in East Prussia. What had happened?

With commendable bravery, one of the conspirators, an officer named Fabian von Schlabrendorff, flew to East Prussia and retrieved the unexploded bomb. He opened the package and found that, incredibly, the bomb had worked. The fuse had performed its function, the glass container of acid had broken, the liquid had dissolved the wire that held back the striker, and the striker had in turn operated correctly, hitting the detonator cap—but the detonator had not reacted and exploded the bomb.[12]

It was once again as if some demonic force had intervened, protecting Hitler and thus allowing him to carry on his work of destruction. Had Hitler been killed in early 1943, it is likely (though we can of course not know for certain) that the Army would have overpowered the Nazis and the SS and then installed a civilian regime that would have ended the war.

Although Britain and America had in January 1943 proclaimed their intention to force Germany to surrender unconditionally, Russia had not yet agreed. Peace in the East would have paved the way for negotiations between a non-Nazi Germany and the Western powers. The immense destruction of the last two years of the war would have been avoided and the eruption of communism into the center of Europe prevented. So much at least would have been possible, perhaps even probable, had Hitler died in March 1943. But it was not to be.

Throughout 1943 and early 1944, several attempts to kill Hitler proved abortive. A plan to shoot Hitler and Himmler was abandoned when Himmler did not appear. An officer acting as a suicide bomber had to hastily dismantle the time bomb he was wearing when Hitler departed earlier than scheduled. Again and again, some trick of fate allowed Hitler to escape death.

On July 20, 1944, the conspirators finally struck. Operation Valkyrie was initiated when a bomb planted in the Führer's East Prussian headquarters by Colonel Count von Stauffenberg exploded during a military conference. The bomb had been hidden inside Stauffenberg's briefcase, which he placed next to Hitler before excusing himself and leaving the conference room. During his absence, someone moved the briefcase a few feet away, behind a leg of the conference table. When the bomb exploded, some of its force was absorbed by the table leg. Four of the men inside the conference room were killed, but Hitler escaped with only minor injuries. Had Stauffenberg used a bigger bomb, most likely everyone in the room would have been killed. Had the briefcase not been moved, it's likely Hitler would have died.

But Hitler survived, and as a result, the conspirators' attempt to seize power in Berlin failed. The last serious attempt to kill Hitler and end the war before Germany was completely defeated had failed to come off.

Hitler died by shooting himself in his Berlin bunker on April 30, 1945, amid the ruins of his "thousand-year Reich." It is astonishing that this man survived so many situations that could—and perhaps should—have led to his death: four years as a combat soldier in World War I, a hail of bullets that killed sixteen of his fellow Nazis in Munich in 1923, a series of assassination attempts including two occasions on which bombs designed to kill him were actually exploded. No outside force, it seems, could end Hitler's life and with it his terrible career of destruction. It is one of the supreme ironies of history that a man who caused so much death could himself be killed only by his own hand.

Adolf Hitler in his Nazi party uniform, which he wore throughout the war

4

THE WAGES OF SEX

Researchers concluded that syphilis was carried from the New World to Europe after Columbus' voyages. Many of the crew members who served on this voyage later joined the army of King Charles VIII in his invasion of Italy in 1495, resulting in the spreading of the disease across Europe and as many as five million deaths.

- New Scientist, January 2008

We come now to a chapter that deals with events as tragic as any described in this book, and perhaps even more ironic. Without sex, the human race could not continue. The great panoply of human history depends upon mating between human males and females; without the basic drive to propagate, our species would not exist. The wisdom of God or Nature is such that almost all humans find pleasure in sexual relations, thereby ensuring that the vast majority of humanity pursues sexual gratification as a basic drive or need. Thus the perpetuation of humankind is assured.

The irony is that along with the pleasure of sex comes the danger of disease. In our own time we have witnessed the ravages of AIDS, a sexually transmitted disease that has killed millions throughout the world. Before AIDS there was syphilis, a deadly bacterial infection. In the centuries before the discovery of penicillin, syphilis was a disfiguring, life-shortening illness. Blindness, madness, or early death awaited many of those who caught this terrible malady.

The Coming of Syphilis

Many important figures in history are known or suspected to have suffered from syphilis. The German philosopher Friedrich Nietzsche's collapse into madness on a street in Turin, Italy, in 1889 probably resulted from his being infected with syphilis years earlier (the syphilis bacteria can remain in the body for years before deadly symptoms occur). He may have become infected when visiting a brothel in his student days, or possibly while treating wounded soldiers as a medical corpsman during the Franco–Prussian War of 1870, for although sexual transmission is the main route of infection, other close contact with an infected person can give one the disease. However, Nietzsche got the disease, it shortened the career of the most important and original philosophical thinker of his time. He was only forty-four years old when he fell ill.

President Abraham Lincoln

Vladimir Lenin almost certainly suffered from syphilis, which probably caused (or at least contributed to) his death at the early age of fifty-three. His demise in turn led to the rise of

Joseph Stalin, one of the most bloodthirsty mass murderers in history.

Abraham Lincoln also is believed to have acquired syphilis, probably from a prostitute, a woman whom he had "a devilish passion".[13] His law partner, William Herndon, stated that Lincoln had told him this. According to Herndon, Lincoln became infected with syphilis in the 1830s. Only one qualified analyst, Dr. John G. Sotos, MD, has accepted that Lincoln was indeed a syphilitic;[14] mainstream academics and historians uniformly reject the idea. This is one instance, however, when the majority opinion of experts and scholars should perhaps be questioned. Recall that for decades—indeed centuries—mainstream opinion vigorously denied that Thomas Jefferson had children by his slave Sally Hemings. Then DNA testing came along. . .

Of course, if Lincoln did have syphilis, we can't point to a major disaster that occurred as a result. His physical ailments did not impair Lincoln in any way during his presidency, though who knows what might have happened had he lived longer into his second term? Of course, all but one of his and Mrs. Lincoln's children died young and without having children of their own, so perhaps syphilis deprived America of the talents of a political dynasty, which might have continued Lincoln's record of service to the Republic.

Another famous syphilitic was Lord Randolph Churchill, the father of Winston Churchill. A son of the seventh Duke of Marlborough, he rose meteorically through the ranks of the Tory (Conservative) Party to become at age forty-five chancellor of the exchequer and effectively deputy prime minister. He married the beautiful American heiress Jennie Jerome in 1874. They had two sons, one of whom, Winston, became world famous.

Lord Randolph's health had begun to deteriorate in the early 1880s. But syphilis in its early stages comes and goes, and Randolph Churchill in the mid-1880s was briefly the most talked about politician in Britain. He resigned from office in 1886 over a political dispute and not because of his illness. Soon thereafter mental deterioration set in, and in early 1895 he died. His final years included embarrassing appearances in Parliament, where his attempts to speak amounted to no more than irrational ramblings. Syphilis had ruined a rising star of British politics.

If we really want to view syphilis against the backdrop of the tiny blunder/great disaster theme of this book, then we should go back farther in time and search for the origins of the disease, or rather its first appearance among Europeans. To do this, we must cast our minds back to the epochal year of 1492, when Christopher Columbus led the Niña, Pinta, and Santa Maria across the Atlantic in search of a new route to Cathay and the spices and other riches of the East Indies.

There is no definite mention of syphilis in the ancient or medieval records of the Old World. On the other hand, it apparently had long existed among the indigenous peoples of the Americas. Spanish chroniclers of the sixteenth century noted that the Indians knew of the disease and suffered from it long before the Europeans arrived.

Did Columbus's crew introduce syphilis to Europe when they returned from the New World? The literature on the origin of syphilis was already extensive when Samuel Eliot Morison, the American naval historian, published his biography of Columbus in 1942.[15]

Morison noted a curious coincidence: the first known appearance of syphilis in Europe was in 1495, during the invasion of Italy by King Charles VIII of France. The pestilence seemed to follow the king's line of march. Was it of French origin, then? Apparently not. According to some contemporary chroniclers, it had first broken out in Portugal and Spain about two years before Charles invaded Italy and had quickly spread to France. It was then carried to Italy by King Charles's troops. That would mean its occurrence in Iberia coincided almost exactly with the return of Columbus from his first voyage (Columbus and the crew of the Niña arrived in Lisbon, Portugal, in early 1493).

The belief grew that a few Spanish and Portuguese women of easy virtue had been infected either by some of Columbus's sailors or (more scandalously still) by Indians brought to Europe by Columbus. Sex being a fact of everyday life and syphilis being highly contagious, it would not be surprising if it spread rapidly across Europe, particularly since the European population of the time had no built-in immunity or resistance to the disease (resistance to any pathogen being a product of previous exposure to that pathogen).[16]

In his book, Morison discusses the development of the theory of an American origin for syphilis as well the countervailing arguments against it. Not being a scientist or medical man, he wisely came to no definite conclusion.[17]

Recently a trained scientist weighed in on the matter. Katherine Wright, a biologist trained at Oxford University, published an essay, "The Revenge of the Americas," which was awarded the British Wellcome Trust science writing prize for 2013. According to her research, no evidence has been found of syphilis in Europe before the time of Columbus.

Late-stage syphilis produces lesions on bone. So far, no European skeleton before Columbus's time has revealed lesions of the right type, whereas hundreds if not thousands of pre-Columbian skeletons in the Americas have them. The preponderance of the evidence, therefore, is that those who returned with Columbus from America brought with them the terrible plague.[18]

Syphilis exploded across Europe in the sixteenth century. By some estimates, 15 percent of the European population became infected. Two famous kings, Henry VIII of England and Francis I of France, may possibly have contracted the disease. Syphilis remained a danger right up until the 1940s, when penicillin was developed. Even today, the possibility that new drug-resistant strains will evolve keeps scientists and medical professionals awake at night.

The extent of the catastrophe is obvious, yet it may be even greater than we can know. How many people destined for greatness were cut down too soon by this dread disease?

Consider General Ranald Mackenzie (1840–1889), who was described by Ulysses S. Grant as the most promising officer in the US Army and promoted by President Lincoln to the rank of brigadier general when he was only twenty-four years old. He was forced to retire at age forty-four by the onset of a violent insanity caused by—yes, syphilis. How many more like him are lost to history?

No Westerner knew about syphilis in 1492. No one in the world at that time knew what a bacterium was or how diseases are transmitted. Sailors after a long voyage are keen to "unwind," and understandably so. Some of Columbus's men took a moment's pleasure on the shores of a new land. A simple and basic human act became a tiny blunder that mushroomed into a global catastrophe.

Of course, the New World's awful gift to the Old was repaid in kind. Smallpox and other diseases unknown in the Americas came west with the Europeans. And the native peoples were ravaged by them. The word syphilis, by the way, was coined by an Italian physician, Girolamo Fracastoro. In 1530 he wrote a poem, "Syphilis, sive Morbus Gallicus" ("Syphilis, or the French Disease"), which told the story of a shepherd, one Syphilis, who so angered Apollo that the god struck him down with a disfiguring disease. Fracastoro later used the name as a clinical term, and it has been with us ever since.

The Coming of AIDS

Syphilis is a terrible disease. Until antibiotics were invented in the twentieth century, it shortened the lives of millions, including some famous figures of history. But it never achieved the virulence of the bubonic plague, which wiped out about one-third of the population of fourteenth-century Europe and made devastating return visits during the fifteenth, sixteenth, and seventeenth centuries (most notably during the Great Plague of London in 1665). The late twentieth and early twenty-first centuries have witnessed another great plague—one that, like syphilis, is caused almost exclusively by sexual contact. Thanks to modern medicine, this plague of our time has proved somewhat less deadly than the medieval Black Death, but it has nevertheless killed at least thirty-five million people since it was first recognized by science in 1981. We are referring, of course, to AIDS (acquired immunodeficiency syndrome).

Those thirty-five million deaths obviously constitute the great disaster caused by AIDS. The tiny blunder that began the AIDS pandemic occurred sometime early in the twentieth century, as we shall soon learn. But first a few facts about AIDS.

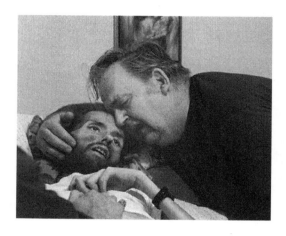

AIDS victim David Kirby

While syphilis is caused by a bacterium, AIDS is caused by a virus, or rather a retrovirus. Retroviruses are composed of RNA (ribonucleic acid) rather than DNA (deoxyribonucleic acid). Most organisms have DNA as a building block, with RNA serving as a messenger that helps to express genetic information. In a retrovirus, the RNA serves as the building block. Retroviruses, upon entering a host cell, transform their RNA into DNA, which then allows them to infect the host. The retrovirus that causes AIDS is called the human-immunodeficiency virus (HIV).

HIV infects the cells of the human immune system. In basic terms, it causes the immune system to weaken and eventually fail. At any one time, most people who are HIV-positive do not have AIDS. Originally this was because it takes years (sometimes as long as a decade) for AIDS to manifest itself. Today we have antiretroviral drugs that in many cases keep HIV from becoming full-blown AIDS, although they do not cure HIV itself.

When the weakening of the immune system caused by HIV reaches a certain point, the infected person is diagnosed with AIDS. People suffering from AIDS cannot fight off certain infections and cancers. Pneumocystis pneumonia (a very serious form of the disease, caused by a fungus), Kaposi's sarcoma (a rare but deadly form of cancer), tuberculosis, and AIDS wasting syndrome are among the consequences of AIDS. The death rate for people with advanced AIDS is, practically speaking, 100 percent.

HIV/AIDS is transmitted by bodily fluids, principally blood, semen, vaginal fluid, and breast milk. In the vast majority of cases, transmission is caused by sexual contact, but other means of acquiring the disease are possible, such as absorption through an open wound or in the womb. In the 1980s many people were infected through blood transfusions, but since then, measures have been taken to prevent the virus from tainting the blood supply. Today there is a less than a one in a million chance of acquiring HIV/AIDS in this way.

AIDS was first recognized in 1981, and the actual virus was isolated by researchers a few years later. Since the 1980s, a great deal has been learned about the origin of AIDS, and we now have a good idea of how it emerged and infected so many people. The facts are both surprising and, needless to say, saddening.

Viruses evolve rapidly, and this is particularly true of retroviruses. Although the human immunodeficiency virus was isolated only about thirty years ago, we know that it's been around longer than that. We know this because scientists are able to trace its evolution through blood and tissue samples that have been preserved for decades, including samples taken from people who were infected long before HIV/AIDS was known to exist.[19]

There are in fact two main types of HIV, which have been labeled HIV-1 and HIV-2. HIV-1, and in particular a subtype known as HIV-1 group M, is the great killer of people. But neither HIV-1 nor HIV-2 originated in human beings. HIV-2 is a mutation of a simian immunodeficiency virus (SIV) found originally in a West African monkey, the sooty mangabey. HIV-1 is a mutation of a simian immunodeficiency virus found in chimpanzees.

The SIV types found in African monkeys (but not in Asian or South American ones, which are apparently SIV-free in the wild) have been around for a long time, possibly millions of years.[20] But the SIV carried by chimps, which eventually mutated into HIV-1, is fairly new, probably only a few centuries old.[21] The SIV carried by chimps is a mutation created when the virus was transmitted from a monkey to a chimpanzee host.

Chimps are not strict vegetarians but rather are omnivores. They enjoy meat, especially monkey meat. Groups of chimpanzees will form hunting parties that kill and consume monkeys. The killing and eating involves ripping the prey apart and devouring the flesh and blood. Under such conditions, it's possible for a virus such as SIV to gain entry to a host via a cut or lesion. It's likely that at some point in the past, a chimp became infected with monkey SIV in this way.[22] The virus then mutated inside the host. Thus the strain of SIV that infects chimpanzees was born.[23] The new strain of virus was transmitted, primarily through sexual intercourse, from chimp to chimp.

The initial jump from chimp to man occurred in a similar fashion. "Bush meat"—that is, monkey and ape meat—

is widely consumed throughout much of sub-Saharan Africa. It's a form of protein that poor Africans can access through hunting, just as chimps derive protein from their monkey prey.

It's also possible that two strains of monkey SIV were acquired by a single individual, and that a new virus deadly to chimps was created when the two strains inside the host exchanged genetic material.

According to many experts, at some point in the early twentieth century, a single bush meat hunter in central Africa killed and butchered a chimp that was SIV-positive and thereby acquired the virus (the chimp's infected blood entering the hunter's bloodstream via an open cut or lesion). Some scientists place this event at around 1910; others say around 1920. The relatively exact dating is the product of genetic sequencing.[24]

In essence, then, the global AIDS pandemic of the late twentieth and early twenty-first centuries resulted from one African hunter with an open wound killing and butchering a chimp infected with SIV. However, that would be an oversimplification. For AIDs to become a global pandemic, there had to be a confluence of events that created the conditions under which the disease could spread globally.

AIDS was first identified in 1981. Research has uncovered a handful of cases outside of Africa prior to that year, but there was no pandemic in the years between 1910 or 1920 and 1980. Certain things had to happen before AIDS could sweep the world.

Had Africa remained in its precolonial, early-nineteenth-century condition, AIDS would have remained a rare disease, confined to a relatively small population of humans in central Africa. But European colonization beginning in the late nineteenth century facilitated the spread of the disease.

Colonization brought urbanization, disrupting traditional tribal societies. Many young, unmarried African men flocked to the new urban centers in search of work. This created a big disparity between the number of men and women in the cities and towns, with males outnumbering females considerably. In such a situation, prostitution occurs; indeed, it flourishes. It has ever been so, regardless of the time or place in which such a disparity arises. Prostitution inevitably leads to an increase in sexually transmitted diseases such as syphilis and gonorrhea. Critically, AIDS is more easily transmitted when a person is already infected with another STD.

Prostitution and increased sexual activity as a result of urbanization became the first factor in the buildup of AIDS cases prior to the onset of the pandemic.

Another factor was improved transportation. As the European colonists built roads and railroads across Africa, it became easier for infected people to move about and spread the disease.

A third factor was the increased access African bush hunters had to guns. Killing a chimp or gorilla is not an easy task for a human. These animals are intelligent and possess tremendous strength. European colonization put more guns into the hands of bush meat hunters, leading to more kills and thereby more exposures to SIV.

A fourth factor, ironically, was improvements in public health. The introduction of vaccines and injectable antibiotics in the 1930s and after actually helped to cause the spread of AIDS in Africa. The reason is that in those days, syringes were not plastic and disposable but were made of glass, expensive, and meant to be reused over and over.

In colonial Africa, there were never enough medical personnel (European or African) to handle the number of patients who presented themselves at clinics and hospitals.

Vaccination programs were carried out by a relative handful of health workers in the cities and countryside. With manpower and equipment in short supply, sterilization measures for syringes amounted to little more than a quick wipe of the needle with a cloth that had been dipped in alcohol. A single needle would be used to prick thousands of people. Needless to say, this contributed to the early spread of AIDS.[25]

After the Congo (present-day Zaire) achieved independence from Belgium in 1960, many Haitians were sent there by international organizations to fill positions in teaching, health care, and other fields that had been vacated when the Belgians left the country. Several thousand Haitians lived and worked in the country over a period of more than a decade. In the early 1970s, the Zairian regime began replacing them with native Africans, and the Haitians returned home. Some of them were, of course, HIV-positive. AIDS probably entered the United States via Haitians traveling to and sometimes settling down in first Florida and then places like New York City.

Travel between Europe and Africa increased with the beginning of the jet age in the 1950s, and AIDS gained a foothold on the former continent too. The cases in Europe and the Americas were rare and as yet unrecognized as a new disease. At this time, the few victims were dying of Kaposi's sarcoma or other known albeit rare diseases. The numbers simply weren't yet high enough to set off alarm bells in the medical and public health communities. Then came the 1980s.

Starting in late 1980, the alarm bells began to sound. Doctors in California and elsewhere were seeing clusters of patients with Kaposi's sarcoma and other end-stage illnesses brought on by what was soon to be named AIDS. At first the patients were mainly homosexual men and Haitians, but soon AIDS was diagnosed in people from other social and ethnic groups. After the human immunodeficiency virus was isolated by researchers a little later, it was learned that many more people were infected, even though they displayed no symptoms of AIDS (it takes several years for HIV to become full-blown AIDS). Then it was discovered that AIDS was epidemic in much of sub-Saharan Africa.

Originally thought of by some as a "gay plague," AIDS turned out to be an equal opportunity virus, with the vast majority of cases in Africa being among heterosexuals. However, the wildly promiscuous bathhouse culture among gays in the 1980s was a big factor in the spread of the disease, which devastated the gay community in America and Europe. The actor Rock Hudson was one of the more famous causalities. In Africa particularly, the disinclination of heterosexual men to wear condoms had an equally tragic effect.

Today, in addition to the thirty-five million people who have died of AIDS, about forty million are living with HIV. Almost two million of these are children. Fortunately, drugs have been developed that allow people to live basically normal lives with HIV, though there is still no cure.

AIDS began when a single bush meat hunter was infected by a chimpanzee he had killed for food. But it turned into a worldwide plague that has killed millions and devastated the lives of millions more as a result of humanity's desire for sex. Sadly, the wages of sex can be death.

5

THE POORLY DESIGNED
BALLOT THAT CAUSED A WAR

What it shows is what we've been saying all along—there is no question that the majority of people on Election Day believed they left the booth voting for Al Gore.

- Ron Klain, Gore's former chief-of-staff

The butterfly effect, as discussed in the author's introduction, is a term used in chaos theory. Basically, it refers to the postulate that a small event can contribute to or produce a big effect in a chain of events. The term gets its name from the supposed ability of a butterfly flapping its wings on one side of the world to affect the weather on the opposite side of the globe.

Whether that's literally true or not is for the scientists to debate, but as this book has shown, it's clear that little things— tiny blunders—can produce major disasters. We've observed how something small and apparently insignificant can set off a domino effect that ends up changing history. And we'll see it again in this chapter, which concerns the butterfly ballot effect.

Enter Theresa LePore. This lady, a Florida native and member of the baby boom generation, had from an early age conceived the ambition to become an election official (that's election official, not elected official). After graduating from college in the early 1970s, she began her career as a clerk in the office of the Palm Beach County, Florida, supervisor of elections.

LePore rose through the ranks to become deputy supervisor and then sought election as supervisor in 1996. Originally registered as a Republican, she switched to the Democratic Party that year because Palm Beach County leaned Democratic (as it still does). She won the election that year and was reelected in November of 2000. But that second election would also bring Ms. LePore national and even global notoriety, for it soon became apparent that, incredibly, she had decided the outcome of that year's presidential election.

Readers will recall that the November 2000 presidential election, pitting then–vice president Al Gore against the governor of Texas, George W. Bush (son of George H. W. Bush, president from 1989–1993), was incredibly close—the closest in US history, in fact. Nationally, Republican Bush lost the popular vote by over half a million votes but won the decisive Electoral College vote by 271–266. His winning margin in the Electoral College was provided by the state of Florida. Bush carried the Sunshine State by a mere 537 votes out of nearly six million cast. As it turned out, a tiny blunder by Theresa LePore made all the difference in the Florida result.

For the November 2000 election, Ms. Lepore, exercising her authority as Palm Beach County supervisor of elections, introduced the butterfly ballot, a form of punch-card ballot. Punch-card ballots came into use in the 1960s, and by the 1990s about one-third of American polling places used them. The punch-card ballot looks just like it sounds: the voter punches a hole in the ballot card next to the candidate of his or her choice. The butterfly ballot, however, is like an open book; it has two pages or sides with names of the candidates for office on each side. Down the spine or middle of the ballot are the holes the voter punches (see illustration).

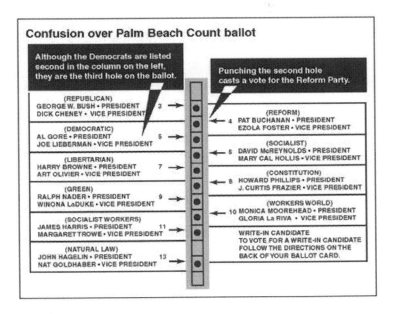

The notorious butterfly ballot

Lepore chose to use the butterfly ballot in 2000 because so many candidates had qualified to run for president in Florida that year. There were ten candidates in all, in addition to which the ballot included a space to write in a candidate. LePore was simply trying to help Palm Beach County's voters, and particularly older voters with impaired eyesight, cast their votes for the candidate of their choice.[26]

Unfortunately, the butterfly ballot's design was flawed in some respects. Looking at the illustration, you will see that there are two holes opposite each candidate's name.[27] A small arrow points to the correct hole to punch for each candidate, but many elderly, visually impaired, and new voters found the setup confusing to say the least. As it turned out, the poor design of the Palm Beach County ballots led directly to the election of George W. Bush to the presidency.

As already mentioned, Governor Bush carried Florida by a mere 537 votes. Palm Beach County is majority Democratic in registration, and in fact Gore won 62 percent of the county's vote. But at least 2,000 people in Palm Beach County who planned to vote for Al Gore wound up voting by mistake for another candidate. How did that happen?

Take another look at the picture of the butterfly ballot. There are two holes to the right of candidate Gore's name. There is also, as already mentioned, a small arrow indicating which hole to punch in order to cast a vote for Gore. However, many people, while meaning to vote for Gore, punched the other hole instead, thereby casting their ballot for Reform Party candidate Pat Buchanan.

Now, how do we know that thousands of people who voted for Buchanan actually meant to select Gore? Well, Buchanan won over 3,400 votes in Palm Beach County, by far his best showing anywhere in Florida. Palm Beach County is majority Democratic; it's utterly far-fetched to think that the very conservative Buchanan did better there than in any other Florida county, including the very conservative ones.

Various statistical analyses have been done indicating that somewhere between 400 and 1,400 Palm Beach County voters actually wanted to vote for Buchanan. Therefore, 2,000 to 3,000 voters who wanted to vote for Gore simply punched the wrong hole.[28] Buchanan himself has been quite open about the fact that many of his Palm Beach voters actually meant to vote for Gore.

The math is easy. Officially, Bush won Florida by 537 votes. But it's as certain as can be that Gore lost at least 2,000 votes in Palm Beach County because of the confusion caused by the butterfly ballot.[29] There's really no doubt: if the true will of the people had been followed, Al Gore, for better or for worse, should have been elected president.

What kind of president Al Gore would have been no one knows, of course. It's highly likely that 9/11 would have occurred no matter who was president. The immediate cause of that disaster was the failure of America's intelligence agencies to share data about the hijackers and their movements before September 11, 2001. While the Bush administration might be blamed for not paying enough attention to the possibility of an al-Qaeda strike on the American homeland, it's the CIA and the FBI that must bear the main responsibility for not preventing the fall of the Twin Towers and the attack on the Pentagon. That said, the events that followed 9/11 were very much owned by George W. Bush and Co.

The initial reaction of the Bush administration to 9/11 was commendable. The president did a solid job rallying the nation in the aftermath of that day's shocking events. The armed forces and the CIA undertook a lightning campaign against the terrorist base in Afghanistan, though the failure to provide enough forces to catch Osama bin Laden at Tora Bora in late 2001 was a lamentable oversight by the higher leadership in the White House and the Pentagon. Only eleven years later was justice finally meted out to the notorious al-Qaeda leader.

In any case, Afghanistan was succeeded by Iraq—a war of choice if ever there was one. The decision to go to war with Iraq was an example of groupthink, in which a prevailing position coming down from key communicators above is agreed to by underlings. No one wants to be the nail that sticks out and is hammered down by the powers that be, so the ideas go unchallenged and unchanged. This has led to some of history's biggest blunders.

Unlike fellow Democrat Hilary Clinton, Al Gore adamantly opposed the war in Iraq from the very beginning. No such war would have taken place if he had become president.

And what was the result? Iraq was destabilized, with parts of it becoming terrorist havens. Over four thousand American soldiers, Marines, and airmen were killed. Over thirty thousand more were wounded, some of them terribly maimed or blinded. Almost two hundred thousand Iraqis, many of them civilians, are estimated to have died as a result of the fighting and terrorist attacks. The financial cost of our Iraq involvement—every penny of it borrowed and therefore added to the national debt—stands at over $2 trillion and counting. Although heavy combat for US forces ended some years ago, we are still involved in Iraq to this day. All this, incredible as it may seem, can be blamed on the butterfly ballot.

Recall also that in the 1990s, as a result of the combined efforts of the Clinton administration and the Republicans in Congress, the United States had achieved a balanced budget. Without the war, the financial ledger of the United States would today undoubtedly be in far better shape.

Theresa LePore was vilified for her role in the election of George W. Bush. She was even reduced to tears on national television when she was blamed for the Iraq War. Yet it should be said that there isn't the slightest evidence that she acted in bad faith or was trying to help a particular candidate become president. In her role as supervisor of elections, she did what she thought was best for Palm Beach County's voters. She simply blundered. Her butterfly ballot was confusing enough to enough voters to change the result of a national election. But could this have been foreseen? Doubtful. The real fault lies with our decentralized system of voting in national elections, with most decisions made at the state and county level.

Some would argue that a consistent, nationwide method of voting and counting the people's votes for president, using the best and most up-to-date technology, is badly needed. The argument against nationwide consistency in the voting process is that it would constitute a violation of the principle of federalism. Fair enough. But when a presidential election is upended by a blunder committed by a minor local official, then perhaps the time has come to forego federalism in this one respect simply to protect the national interest.

The unfortunate Ms. LePore will go down as a modern-day Pandora. Pandora's tiny blunder was opening a box she'd been told to keep closed. How could a box contain so many ills? But it did. Theresa LePore created the butterfly ballot. How could such a simple thing change the course of history? But it did. Tiny blunders, big disasters.

6

CHAPPAQUIDDICK:
THE FATAL BRIDGE

The Kennedys are one of America's most prominent political families, rivaled only to a limited extent by the Adamses, the Roosevelts, and the Bushes in our national history. They have also known more tragedy than any political family in modern memory. Of Joseph P. Kennedy Sr.'s four sons, the first, Joseph Jr., was killed on active duty in World War II; the second, John, was elected to the presidency, only to be struck down while in office by an assassin's bullet; the third, Robert, was murdered by an assassin while seeking the office of president. This left the youngest son, Ted, to carry on their legacy.

He nearly died when he broke his neck in a plane crash in 1964. But the youngest Kennedy brother survived into old age and served for almost five decades as a US senator, though never reaching what many saw as his full potential as a political figure and leader. Tragedy would befall him as well, but in his case, it was entirely of his own making. He committed a series of blunders—some small, some perhaps not so—that caused the tragic death of a young woman, while at the same time dooming his presidential ambitions and crushing the hopes of millions of Americans who wanted to see a Kennedy in the Oval Office again.

The question of character has dogged the Kennedys for decades—indeed generations. Joseph Kennedy Sr. made his fortune through stock manipulation and bootlegging during Prohibition. He was a serial womanizer who made little effort to hide his infidelities from his wife and children. He had his own daughter lobotomized in order to keep her from creating any scandal that might affect the family's political fortunes. He was, quite simply, a scoundrel.

Joe Jr., a decorated war hero, was also a bully whose other character flaws were muted by his early death. His brother John was, like his father, a serial adulterer who apparently gave little thought to his long-suffering wife's feelings. Although intelligent, brave, charming, and funny, he was also selfish and quite ready to use others in the furtherance of his own ambitions. Bobby had a reputation for ruthlessness and, while attorney general during John's presidency, showed no compunction about strong-arming anyone, including members of the press, who stood in the way of the Kennedys. Although the father of eleven children, Bobby was also known to stray.

To this day, it remains unexplained why he twice visited Marilyn Monroe's home on the night of her death.

Then there was Ted. As the youngest brother growing up in the shadow of his older siblings, he might have felt compelled to push himself in order to shine. But on the contrary, he again and again displayed laziness, poor judgment, and a lack of character. In 1951 he was expelled from Harvard for cheating. He was later readmitted, no doubt, as a result of his family's power and influence. In the interim, he enlisted in the US Army but had strings pulled by his father to keep him far away from the battlefields of the Korean War. During the 1950s he was repeatedly cited for motor vehicle violations.[30]

Ted inherited his brother John's Senate seat in 1962 when he was only thirty.[31] To this point, his real accomplishments were few and far between. He had risen because of his family name and through the influence brought to bear by his father and older brothers. He was a heavy drinker and, like his brothers, a womanizer. There was at this time some talk of a succession of Kennedy presidents—John would be followed by Robert and Robert by Ted.[32] Such talk had substance when it came to John (who was of course already president) and Robert, but Ted's name was included only because of his fraternal relationship to the other two.

JFK resigned his Senate seat after his election to the presidency in 1960. A Kennedy family friend was appointed to fill the vacancy as placeholder until a special election for the seat was held in 1962.

By 1963, Vice President Lyndon Baines Johnson was becoming ensnared in the TFX and Bobby Baker scandals, and the Kennedys were quietly letting it be known to political insiders that Johnson would not be on the ticket in 1964. With JFK's assassination, the scandals threatening Johnson fell by the wayside. LBJ of course went on to win election to the presidency in his own right in 1964.

To his credit, Ted did go on to master the legislative craft, particularly after he was elected to a full term as senator in 1964. He endured the violent deaths of JFK in 1963 and RFK in 1968, as well as his own near-fatal plane crash in 1964 and two miscarriages suffered by his wife, Joan. But these tragedies did not sober him sufficiently to curb his wild streak. The drinking and partying continued, and it may be that, having suffered so much loss, he was incapable of maturing into a full adult, much less a statesman. Nevertheless, the magic of the Kennedy name was such that Ted was seen as an almost inevitable president, the coming man who would dominate American politics as soon as he got the chance—perhaps as soon as 1972, when the despised Kennedy rival Richard M. Nixon would be up for reelection as president. Then came the night of July 18–19, 1969.

The Kennedys owned a compound at Hyannis Port on Cape Cod in Massachusetts. They also owned land on Martha's Vineyard, an island off Cape Cod's south coast. Chappaquiddick Island is opposite Edgartown on Martha's Vineyard. It is actually connected to Martha's Vineyard by a narrow peninsula, but this land connection is sometimes severed for considerable periods as a result of storms.

On July 18 (two days before Apollo 11's historic landing on the moon), Ted Kennedy checked into the Shiretown Inn in Edgartown. Ostensibly he was there to skipper his boat in the Edgartown Sailing Regatta, an annual event in which the Kennedys, who were well known as sailors, typically participated. The regatta began that afternoon. After the race, Kennedy remained on Chappaquiddick, for there was another event planned for that evening—a private party in which Kennedy and five other married men would be accompanied by six young, attractive, and single females, all of whom had worked for Bobby Kennedy during his 1968 presidential run. They were referred to as the "boiler room girls," because their principal duties were tracking delegate counts during the Democratic primaries. They also performed secretarial work. These young ladies included a twenty-eight-year-old blonde named Mary Jo Kopechne.

Ms. Kopechne had worked for Democratic causes and officeholders since graduating from college in 1962. She had joined Senator Robert Kennedy's staff in 1965. His death devastated her. She was a devout Roman Catholic and did not have a reputation as a party girl.

Nevertheless, she was at the party on that fateful evening of July 18. The party began about nightfall, which comes late in July. Steaks were grilled and eaten, and there appears to have been considerable consumption of alcohol. Mary Jo was later found to have a blood alcohol level of 0.9, which indicated that she had consumed several drinks over a relatively short period.[33] According to Kennedy, he and Kopechne left the party at about 11:30 and drove off in the senator's car, a black Oldsmobile Eighty-Eight.[34] According to Kennedy, he was driving her to the ferry that would bring them back to their hotel rooms in Edgartown. However, Ms. Kopechne left her purse and her room key at the party, which indicates that she was either very forgetful indeed or had simply agreed to spend some time alone with the senator.

Actually, the pair almost certainly left the party about an hour later. Between 12:30 and 12:45 a.m., a deputy sheriff spotted what was probably Kennedy's car near the spot where the accident would take place. Kennedy had to maintain that he and Kopechne had left by 11:30 because the ferry that would have taken them to Edgartown stopped running at midnight. A later departure would indicate that they left the party with a different purpose in mind.

Whether a tryst was about to occur we'll never know because on the way to wherever the senator and Mary Jo were going, an accident occurred—an accident that would profoundly affect both of their lives, as well as the future of American politics and, perhaps, history itself.

Kennedy turned onto Dike Road, a dirt road that lacked any street lighting. In turning onto Dike Road, Kennedy was traveling away from the ferry landing and toward a deserted beach. He later claimed that he had simply taken a wrong turn in the dark.

After driving some distance down Dike Road, Kennedy came upon Dike Bridge, a wooden bridge without guardrails that angled to the left of the straight path the car had been traveling on. By Kennedy's account, he was traveling at about twenty miles per hour. He failed to see the bridge until it was too late and drove the car straight into Poucha Pond, an inlet on the east side of Chappaquiddick Island. The car overturned as it plunged into the water, which was about six feet deep, and came to a rest on its roof.

No one knows exactly what happened over the next several hours because Senator Kennedy's story lacks corroboration on most points, including the most crucial ones. Somehow, he escaped from the car while Mary Jo remained trapped inside. According to Kennedy, he made seven or eight rescue attempts, diving into the water and trying without success to reach her.

One would think that his next move would be to alert the police, who might have been able to get a diver down into the car and rescue the trapped Kopechne. But instead, Kennedy returned to the party and alerted two of his friends, Joseph Gargan and Paul Markham, to what had happened. While returning on foot, Kennedy passed several houses at which he might have stopped and phoned the police.[35]

Gargan, Markham, and Kennedy drove to the scene of the accident, and more attempts were made to rescue Kopechne. These having failed, Kennedy's friends drove him to the ferry landing. Here Kennedy supposedly jumped into the water and swam the five hundred feet to Edgartown. He was, he said later, in shock. Yet during the course of the morning, he made a series of phone calls to longtime family advisors and retainers. One call he did not place was to the police. Nor did Markham or Gargan contact the police. They stated later that, after their attempts to rescue Kopechne had failed, they told Kennedy that he must report the accident and that Kennedy had assured them he would. Whatever the truth of the matter, approximately ten hours passed after the accident before Kennedy reported it to the police.

A police diver was dispatched to the scene and was able to remove the body of Mary Jo in a matter of minutes. She was, of course, dead—but not from drowning. It was apparent from her position that she had survived for some hours, sustained by an air pocket at the top (actually bottom because the car was upside down) of the rear window of the car. She had suffocated in agony after waiting in vain to be rescued. The failure to report the accident had doomed Kopechne, whereas had it been promptly reported, she would almost certainly have survived.

Kennedy claimed that his failure to report the accident was due to shock, exhaustion, and disorientation. Given that soon after the crash he supposedly swam the five hundred feet to Edgartown, and given his extended phone conversations with lawyers and advisors in the morning, it stretches credulity to think that he was incapable of reporting what had happened.

To an objective observer, it appears that he was quite deliberately negligent and callous. Many have speculated that he was intoxicated and couldn't have passed a breathalyzer test that night. Others think that a plan was hatched to have one of his friends take the blame by claiming to be the driver of the car (this, however, would have required the cooperation of the other ten people at the party who had seen Kennedy and Kopechne drive off together). Whatever the truth may be, it doesn't reflect well on Edward Kennedy. Above all, it should be remembered that his failure to promptly report the accident led to the death of Mary Jo Kopechne. Under the circumstances, he could very well have faced a charge of manslaughter.

But as so often happened with the Kennedys, his misdeeds were lightly punished. The Massachusetts authorities had no desire to conduct a full investigation. No autopsy was conducted on the body of Mary Jo Kopechne, an oversight that left many questions unanswered. Kennedy was allowed to plead guilty to leaving the scene of an accident and received a two-month suspended sentence. An inquest was belatedly held in 1970 and concluded that Kennedy's turn onto Dike Road (away from the ferry slip) had been intentional and that his operation of the vehicle had been negligent. But although the inquest found that there was probable cause that Kennedy had committed a crime, the authorities refused to prosecute. Kennedy was reelected to the Senate that November by a large majority and won his next six elections as well. He died in office in 2009.

A week after the tragedy, Kennedy gave a nationally televised speech in which he tried to explain his actions (and nonactions) on the fatal night. It was surprisingly well received by the public (especially, of course, by Democrats) but excoriated by more sophisticated viewers in the media and elsewhere. There simply was no good reason for his waiting until the next day to report the accident. It was not revealed until the inquest held the following year that Mary Jo had probably survived for several hours while trapped in the car. Had this been known in July 1969, perhaps not even the Kennedy name and the family's power and influence could have saved Ted from a criminal indictment and possibly even prison time.

As it was, he got off, for all intents and purposes, scot-free. Five years after Chappaquiddick, when President Gerald Ford pardoned Richard Nixon for the crimes that had caused the latter's resignation, Kennedy made the following statement on the Senate floor: "Do we operate under a system of equal justice under the law, or is there one system of justice for the average citizen and another for the high and mighty?" The hypocrisy and tone-deafness of these words stagger one who reads them today, even after the passage of almost fifty years. But insouciance rather than true contrition has ever been the Kennedy way.

It remains to define Chappaquiddick within the tiny blunder/great disaster theme of this book. Peccadillos such as drinking too much and marital infidelity (or the intention to be unfaithful) were almost certainly among the small blunders Kennedy committed that night. A bigger blunder, of course, was his failure to report the accident, which doomed Mary Jo Kopechne to a horrible death.

Her death was obviously a tragedy for Mary Jo and her family, and it was certainly a great disaster in political terms for Edward Kennedy. We can see clearly that the stain of Chappaquiddick prevented him from seeking the presidency in 1972 and 1976, and severely hampered his unsuccessful attempt to wrest the Democratic nomination for president from Jimmy Carter in 1980.

After 1980, Kennedy never again sought the presidency. Take away Chappaquiddick and he might've beaten Nixon in 1972, while it seems all but certain that in 1976 a scandal-free Ted Kennedy would have easily been elected president.

Was Ted Kennedy's failure to reach the highest office a disaster for the nation and the world? Although Kennedy became a skilled and accomplished legislator, he never displayed real insight into many big problems or the character and judgment required of a great leader. The Kennedys, of course, were surrounded by clever and able advisors. Would a President Edward Kennedy have performed well when confronted with the decline of détente during the 1970s or the crisis that erupted in Iran and doomed the presidency of Jimmy Carter? Would the economic challenges of that time, such as the oil shocks and inflation, have been better managed if he and the Kennedy team had been in power? Would he have been able to inspire the nation and the world as his brothers John and Robert had? We can never answer these questions definitively. But in the harsh light cast on the man by Chappaquiddick, we would have to say that he likely would have fallen short, and perhaps far short, of greatness.

7

VICTORY DISEASE
ON THE TEXAS FRONTIER:
THE BATTLE OF SAN JACINTO

Much has been written relative to this celebrated battle, in which the flower of the Mexican army perished and when Santa Anna was made prisoner, but I beg to introduce the following as given to me by an officer who engaged in it—given in his own words -"The Battle of San Jacinto was probably lost to the Mexicans, owing to the influence of a Mulatto girl (Emily) belonging to Col. Morgan who was closeted in the tent with General Santa Anna at the time the cry was made 'The enemy they come! They come!' & detained Santa Anna so long that order could not be restored readily again."

- William Bollaert, "Texas 1842 by a Traveler"

Arthur Schlesinger Jr., Pulitzer Prize-winning historian and special advisor to President Kennedy, made the observation that kings, generals, and presidents tend to make their biggest mistakes immediately following their greatest victories. History provides many examples of this pattern of self-destruction, which has been found in some of the world's most successful leaders.

This phenomenon bears a close relationship to what the Japanese call *senshoubyou*. In the English-speaking world, it goes by the name of victory disease. It refers to the

95

overconfidence and emotional rush that come after a series of victories, which leads to dangerous overreaching and a carelessness that then results in a major defeat. Several notable examples of these self-inflicted reversals of fortune are summarized as follows:

Napoleon's Russian Campaign

After taking power in France in 1799, Napoleon won a string of victories that gave France control of Belgium, Holland, Italy, Croatia, and a number of states in Germany. He also had dependencies established in Switzerland, Poland, and Spain. Austria, Prussia, and Russia were forced into treaties of alliance.

Feeling betrayed by the czar in 1812, Napoleon made the fatal error of crossing the Niemen River into Russia with the Grand Armée of 600,000 men. Within six months, only 93,000 remained. Napoleon did not lose any pitched battles against the Russians and did manage to capture Moscow. However, the French army was nevertheless destroyed by the intense cold of the Russian winter, food shortages, disease, and harassing attacks from the czar's army.

This epic defeat marked the beginning of the end for Napoleon's empire. He lost such a large part of his army in the Russian campaign that he was never again able to stabilize his regime. He later was defeated by to the Duke of Wellington at the Battle of Waterloo in 1815.

George Armstrong Custer

Even as a West Point cadet, George Armstrong Custer tested the limits of the academy's rules and simple common sense. His record of 726 demerits still stands today as one of worst in the over two-hundred-year history of the academy. Many of the infractions were for practical jokes that he played on his fellow classmates. "Auty," as he was called by his family, seemed to be bored with his studies and graduated last in a class of thirty-four.

However, the raucous and high-spirited behavior that nearly got Custer expelled from West Point on multiple occasions served him well outside the classroom. His bravado helped to make him a highly effective cavalry officer when facing the enemy in the field. He was involved in many of the key battles of the Civil War.

Custer would brazenly charge into battle with "a hoop and a holler" (in Lincoln's words), exposing himself to enemy fire and having one horse after another shot out from under him. Many people spoke of "Custer's luck" because he seemed to always win, and he never suffered any career-ending injuries.

Custer's superiors recognized and rewarded his success. He was promoted to the rank of brevet brigadier general at the age of twenty-three and was called "the Boy General" by the northern press. Because of his daring counterattack that stopped

Jeb Stuart's flanking movement at Gettysburg, he was promoted again to the rank of brevet major general.[36]

Custer never really knew serious defeat until the age of thirty-eight, when he was fighting in the Dakota Territory. Throughout his career he had followed a policy of charging into battle, getting himself into trouble, and then fighting his way out of it. But at the Battle of the Little Big Horn, his famous luck finally ran out.

Custer was warned by Native American scouts not to go into the Greasy Grass Valley because there were "many warriors there." They told him that if he went into the valley on the Little Big Horn River, he would "go home by a way that he did not know." [37]Having never yet tasted defeat, he ignored the warning and was massacred along with all of the men in his detachment.

General Douglas MacArthur

Top of his class and first captain of the Cadet Corps, Douglas MacArthur's classmates at West Point were of two opinions regarding his bearing and behavior: one group believed him to be an insufferable egomaniac, and the other

group believed that anything other than very high self-esteem in someone so extremely talented would have been pure hypocrisy.

Unlike George Custer, Cadet MacArthur applied himself with mature purpose to the academic program: he achieved the third-highest total score in the history of the academy. He was a success with his athletic endeavors as well. He played third base on the baseball team and was student manager of the football team.

In World Wars I and II, MacArthur amassed a long series of victories over his German and Japanese opponents. Considered by historians to be one of the best generals that the United States ever produced, few military leaders ever had such an admirable record.

Perhaps his greatest triumph came in the Korea War with the invasion of Inchon. A large amphibious landing deep behind North Korean emplacements that led to a collapse of the enemy's lines of defense was a masterpiece of military planning. This great victory created a complete reversal of the United Nations' fortunes, which up to that time had been in dire straits.

However, MacArthur's already bloated ego might have become even more inflated by this triumph. When asked what he would do if the Chinese invaded Korea after Inchon, he is reported to have said that he would then initiate "the greatest slaughter in military history." His ego was beginning to interfere with his good judgment.

The Chinese did invade, and they threw Allied forces far back from their forward positions. It was a major reversal of fortunes for the United Nations and a crushing defeat for MacArthur. It took Matthew Ridgway taking over as MacArthur's field commander to eventually stabilize the situation along the 38th parallel.

The Battle of San Jacinto

Nothing but little chickens . . .

- Santa Anna, after the battle of the Alamo, referring to both Texian and Mexican causalities

In the words of one analyst, Antonio López de Santa Anna is remembered today as one of the Western world's most "authentically vainglorious villains." He was guilty of many war crimes and seemed to be psychopathic in his disregard for human life. The generalissimo costumed himself and the

officers around him in flashy uniforms with gold braid, ribbons, and hanging metals like military peacocks. He styled himself as "the Napoleon of the West" and did everything within his power to emulate the French military icon.

El Presidente Santa Anna

In 1834, Santa Anna exerted his power as El Presidente of Mexico and scrapped the federal constitution of 1824. In doing so he also dissolved both the Congress and all the state legislatures and granted himself the full power of a supreme dictatorship.

This commandeering of power without democratic support triggered a rebellion in all seven of the Mexican states, including Texas. The generalissimo then began systematically crushing all opposition in the various states with remarkable cruelty. By February of 1836, all the insurrections had been extinguished except one: the provisional state government of Texas. The time had come for the dictator to march north.

In February, Santa Anna's army of approximately 4,500 men crossed the Rio Grande and began moving toward San Antonio de Béxar. This was earlier than the Texians had expected.

There followed the massacres at the Alamo and Goliad. Santa Anna ordered all survivors shot and their bodies burned. The general saw no particular need for mercy. The brutality, he thought, would send a scare through the English-speaking settlers and send them retreating to the eastern border. "The Runaway Scrape," as it was known, turned into a desperate panic.

The battles against the settlers had been fierce and costly, but they did not pose any real threat to the success to Santa Anna's campaign. Neither Travis at the Alamo nor Fannin at Goliad had any real chance of survival once the battles had become engaged.

At this point Santa Anna had grown accustomed to winning. It happened so often that he was beginning to take it for granted. For two years now, he had defeated one opponent after another in Mexico and in Texas. He reviewed in his mind his victories against the English-speaking settlers. They had been overwhelmingly defeated at San Patricio, Agua Dulce, the Alamo, and Goliad. All surviving Texians, he believed, were demoralized and in retreat.[38]

Based on this series of successes, Santa Anna then engaged in some of history's greatest military miscalculations. From his perspective, it was simply a question of chasing down the scattered remnants of the defeated rebels.

Orders were therefore given to divide his army into four groups, sending them separately across the state like hounds chasing after wounded rabbits. He was informed that the largest group of the retreating rebels seemed to be led by a man named Sam Houston.

Everything in the northern campaign was well in hand for the sad-faced dictator. Only a mopping-up operation remained. It was just a question of running the enemy to ground. One or two more victories and all would be over. Santa Anna would then be able to go home to his haciendas (large estates) in Mexico.

Santa Anna and his officers traveled in style and lived well. He would send his staff out looking for young women to bring to him. He was a known user of opium. He enjoyed rich foods and liquor and would sometimes entertain the young ladies in the privacy of his tent.

Sam Houston, for his part, was not suffering from excessive optimism—or excessive anything. Some of his men had no shoes, and there was not even a single tent in his entire army. The soldiers were eating rations of raw corn, and many of them were suffering from camp fever.

Houston was leading what was little more than an armed mob of seven hundred men. At times they seemed on the verge of mutiny. As one biographer put it, "All new states are infested more or less by a class of noisy, second-rate men who are always in favor of rash and extreme measures. But Texas was absolutely over run by such men."

Rather than taking a stand and fighting against the invading army, Houston insisted on retreating farther and farther into East Texas. "We cannot fight the enemy 10 to 1 in their home territory." He was looking for just the right time and just the right place, hoping that his enemy would make a fatal mistake.

The officers in his ragtag army accused Houston of cowardice and questioned his competence. Criticism came down from above as well. During his retreat, he received a note from his main political rival, David Burnet, president of the Republic of Texas, which stated the following: "Sir: The enemy is laughing you to scorn. You must fight."

Angry at what he considered to be ill-informed interference, Houston put the dispatch in his pocket and went about his business. In response to those talking insurrection against him, he had two graves dug and posted notices that they would be filled with mutineers.

General Sam Houston

During this time, Santa Anna was moving in a leisurely fashion across the plains of East Texas. Based on the lack of resistance and his earlier successes, he was continuing to jump to conclusions about his "beaten" enemy. They were scattered and demoralized and unable to mount an effective defense. It did not concern "the Napoleon of the West" that his large army was spread out widely across the territory and had not been concentrated to face the still dangerous Texian army.

Finally, after weeks of hardship and bad luck for Houston and his army, a ray of hope penetrated the darkness. Santa Anna stumbled into a trap of his own making.

Maybe it was the result of overconfidence. Maybe it was from the dreamy spin of his opium use. Or maybe it was the distraction of the multiracial Emily West (Morgan), later known as the "Yellow Rose of Texas," after all.

The Napoleon of the West placed his army so that it was hemmed in on three sides by water: Buffalo Bayou to the north, the San Jacinto River and McCormick's Lake to the east, and Galveston Bay on the south, with the Texian army on the remaining side.

When Houston learned of his enemy's disposition through an intercepted dispatch, he was ecstatic. "We have the monkey up a tree," he said to one of his officers. "With this we may win the war." General Houston had his key scout Deaf Smith cut down his army's one escape route, the bridge over Vince's Bayou. The removal of the bridge was announced to the Texian troops, and the awareness spread from man to man. The destruction of the bridge meant that there was no escape from the battlefield for the men on either side. The time of reckoning had arrived. The two armies would be locked in deadly and decisive combat.

On April 20, 1836, Houston moved his troops quietly across Buffalo Bayou on rickety boats. He then located them at the fork of the bayou and the San Jacinto River. He positioned his troops in thick oak groves along the edge of the bayou and told them that they could build small campfires for breakfast. Cows had been found in local fields and then slaughtered. Their meat was cooked over the fires on green sticks. That night there was skirmishing between the two armies but no major engagement.

Many on both sides expected Houston to attack at dawn. But the general slept late, and no attack was ordered. When would he attack? What was he waiting for? Many of Houston's officers felt a ripe opportunity was being left to go begging. They believed that now was the time to attack.

Houston called a council of war and permitted the officers to advance one plan and then another. He listened to their haranguing and complaints and then, saying nothing, he simply walked off, leaving the issue unresolved. There was much grumbling among his men about what seemed to be his lack of resolution.

George Hockley, one of Houston's top aides, approached him and asked, "Why don't you tell them your plan, General? You could stop all of this quarreling."

His answer contained the key to Houston's personal thoughts and the inner core of his entire campaign:

"Hockley, I've kept my own council from the start, and I keep it now. I grant you we could have won. (If we had attacked earlier). Probably. But we would have done it with heavy losses. When I attack, I will win and I will win without losing a dozen men. I retreated from Guadalupe to the Brazos and advanced from the Brazos to the San Jacinto without losing a man or an animal. The stakes are too great, Hockley, and our forces too small, for me to take any chances. If I took a needless risk with our few men merely for the sake of a pleasant atmosphere in our camp, I would prove myself as great an enemy of Texas as Santa Anna.

"Believe me, Hockley in all our 700 odd men, those I can trust can be counted on my two hands (holding his large hands out in front of him). If it's any comfort to you, you are among them. But with all our hotheads, so hungry for personal glory and so impatient with the processes of war, I cannot risk my plans being known: Patience, Hockley, patience and fortitude."

The burden of great worry had weighed heavily upon the general. His weathered face showed signs of the stress of the long campaign. But still he stayed true to his unspoken plan and kept his own counsel. He turned and walked away.

Without prior warning, at 3:30 in the afternoon on April 21, 1836, General Sam Houston gave the order for his men to assemble into fighting ranks. The order came as a well-kept surprise. Everyone on both sides of the line had expected an attack at dawn. Everyone was wrong.

The sun was starting its downward arc, and afternoon shadows were growing long across the spring grass. The Mexican army would be facing into the setting sun. The attack that Santa Anna and his officers had expected at dawn had not come. Perhaps they thought it would never come from their beaten enemy. It was time to relax. Many in the Mexican army would be taking their afternoon siestas.

Houston rode his large white stallion back and forth in front of his troops. He raised his sword and signaled for the advance to begin. In the back, a lone flute played an old romantic ballad—an odd choice for a battle hymn, but maybe it was the only song the player knew:

> Come to my bower and lie down with me
>
> Come to my bower shaded by the tree
>
> There in the roses and lilacs we'll lie
>
> You'll have a blush on your cheeks

But a smile in your eye.

Surprise was total. There was immediate disarray among the Mexican troops, who scattered in retreat. Furthermore, the Texians had the advantage of very accurate long rifles that were effective at a considerable range. The smooth-bore British Brown Bess used by the Mexican army was only accurate at a short distance against a concentrated mass of troops. The broken-field combat of Houston's army made the muskets ineffective.

But the biggest advantage Houston's men may have had was their possession of Bowie knives, sharpened to a razor edge. In close-quarter combat, they were a deadly and effective weapon.

As Houston expected, Santa Anna was in his tent asleep, or perhaps distracted when the attack began. He finally came out from his quarters wearing red carpet slippers and rubbing his eyes.

Santa Anna surrenders to Sam Houston

Santa Anna called for his drummer to beat the drums to assemble his troops. The drummer replied that he had been shot.

The generalissimo called in anger for his bugler to sound assembly. He too called out that he had been shot. Santa Anna then saw one of his best divisions in full retreat. His army in collapse, the Napoleon of the West jumped on a black horse and rode away, looking desperately for a way to escape.

In eighteen minutes, the battle had turned into a rout and then into a terrible slaughter. Houston's soldiers did not allow many of the Mexicans to surrender. The men, most of them farmers in peacetime, had turned into maniacal killers shouting, "Remember the Alamo!" and "Remember Goliad!" When some of Houston's officers tried to stem the carnage at McCormick's Lake, they too were threatened.

Order was finally restored. Santa Anna, who was trying to pass himself off as an ordinary soldier, was identified and brought before a wounded Houston. The general's leg had been shattered by a bullet and he was resting under a tree. Most in the Texian army wanted to hang the dictator, the man who had massacred so many of their fellow Texians. However, exercising the restraint and good judgment that had just won a pivotal battle, Houston decided to spare the dictator's life. He needed a living Santa Anna to serve as a bargaining chip in peace negotiations with the Mexican government.[39]

In summary, Santa Anna had frittered away what should have been an easy and conclusive victory. If he had won at San Jacinto, he would have banished the *Norte Americanos* from the Mexican province of Texas for a long period of time. However, distraction, overconfidence, lack of discipline, sexual self-indulgence, or some mixture of all four of these, along with a little bad luck, had led to his downfall.

The Japanese would call it *senshoubyou*. But by whatever name, it is remembered by historians as one of the world's most decisive battles. Because of it and events that followed, the United States would stretch from the Atlantic to the Pacific Ocean. For good or for ill, Manifest Destiny would be realized. And the world as we know it would never be the same again.

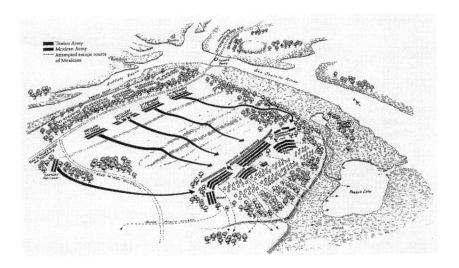

FROM LONG, LONG AGO

Jared Knott

8

WHEN ANCIENT EMPIRES CLASHED

O man, whoever you are and wherever you come from, for I know you will come, I am Cyrus who won the Persians their empire. Do not, therefore, begrudge me this bit of earth that covers my bones.

- From the tomb of Cyrus the Great

Cyrus the Great, king of the Persians, lord of Asia, and the liberator of the Jews from their Babylonian captivity, was the first great conqueror-hero in history. Before Alexander the Great, Caesar, Genghis Khan, Tamerlane, and Napoleon, there was Cyrus.

Cyrus founded the Persian state (now Iran) over 2,500 years ago. Not much is known for certain about his origins or early life. Just before 550 BC, he was the king of Anshan (in what is now southern Iran) and a vassal of the king of the Medes, Astyages.[40]

Media in the mid-sixth century BC was the largest kingdom west of China. The Median Empire stretched from eastern Asia Minor (now Turkey) to the lands that we know today as Afghanistan and Pakistan. A little before 550 BC, Cyrus rebelled against Astyages and defeated him after three years of war. Cyrus was now king of the Persians and the Medes (Persians and Medes were closely related peoples, rather like, for example, Germans and Austrians).

After his victory over Astyages, Cyrus turned his eyes westward toward the other great powers of the day, all of which viewed his sudden rise with apprehension. These powers were Egypt and Babylon of ancient fame, and the kingdom of Lydia in Asia Minor, ruled by King Croesus. Croesus was renowned for his wealth; the saying "as rich as Croesus" refers to him. It was in Lydia that gold coins were first minted.

Croesus took the lead in forming an alliance against Cyrus among Lydia, Babylonia, and Egypt. He even persuaded Sparta, the strongest Greek state of the day, to join. He considered taking the offensive against Cyrus rather than waiting for the Persians to attack.

Croesus sent emissaries to the famous Oracle of Delphi in Greece, hoping to receive a prophecy that would support his plan to attack Cyrus. To the question the Lydians put to the oracle—whether to go to war with Persia or not—the pythoness (the priestess who voiced the prophecies) replied, "If Croesus attacks the Persians, he will destroy a mighty empire." Delighted by this answer, Croesus assembled his army and marched forth to meet Cyrus in battle.

The two armies met at the river Halys in Asia Minor. A long and bloody battle followed, ending in a draw. Winter was approaching, and Croesus decided to return to his capital, Sardis, and disband his army for the winter, which was the practice in those days. Today we would call it "going into winter quarters." But Cyrus had other ideas.

One of the qualities that made Cyrus great was his imagination and willingness to defy conventional wisdom. Fighting a winter campaign in the mountains was unheard of in those days. But this is exactly what Cyrus decided to do. Instead of returning to Persia to rest and replenish his army for the spring campaign to come, he marched into Lydia and advanced on Sardis, taking Croesus completely by surprise. A second battle was fought outside the city walls, and after a great slaughter on both sides, the Lydians were compelled to retreat into the city. Cyrus now laid siege to Sardis.

For the Persians, there remained the problem of how to breach the walls and enter the city. A long siege was out of the question, for the Persians were far from home and lacking supplies that would sustain them if they tried to starve Sardia into submission. As it was winter, the Persians couldn't live off the land, the crops having already been harvested. A quick capture of the city seemed impossible since the Persians had no siege equipment such as catapults that would allow them to break down the walls.

Had Cyrus led his army on a fool's errand? Were the Persians doomed to abandon the siege and retreat across the mountains to their home country, with all the hardships and losses that such a withdrawal, especially when conducted in winter conditions, would entail? It seemed possible that the Persian Empire would fall almost before it was born, and that Cyrus would go down in history as just another would-be conqueror who tempted fate and perished ignominiously through hubris and miscalculation.

Croesus certainly must have thought so as he looked down on the Persians from the walls of his capital. No doubt he recalled the prophecy of Delphi and imagined that a mighty empire was on the brink of destruction. A mighty empire was indeed about to be destroyed, but not in the way Croesus imagined, for now a small blunder occurred that was to change the course of the war between Lydia and Persia, and of history itself.

The citadel of Sardis stood upon Mount Tmolus and was considered impregnable. One part of the fortifications was a sheer rock face, impossible to climb and therefore left unguarded. But there was a hidden path, impossible to see from the outside, by which one could travel from ground level to the fortress above. One day a Lydian soldier dropped his helmet outside the walls and retrieved it by traveling down the path, after which he returned back up again. One of Cyrus's soldiers, a man called Hyroeades, observed the Lydian soldier and thereby discovered the one weak spot in the defenses of Sardis. The next day, the Persians entered the citadel via the hidden track, and the city was taken.

So at least is the story told by the Greek historian Herodotus, who is sometimes called "the father of history." Herodotus had (and still has) a reputation for liking colorful stories, but his account of the fall of Sardis is the oldest one we have, closer in time to the actual event than any other. Thus, it deserves, perhaps, the benefit of the doubt. In any case we know that Cyrus took the city and added the lands of Croesus to his own empire. As he witnessed the fall of his capital and the end of his mighty empire, Croesus realized that the Oracle of Delphi had prophesied correctly—he simply had not imagined that his empire would be the one to be destroyed.

The fate of Croesus is uncertain. According to Herodotus, Cyrus spared his life and made the former king his close companion and advisor. Other sources say that Cyrus had Croesus put to death.

Cyrus next marched against mighty Babylon, which fell to him in 539 BC. The Jews had been held captive in Babylon since 587 BC, when the Babylonian king Nebuchadnezzar, familiar to us through the Old Testament, conquered Judea and forced the people to leave the land and go into exile. By proclamation, Cyrus freed the Jews and allowed them to return to their ancestral home in Palestine.

Cyrus had meant to conquer Egypt as well, but before he could do so, he died while fighting the fierce Massagetae tribesmen, who lived as nomads in the far eastern regions of his empire. His son Cambyses eventually subdued the ancient kingdom of the Nile. The last of Croesus's allies, the Spartans, together with the other peoples of Greece, became the target of Cambyses's successor Darius and Darius's son Xerxes. The Persian campaigns against the Greeks had a much different outcome, but those events are another story for another time.

Cyrus the Great was known as the father of the Persian people and is so regarded in Iran even today. He built the greatest empire the world had known up to that time, and one that has rarely been surpassed since. Many of the people he conquered viewed him as a liberator, for he was a just and tolerant ruler. Yet Cyrus probably owed his fame to the fact that an unknown Lydian solider dropped his helmet outside the walls of Sardis.

Jared Knott

9

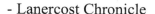

THE DEATH
OF A RANDY KING

Alexander did not spend his decade as a widower alone: he used never to forbear on account of season nor storm, nor for perils of flood or rocky cliffs, but would visit none too creditably nuns or matrons, virgins or widows as the fancy seized him, sometimes in disguise.

- Lanercost Chronicle

ALEXANDER II.

Alexander III, king of the Scots, was one of the greatest Scottish monarchs, his fame exceeded only by that of Kenneth MacAlpin (the semi legendary founder of the Scottish kingdom), David I, and Robert the Bruce. His reign, which lasted from 1249 to 1286, was the last of the Dunkeld dynasty, which began in 1034 and included such kings as Macbeth and David I.

Alexander succeeded to the throne at the age of seven, following the death of his father, King Alexander II, and was crowned at Scone on July 13, 1249. On December 26, 1251, he married Margaret of England, the eleven-year-old daughter of

King Henry III (the son of "Bad King John," who signed Magna Carta).

At a meeting between the two kings in 1255, Henry III attempted to force the young Alexander to recognize him as overlord of Scotland, but Alexander refused to submit. Alexander's youth was dominated by a struggle between two noble factions—one pro-English, one not—for control of the boy king and the government of Scotland. In 1257, Alexander was kidnapped by the anti-English group, but a compromise was worked out, and the peace of the realm maintained.

Alexander became king in fact as well as name when he turned twenty-one in 1262. At once he declared his intention of winning for Scotland the Western Isles (the Hebrides and the Isle of Man), something his father had tried and failed to do. The isles had been ruled by Norway for centuries, a legacy of the Viking Age when Scandinavian fleets dominated the North Sea and terrorized the coastal towns of Scotland, Ireland, England, and France.

At the time, Norway was ruled by King Haakon IV (reigned 1217–1263). Norway was at the height of its power and influence, and Haakon's fleet was the largest in northern Europe. Nevertheless, Alexander boldly laid claim to the islands and then sent an expedition to attack the Isle of Skye. Furious and determined to teach Alexander a lesson, in 1263 Haakon personally led a force that might have been as large as 200 ships and 15,000 men to the Western Isles.

Just how clever and resourceful the young Alexander was now becoming evident. In the summer of 1263, Haakon's fleet anchored off the Isle of Arran. Unable to meet such a large force on equal terms, Alexander began negotiations. He artfully prolonged these until autumn, when stormy weather set in. When some of Haakon's ships were driven aground off Largs in the Firth of Forth and the Norwegian forces made a landing, the Scots launched a surprise attack on them (October 2, 1263). The Battle of Largs was a draw, but the lateness of the season forced Haakon to return to Norway. The Norwegian king died at Orkney while on his way home, a great stroke of luck from Alexander's point of view.

Alexander conquered the Hebrides in 1264, and by the Treaty of Perth in 1266, Norway ceded the islands to Scotland in return for a sum of money. In 1275, Alexander definitely won the Isle of Man for Scotland after the Scots were victorious at the Battle of Ronaldsway. The young king had added the Western Isles to his possessions, succeeding where his father Alexander II had failed.

After Alexander came to the throne, his relations with England and his father-in-law, Henry III, were amicable. This state of affairs continued under Henry's son, the formidable warrior King Edward I (who succeeded his father in 1272 and was later to become known as the "Hammer of the Scots"). Alexander and Margaret had three children—two sons, Alexander (born 1264) and David (born 1272), and a daughter, Margaret (born 1261), who married King Eric II of Norway in 1281. At the time of his daughter's marriage, Alexander III was just forty years old, and Scotland was prosperous and at peace.

Then, a series of disasters struck.

First Alexander's youngest son, David, died. Then his other son, Alexander, the heir apparent, died in 1284. Prince Alexander had been married but died childless. The king's other child, Margaret of Norway, died in childbirth in 1283, leaving an infant daughter, also named Margaret and later called the Maid of Norway. In Scotland the succession passed through the male line, but Alexander III persuaded the Scottish nobles to name little Margaret his successor. However, an infant girl as heir presumptive was leaving much to chance, so King Alexander decided to remarry and, hopefully, produce more sons.

Queen Margaret, the mother of the king's three children, had died in 1275 when she was not yet thirty-five years old. That life in the Middle Ages could be cruel and harsh is clearly revealed by the many early deaths in Alexander's family. Since the queen's death, Alexander had not been lacking in female companionship. According to the *Chronicle of Lanercost*, a contemporary history, he was a womanizer who "used never to forebear on account of season or storm, nor for perils of flood or rocky cliffs but would visit, not too creditably, matrons and nuns, virgins and widows, by day or by night as the fancy seized him." He was, in plain English, a randy king who took his pleasure with any woman he fancied.

Now, with his wife and all his children dead, the king resolved to remarry. He chose as his new wife Yolande de Dreux, the daughter of a French count. She was also related to the Capetian kings of France. Alexander and Yolande were married in October or November of 1285 (sources differ). She was twenty-two; he was forty-four.

In March 1286, Queen Yolande was staying at Kinghorn on the Firth of Forth, across the water from Edinburgh. The king spent the day of March 18 in council with his nobles. When their business was finished and the king had dined, he resolved to set out at once to see the queen, whose birthday was the next day. It was a dark and stormy night. *The Chronicle of Lanercost* tells us what happened:

The protracted feast having come to an end, he would neither be deterred by stress of weather nor yield to the persuasion of his nobles, but straightaway hurried along the road to Queensferry, in order to visit his bride. . . . For she was then staying at Kinghorn.

When he arrived at the village near the crossing, the ferry master warned him of the danger, and advised him to go back; but when [the king] asked him in return whether he was afraid to die with him: 'By no means,' quoth he, 'it would be a great honor to share the fate of your father's son.' Thus he [i.e., the king] arrived at the burgh of Inverkeithing, in profound darkness, accompanied by only three esquires. The manager of his saltpans, a married man of that town, recognising him by his voice, called out: 'My lord, what are you doing here in such a storm and such darkness? Often, I have tried to persuade you that your nocturnal rambles will bring you no good. Stay with us, and we will provide you with decent fare and all that you want till morning light.' 'No need for that' said [the king] with a laugh, 'but provide me with a couple of bondmen, to go afoot as guides to the way.'

And it came to pass that when they had proceeded two miles, one and all lost all knowledge of the way, owing to the darkness; only the horses, by natural instinct, picked out the hard road. While they were thus separated from each other, the esquires took the right road; but [the king] at length . . . fell from his horse, and bade farewell to his kingdom in the sleep of Sisara.[41]

Alexander's horse had presumably stumbled and the king had been thrown, possibly falling off a cliff. His dead body was found on the morning of March 19. Soon after his death, it was learned that Queen Yolande was pregnant, but either she suffered a miscarriage or the child was stillborn or died in infancy. Scotland was without a leader. Alexander's sole surviving heir, his granddaughter, Margaret, the Maid of Norway, thus became queen of the Scots. She left Norway for Scotland in 1290 but died on the way at Orkney, just as her great-grandfather Haakon IV had done while returning from Scotland to Norway in 1263. She was only seven years old.

The death of Alexander III plunged Scotland into a difficult period known as the Wars of Scottish Independence, which lasted from 1296 to 1357. This was the time of William Wallace, Robert the Bruce, and the Battle of Bannockburn, a famous Scottish victory of 1314. The earlier part of this history is covered, with occasional accuracy, in the Mel Gibson movie Braveheart.

For the next 250 years, until the Scottish king James VI became king of England as James I, Scotland rarely knew the peace and prosperity it had achieved under Alexander III. King Alexander, keen to be with his new young bride, had committed a small blunder by riding out on a pitch-black and stormy night. The accident that followed and ended his reign was a great disaster for Scotland, one that took the Scots centuries from which to recover.[42]

10

THE LOST TREASURE
OF BAD KING JOHN

Somewhere near Lincolnshire and Norfolk in 1216, 'Bad King John'—a monarch so incompetent and evil that his name is still preserved in East Anglia folklore, films and nursery rhymes—was running from his enemies. When his army tried to cross the mudscapes of the tidal estuary that Britons call the Wash, rising waters caught his baggage train. The wagons and their contents, including the king's treasure, were lost. King John of England, "Bad King John" as he is often called, reigned from 1199 to 1216.

He is perhaps best known as the king who signed Magna Carta, the foundational document of English (and therefore American) liberty. He's also the king referred to in the tales of Robin Hood. Although generally considered to be the worst monarch ever to reign over England (even worse than Richard III, who, by the way, wasn't as bad as Shakespeare made him out to be—but that's another story), Bad King John was probably a more complex figure than popular histories would have us believe. His reputation has undergone various permutations over the centuries. The current consensus is that he was a capable soldier and administrator, though cruel and capricious.

It seems worthwhile to examine King John's background and reign before we discuss the tiny blunder that caused a great disaster for this particular monarch.

John was the youngest son of King Henry II (reigned 1154–1189), one of England's greatest kings, and his queen, Eleanor of Aquitaine, the widow of the king of France, who, when she married Henry, was the wealthiest woman in Europe and probably the most accomplished as well (she was well educated, was a patron of the arts, and had even gone on a crusade to the Holy Land).[43]

Bad King John

John's oldest brother, Henry, died when John was a teenager. This made Richard—later King Richard the Lionhearted—Henry II's heir. Another brother, Geoffrey, also stood between John and the throne. Probably no one thought that John would ever become king considering that he had two older brothers ahead of him in the succession. Nevertheless, John eventually did ascend to the throne, and at a relatively young age (he was in his early thirties when he became king).

Richard the Lionhearted, as most people know, was a great warrior.[41] Soon after succeeding his father, he led a crusade to the Holy Land (1189–1192), where he battled the famous Saladin. Victorious in battle but unable to recover

Jerusalem from Saladin, Richard set out for England but was captured by Leopold V, duke of Austria, who had a personal grudge against the king. During Richard's captivity, John began a rebellion against his brother; he also joined the king of France in attempting to bribe Richard's captors to keep the king imprisoned.

Nevertheless, on his return, Richard pardoned John and confirmed him as his heir (their brother, Geoffrey, had died in 1186). In 1199, Richard was killed by a crossbowman while besieging a castle in France[40] John then became King of England and of large parts of France and Ireland, which together constituted the so-called Angevin Empire founded by Henry II.

John's reign proved a time of trouble for England. On his accession he found himself at war with King Philip II Augustus of France (reigned 1180–1223) and with his own nephew, Arthur of Brittany, the son of his brother Geoffrey. Both men had designs on John's French possessions. A truce was patched up in 1200, but war broke out anew in 1202. At the same time, the English barons demanded that John recognize their privileges or else they would refuse to serve in France. This was the beginning of the struggle between the English monarchy and its subjects that was to continue off and on for centuries.

After winning an initial victory at the Battle of Mirebeau on August 1, 1202, the fortunes of war deserted John. In 1203, he had Arthur of Brittany, whom he had captured, put to death. Some chronicles say that John killed his nephew with own hands. In any case, the murder of Arthur further darkened John's reputation and damaged his popularity among his subjects, especially in his French possessions.

In 1204, Philip conquered most of John's French lands. Then John came into conflict with Pope Innocent III (England was of course still a Catholic country in those days) over the election of Stephen Langton as archbishop of Canterbury (Langton, by the way, is credited with arranging the Bible in the form we have today). This conflict was even more portentous than the breakdown of John's empire in France, for it triggered the confrontation between king and nobles that led directly to the signing of Magna Carta.

John preferred a different candidate for Canterbury and refused to accept the election of Langton. In response, the pope first laid England under an interdict. Then, after prolonged negotiations failed, he excommunicated John and absolved England from its from allegiance to him. This finally brought John to heel. Langton was installed as archbishop in July 1213, whereupon he absolved John (in effect ending the king's excommunication and telling his subjects to resume their allegiance). John, however, was required to swear an oath that the liberties enjoyed by English subjects under his father would be restored, and that any unjust laws he had made would be repealed. But John was better at making promises than keeping them.

A power struggle between king and archbishop ensued, a struggle reminiscent of the one between John's father, Henry II, and Archbishop Thomas Beckett. In 1213, Langton summoned a council of clergy and barons to confer about the king's inequities. At the same time, John also summoned representatives of both nobles and commons for consultations. Historians have seen these councils as the forerunners of Parliament.

Be that as it may, the firm leadership of Langton and, crucially, the support he received from the barons decided the issue in the archbishop's favor. The conflict between Henry II and Archbishop Beckett had been decided when four barons who supported the king murdered the archbishop in Canterbury Cathedral. But John, thanks to his tyrannous ways, was opposed by most of his nobles. The combined pressure of Archbishop Langton and the barons forced John to put his seal upon Magna Carta at Runnymede on June 15, 1215, a historic event in the long struggle for liberty and democracy.

Rather than accept this compromise, John persuaded the Pope (who had switched to John's side because the settlement of 1213 had made John, and with him England, the pope's fief) to annul Magna Carta. The barons thereupon began a civil war.

Meanwhile Philip of France had won a decisive victory over the English at Bouvines (July 27, 1214). The French now came to the aid of the English barons against John. In 1216, Philip's son, Louis, entered London with a French army, the last foreign prince but one to do so.

John was down but not out. He began a vigorous counteroffensive against the rebels and the French. But while campaigning in the east of England, he fell ill with dysentery. There were of course no antibiotics in those days, and the king grew weaker as he marched his army from Bishop's Lynn (now King's Lynn) toward Newark Castle, where he hoped to rest and reorganize his forces.

John's baggage train included all of his portable wealth—gold plate, coins, and the crown jewels of England. With his capital occupied by his enemies, there was nothing for John to do but carry his treasure about with him; the alternative would have been to let it fall into the hands of the barons or the French. A penniless king would have been deserted by his mercenary troops and even by many of his English followers.

The king's march skirted the "Wash," a vast area of tidal marshes and mudflats, treacherous to cross. But he ordered his baggage train to travel by a causeway directly across the Wash—whether to save time, for safety's sake, or both is uncertain. In any case the order amounted to a tiny blunder that led, unfortunately for John (and for the English treasury), to a big disaster.

Safety was a matter of timing. The Wash was traversable only during low tide. The horse-drawn carts containing the treasures of England were too slow moving across the causeway to safety. The incoming tide swallowed up the heavily laden carts, and, according to most accounts, the whole of the treasure was lost, disappearing into the mud.[45]

Some accounts say that, rather than taking the roundabout way, John traveled with his wealth across the Wash and that he barely escaped suffering the same fate as his wealth. Traveling with his treasure would have made sense in that John probably couldn't trust even his closest retainers, who might well have absconded with it in his absence.

It has been estimated that the lost treasure would be worth about $72,000,000 in today's money. We shall probably never know. If the treasure truly was lost in the Wash, it would today be sitting somewhere under twenty feet or more of mud and virtually impossible to find and recover.

The loss of the treasure was a huge disaster. The king could no longer pay his troops. Supplies would have to be obtained by requisitioning, a means sure to provoke resistance and render the king even more unpopular with his subjects. For John, the loss of his treasure—England's treasure—was the final straw. His illness worsened, and he died just five days after all his wealth had been swallowed by the mud.

John compares poorly to his father, a truly great king, and to his brother, the warrior Richard. He was not without ability as a soldier and a king, but his personal defects overshadowed his virtues. His tumultuous reign ended on a bizarre note as a tiny blunder precipitated a great disaster—the loss of a king's treasure in gold, coins, and jewels to the bottom of the wash.

King Richard The Lionheart

TECHNICAL SNAFUS
AND MISCALCULATIONS

11

MEDICAL MISTAKES

Based on an analysis of prior research, the Johns Hopkins study estimates that more than 250,000 Americans die each year from medical errors.

- "Health News" from NPR

We come now to two chapters that vary our theme somewhat. Rather than tiny blunders leading to big disasters, "Medical Mistakes" and "Political Mistakes" deal with some might-have-beens of history—tiny blunders that have left posterity wondering what might have happened had they been avoided. In "Medical Mistakes," I focus first on the father of our country, George Washington, and the circumstances surrounding his death.

I then discuss two people who could possibly have changed the course of American history in the twentieth century. The first is Huey Long, the Louisiana Kingfish. The second is Rosemary Kennedy, the sister of John and Robert Kennedy. Rosemary Kennedy's ability to become a changemaker is more speculative in nature, but still worth exploring. We begin with George Washington.

George Washington

In the late afternoon of December 12, 1799, returned home after several hours riding around his property, Mount Vernon. During his ride, the weather had been foul, the temperature slightly below freezing with intermittent rain and snow.

The next day, Friday the 13th, Washington felt a cold coming on. During the day, he developed a severe sore throat and hoarseness. However, he did not take to his bed and carried on as usual, refusing any treatment.

Washington awoke in the early hours of December 14th. His condition had worsened. He could hardly swallow and had trouble breathing. Doctors were sent for: Washington's personal physician, Dr. James Craik; Dr. Elisha Cullen

George Washington

Dick; and Dr. Gustavus Richard Brown. These men were capable medical practitioners, at least for their time. Of course, medical science in the late eighteenth century had hardly advanced from the days of Hippocrates and Galen centuries earlier.

At his own direction, Washington had already been bled, a procedure that in his day was a common treatment for many illnesses. The attending physicians proceeded to bleed him further. They drew almost half of the blood from his body.

For a man of Washington's age (he was almost sixty-eight years old), such blood loss was bound to be dangerous and possibly fatal. That older people often fared less well when bled than younger ones was known even at the time, yet the doctors proceeded.

Washington's condition worsened. He appeared to be suffocating. Dr. Dick recommended that Washington's trachea be perforated, a procedure much like the tracheotomy doctors perform today. But the other two physicians vetoed the idea. Perforating the trachea was a relatively new procedure, but it had already saved lives. In retrospect we can see that it represented a last chance to keep Washington alive. But nothing was done, and the ex-president died in considerable agony that night.

The nature of Washington's illness remains in dispute. He clearly suffered from an acute swelling of the larynx and epiglottis, probably brought on by a bacterial infection in the throat. The swelling apparently was severe enough to cut off the airway leading to his lungs, causing death by suffocation.

In the absence of antibiotics (not discovered until nearly a century and a half later), Washington would have had to rely on his own body's powers of resistance to overcome the illness. Yet his ability to fight the disease was fatally compromised by the excessive bleeding performed by his doctors. Had he not been bled and had Dr. Dick been allowed to perforate the trachea, Washington might have had a fighting chance at survival. But medical mistakes sealed his doom.

Washington's days as commander in chief of the Continental Army and president of the fledgling United States were behind him at the time of his death. But he hadn't retired completely from public affairs. In fact, he planned to become involved in the election of 1800, to help to reelect John Adams to a second term. Whether Washington would have affected the outcome of the election, in which Thomas Jefferson defeated Adams by seventy-three electoral votes to sixty-five, is of course unknown.

Jefferson's victory heralded the end of the Federalist Party and inaugurated a sixty-year period in which his party, the Democratic-Republicans (forerunners of today's Democrats) dominated American politics.

The key state in 1800 was New York, which voted for Jefferson after having supported Adams in 1796. The switch in New York's vote was due to the machinations of Aaron Burr, Jefferson's running mate. Whether Washington could have done anything to counter Burr is perhaps unlikely. But we'll never know because medical mistakes removed Washington from the national scene before any votes were cast.

Huey Long

Huey Long would have been only fifty-five years old in 1948. Harry Truman won that year's election despite a three-way split in the Democratic Party, with Strom Thurmond running on the Dixiecrat ticket and carrying four states with thirty-nine electoral votes. Could Long have done better than

Thurmond, perhaps tilting the election to the Republican Thomas Dewey? We'll never know.

Despite his remarkable abilities and his successes as governor of Louisiana, Huey Long achieved nothing of substance on the national scene. His share-the-wealth plan has been dismissed by economists as pure pie in the sky. Had he survived, it's likely that his power and popularity would have diminished rather than grown. But he might have been a major disruptive force in America during a critical time in our history. Just how disruptive will always be a matter of speculation since medical mistakes prevented him from fulfilling whatever his destiny would otherwise have been.

Huey Long is almost forgotten today, at least outside of his home state of Louisiana, but in his lifetime his impact on America was both spectacular and substantial. Had he lived longer, he might have played a big role in American and world history.

Huey Long was a man of tremendous natural ability. He was also corrupt, abrasive, and at times sadistic. He made many enemies. Unlike many white southerners of his time, he was not a racist, though he was constrained throughout his political career by the racial attitudes of his time. He rose to become a national figure before he turned forty. Had he not been cut down by an assassin's bullet at age forty-two, he might have become president. Let's briefly examine his life and career.

Long was born in rural northern Louisiana in 1893. The area of Louisiana he grew up in suffered from extreme poverty, and the people there harbored a deep dislike for their more well-to-do fellow citizens in the southern part of the state and the plutocracy that marked Gilded Age America. Today we tend to think of the South as a deeply conservative place, but during

Long's childhood and youth, Winn Parish, Louisiana, his home territory, was a stronghold of the Populist Party. Strange as it may seem today, in the election of 1912, Winn Parish gave a majority of its votes to the Socialist candidate for president, Eugene Debs.

The Long family was a large one—Huey had eight siblings. His family was, by Winn Parish standards, fairly well off, but he grew up resenting his "betters" as much as his poorer neighbors did. This attitude was to remain with him throughout his life and affected his political career and persona.

Highly intelligent but unable to afford college, Long embarked upon a career as a traveling salesmen. Eventually he entered Tulane University Law School in New Orleans, and after attending for only a year, he was able to pass the state bar exam, a remarkable achievement that underscored his unusual intelligence and ability. He entered private practice and took many cases in which he represented the "little man" against large corporations. He was elected to the Louisiana Public Service Commission at the age of twenty-five. At age twenty-nine, he argued and won a case against the Cumberland Telephone and Telegraph Company, which had been systematically overcharging its customers, before the US Supreme Court.

Huey Long was elected governor of Louisiana in 1928, when he was only thirty-five years old. A Democrat, he pioneered many modern techniques of political campaigning: sound trucks, speeches delivered on the radio, and a frenetic schedule of personal campaign stops. Some of these same techniques were employed by Franklin Roosevelt in his successful campaign for the presidency in 1932—and by Adolf Hitler in his unsuccessful bid for the presidency of Germany in that same year. In time Long would evoke comparisons to both of these men. And he might have risen just as high as they did had he not been shot and killed by the relative of a political opponent one month after declaring himself a candidate for the presidency.

Upon becoming governor, Long implemented the spoils system on a massive scale, firing hundreds of state employees and replacing them with his own political supporters. He also implemented a popular program of public works that provided employment for Louisiana workers and greatly improved the state's infrastructure. In this he was a forerunner of FDR and the New Deal. He instituted other progressive measures, such as providing free textbooks for schools.

This won him the love and loyalty of those at the bottom of the economic ladder while provoking the resentment and hatred of many of the well-to-do. Eventually Long was impeached by the Louisiana House of Representatives, but he never came to trial before the state Senate, probably as a result of his exercising improper influence over some members of that body. At this point he began receiving death threats and was forced to hire bodyguards for protection, making him the only elected official in the United States other than the president to have a personal security detail. Nevertheless, he went on to run for the US Senate, winning an easy victory in the 1930 election.

It's said that as a young man Long planned his political ascent: first he would be elected to local office, then governor, then senator, and finally president. He nearly achieved that grand slam, which is a tribute to his ability and political acumen. His great weakness was the ease with which he made enemies. Given his personality and political program, he was bound to evoke both love and hatred. His vast ego, abrasive personality, and radical economic views caused powerful and influential figures in both Louisiana and Washington, DC, to oppose him. The consequences of this for Long were eventually fatal.

Arriving in Washington as a freshman senator during the depths of the Great Depression, Long focused his political oratory on the wealthy and the politicians who seemed to serve at their beck and call. He ardently supported Franklin Roosevelt for president in 1932.

But Long was too much of a young man in a hurry. At a meeting with FDR at the White House in June 1933, he behaved disrespectfully toward the president, even calling him "Frank" rather than "Mr. President." As a result of this and other confrontational behavior, he was cut out of all patronage in Louisiana, a blow to his political power and prestige.

The two men became fierce opponents. Roosevelt instigated investigations into Long's political machinations in Louisiana and his personal finances. Meanwhile, Long's Senate career was proving to be short on substance. Far to the left of the president and his party on economic issues, he was unable to muster majority support for any of his legislative initiatives.

As a result, he became more demagogic, culminating in his "Share Our Wealth" plan, which he unveiled in a radio address in 1934. In substance this was a soak-the-rich plan, with the monies confiscated from millionaires being redistributed to the less well off. Although abhorred by the political and financial establishments, many common people, their lives ruined (or nearly so) by the ravages of the Depression, saw the plan as the road to salvation.

At about this time, FDR mused that the danger of dictatorship in America came from two men—General Douglas MacArthur on the right and Huey Long on the left. That such currents underlay American life at this time of crisis is undeniable. Whether Long ever imagined himself as dictator of America is unknown, but his personality was such that some people began to refer to him as Der Kingfish. Hitler, by this time dictator of Germany, was of course known as Der Führer. (Kingfish was a nickname given to Long by his supporters in the 1920s).

Long's influence over the masses had now reached its height. Share Our Wealth clubs existed throughout the nation, with millions of members. Long's radio addresses drew as many as twenty-five million listeners (at the time radio was the means of mass communication in America). He was allied with the demagogic, anti-Roosevelt, and anti-Semitic Catholic priest Father Charles Coughlin, whose radio audience was even larger than Long's. Long had already published an autobiography, *Every Man a King*. He now came out with a second book, *My First Days in the White House*. In August 1935, Huey Long declared himself a candidate for the presidency.

It's uncertain just how Long planned to approach his run for the White House. Would he challenge Roosevelt for the Democratic nomination in 1936 (a contest he was certain to lose) and then run as a third-party candidate? Would he put off a presidential run until 1940? It seems certain that Long could not have beaten Roosevelt in 1936 (Roosevelt won 61 percent of the popular vote and carried forty-six of forty-eight states that year). Whether he could have taken enough votes away from FDR to elect the Republican candidate, Alf Landon, or throw the election into the House of Representatives is almost as doubtful. But we'll never know for sure because Huey Long was shot by an assassin on September 8, 1935 and died two days later.

According to the official theory, Long was killed by a shot from a .32 caliber handgun fired by Dr. Carl Weiss, a former president of the Louisiana Medical Society. Weiss was the son-in-law of a Louisiana judge Long was seeking to have removed from the bench.[46] An alternative theory holds that Weiss actually punched Long, and both men were then killed in a hail of bullets fired by Long's bodyguards. It's not my purpose here to examine the circumstances of Long's assassination—did Weiss indeed fire the fatal shot, and if so, did he act alone? Readers interested in this aspect can consult sources that discuss the controversy.[47]

The shot that hit Long was fired in a corridor of the state capitol building in Baton Rouge. Long suffered a through-and-through wound in the upper right abdomen just below the ribcage. He was rushed by car to a nearby hospital. He was conscious on arrival, though the wound was clearly a serious one, and Long appeared to be on the verge of shock.

The admitting physician was Dr. Arthur Vidrine, the dean of the Louisiana State Medical School in New Orleans, who happened to be visiting Baton Rouge. Ironically, Dr. Vidrine had been appointed dean of the medical school in 1931 by then-governor Huey Long. Although professionally competent, he was by no means an outstanding physician, as his treatment of Long was to prove.

Long's wound was cleaned, and he received a blood transfusion. According to some accounts, Vidrine told Long that he would need an operation, and Long, still conscious, agreed. Other accounts say that the decision to operate was made by committee, with Long's aides and others participating.

Long asked that Dr. Urban Maes, a top surgeon in New Orleans, be sent for. But Maes was involved in a minor traffic accident – a tiny blunder – while he was traveling to Baton Rouge. Long's deteriorating condition made it inadvisable to wait for the arrival of Maes, so the operation proceeded with Vidrine and Dr. William Cook, a Baton Rouge surgeon, sharing surgical duties.

Certain preliminary procedures, such as x-rays and catheterization to remove urine, were not performed; whether through oversight or to save time is unclear. Spectators, such as Long's aides and bodyguards, were allowed in the operating room. Some put on surgical scrubs; others were in street clothes.

Midway through the operation, Long's personal physician, Dr. Clarence Lorio, arrived and took Dr. Cook's place. Thus, three surgeons were involved in operating on Long, an unusual procedure. Surgery revealed that vital organs such as the liver and stomach were undamaged. There was minor damage to the colon, which was repaired. Then the incision was closed, and Long was sent to recovery.

Somehow Vidrine and the other doctors had failed to notice that one or both of Long's kidneys had been damaged. Catheterization was now performed, and blood was found in Long's urine. Another operation was called for, but Long's deteriorating condition led the doctors to decide against one. In fact, only another operation could have saved Long. But the initial mistakes had probably doomed the Kingfish anyway. Long lapsed in and out of consciousness, and his pulse became rapid and faint. Infection was clearly present, but antibiotics were not yet available in 1935. Repeated blood transfusions failed to improve his condition. Early in the morning of September 10, 1935, Huey Long died.

No autopsy was performed, and it remains uncertain whether Long died as a result of internal hemorrhaging or peritonitis caused by infection. What is clear is that repeated mistakes by the medical professionals present—no x-rays taken, failure to catheterize the patient, failure to follow sterile procedures in the operating room, and especially the cursory nature of the operation itself—doomed the Kingfish to an early demise. Had Dr. Urban Maes arrived in time, his expertise might have saved Long. But we will never know.

The "what-ifs" surrounding Huey Long are numerous. While it seems highly unlikely that he could have affected the outcome of the 1936 presidential election, 1940 might have been a different matter. The recession of 1937 cut into the economic gains of Roosevelt's first term, and this might have increased the popular appeal of Long's share-the-wealth policies.

Isolationism was a strong force in America in 1940, and Long might have been able to harness it to his political advantage. The tradition that presidents should not seek a third term could have been exploited by Long, a formidable demagogue. A three-way race in 1940 might have taken enough votes away from FDR to put Republican candidate Wendell Willkie in the White House, with consequences about which we can only speculate.

Rosemary Kennedy

The Kennedy family has been called "America's first family" and even its "royal family." The term dynasty is often used in reference to the Kennedys. These names may sit well with people who remember John F. Kennedy's inaugural address or his handling of the Cuban Missile Crisis. They may resonate with those who are rightly thankful for the 1963 test ban treaty or who become sentimental at the memory of Robert Kennedy's last campaign. But despite the service rendered to America by the Kennedys in both war and peace (about which see other chapters in this book), the elevation of this family to near-mythical status seems a bit out of place.

The Kennedys were clannish and arrogant; it's a not-so-well-kept secret that they treated their perceived social inferiors with callousness and even, at times, cruelty. They committed major blunders in both their public and private lives. And they committed crimes as well. The family patriarch, Joseph P.

Kennedy Sr., was a bootlegger, a stock manipulator, and a serial adulterer who was capable of forcing himself on any woman who hesitated to accept his advances. Some of Joe Kennedy's rough edges were smoothed out in his sons but not all of them.

The seamy side of Camelot was suppressed for a time after John's and Robert's untimely deaths, but beginning in the 1970s and continuing to this day, the dark side of the Kennedy family has come into public view.

The Kennedys are of course known for the many tragedies that have overtaken them. Some of these tragedies were, in whole or in part, self-inflicted, the products of hubris. John Kennedy's decision to ride through downtown Dallas ("nut country" as he himself called it) in an open convertible is an example. Others were products of ignorance or stupidity, such as John F. Kennedy Jr.'s decision to fly over the ocean at night despite his lack of experience in instrument and night flying.

One Kennedy, who to this day is hardly known to the public, suffered tragedy at the hands of her own father. Her life was changed dramatically and for the worse not by her own bad judgment or miscalculation, but by a decision taken by her father in the name of protecting the family's reputation.

This story reads like a Greek tragedy. It is the story of Rosemary Kennedy, who became a victim of medical malpractice at the instigation of her ambitious and ruthless father, Joseph P. Kennedy Sr.

Actually, the unfortunate Rosemary was twice victimized by a medical mistake, the first time occurring at the hands of a nurse present at her birth.

It was the late summer of 1918. World War I was approaching its climax, and the Spanish influenza pandemic was raging around the world—including in Brookline, Massachusetts, where Rose Fitzgerald Kennedy, the wife of Joseph Kennedy, was going into labor. Because of the flu pandemic, doctors in Brookline, as elsewhere, were overburdened by the extraordinary number of sick and dying patients requiring their attention. The doctor who was to deliver Rose's baby was running late. A nurse was present who, all accounts agree, was perfectly capable of delivering the baby.

Yet she refused to do so, first telling Rose to keep her legs tightly closed, then actually pushing the baby's head back in the birth canal rather than letting the infant emerge. The nurse continued to prevent the birth from occurring until the doctor arrived some two hours later.

We can surmise that the baby was deprived of the full amount of oxygen she would have received during a normal delivery. She might also have been traumatized by the unnatural actions of the nurse. In any case, there were noticeable effects on young Rosemary's development. She learned to crawl, walk, and talk later than her siblings. At school she was a slow learner and failed to advance intellectually beyond the level of a ten-year-old.

For a family like the Kennedys, always striving for position and success, such characteristics were shameful and to be kept hidden. Rosemary, even with her mental capacity diminished, felt the disappointment and shame of her parents keenly. Letters to her father reveal an almost pathetic desire to please him and see more of him than the little time he spared for her.

When her father was appointed ambassador to Great Britain in 1937, Rosemary's life brightened somewhat. She was presented at court and enrolled in a Montessori school, where the environment was more pleasant and conducive to learning than what she had known in her previous schools or for that matter at home.

As she approached her twenty-first birthday, Rosemary was a cheerful, pretty, full-figured girl who was bound to attract attention. But Joseph and Rose attempted to shield her from life and its temptations, no doubt in part because they were worried about her, but also because they were concerned about maintaining proper appearances.

Rosemary in turn became somewhat rebellious and moody. She was now attending school at a convent in Washington, DC. She began sneaking out at night, which prompted fears that she might get pregnant or become involved in some other kind of scandal. Joseph Kennedy, concerned first and foremost for his political future and that of his sons, decided to act.

Without informing his wife, Kennedy had doctors perform a lobotomy on Rosemary. At the time, this was a relatively new procedure and was claimed by its advocates to be a cure for some mental illnesses. It involves drilling into the patient's skull and then literally destroying living tissue in the frontal lobe of the brain. Needless, to say, this "psychosurgery" amounts to little more than quackery. After the 1950s, it was recognized as such and discarded as a legitimate procedure. Many thousands of people suffered permanent impairment as a result of undergoing a lobotomy.

Rosemary Kennedy was one of those thousands. After being lobotomized, she could no longer walk or speak more than a few words. She was placed in an institution, where she remained for the rest of her life. She died in 2005 at the age of eighty-six.

Rosemary was just a year younger than her brother John, the future president. Could she too have affected American and world politics, as her older and younger brothers did? Certainly under the patriarchal conditions that prevailed during most of her lifetime and in the household in which she was raised, girls were not encouraged to enter public life. But there were exceptions, such as Margaret Chase Smith (1897–1995), the long-serving US senator from Maine (who, by the way, voted against President John Kennedy's nuclear test ban treaty).

Had Rosemary not been twice betrayed by health care providers, could she have made a mark in politics or other worldly matters? A healthy Rosemary would have had many advantages—such as wealth, good looks, and a family background in politics—that might have spurred her to enter and succeed in public life. But medical mistakes first hindered her development and then incapacitated her for life. Her ability to contribute to America and the world will forever remain among the might-have-beens of history.

12

MURPHY'S LAW RUN AMOK

Anything that can go wrong will go wrong.

- Murphy's Law

We come now to a chapter that describes how Murphy's Law—anything that can go wrong will go wrong—has played a role in some big and very famous disasters. These particular disasters may not have changed the world, but they illustrate how one little thing, one tiny blunder, can sometimes lead to catastrophe.

The origin of the idea that whatever can happen will eventually happen is lost in the mists of time. It was undoubtedly first thought of centuries or perhaps even millennia ago. The term Murphy's Law was coined in the late 1940s. Air Force Captain Ed Murphy, an engineer at Muroc (now Edwards) Air Force Base in California, complained about a technician who persistently wired a transducer incorrectly, causing repeated malfunctions. In referring to this particular technician, Murphy told colleagues that "if there is any way to do it wrong, he will." So at least goes the story.

Murphy's Law is all about human fallibility. Imperfect human beings working under pressure allow urgency to crowd out or overshadow matters that turn out to be of great importance, or the importance of little things is forgotten as we try to bring great projects to fruition.

Corners are cut. Penny-wise and pound-foolish economies lead to big losses—losses of money and sometimes of lives. Occasionally pure negligence or incompetence leads to tragedy. Disaster lurks around the corner in almost any human endeavor. What follows are some famous examples of Murphy's Law run amok.

The Johnstown Flood

The Johnstown Flood of May 31, 1889 is the quintessential American disaster, or at least it was until Hurricane Katrina and then Hurricane Harvey came along in 2005 and 2017, respectively. On that May 31st, the steel town of Johnstown, Pennsylvania, was hit by a wall of water sixty feet high that flattened most of the town and killed more than 2,200 of its residents. And it was all so preventable.

Johnstown was founded in 1800 on the banks of the Conemaugh River in southwestern Pennsylvania, about seventy miles east of Pittsburgh. During the Industrial Revolution of the nineteenth century, Johnstown became a major center of steel production. It was home to the Cambria Iron Works (later named the Cambria Steel Company), an enterprise known for the high quality of its steel. By 1889, Johnstown had a population of about 30,000.

The town's location in a river valley made it prone to flooding, though there was no precedent for the terrible event that occurred in 1889. That disaster was not simply an act of nature but came about largely through the action (and inaction) of men—specifically, some of the so-called robber barons who dominated the early industrial era in America.

Construction of an earthen dam upriver from Johnstown
was begun in the 1830s. Its purpose was to collect water that
could be fed through sluice pipes at the base of the dam into a
canal that had been built to connect Johnstown to Pittsburgh.
The water level frequently became too low for the canal to be
navigable, particularly during periods of drought. When
completed in 1852, the South Fork Dam, as it was called, was
over seventy feet high and nine hundred feet long. It held back
the waters of an artificial lake that in 1889 held about twenty
million gallons of water. The release of water through the sluice
pipes was controlled from a wooden tower beside the dam.

As fate would have it, the dam was obsolete almost
before construction ended. A railroad connecting Johnstown
and Pittsburgh was completed just a few months after work on
the dam ended. The canal system and the dam were no longer
needed, and the state of Pennsylvania, which owned them, put
them up for sale. The railroad itself purchased the canal and the
dam in 1857, mainly to obtain the rights of way.

Earthen dams, if properly built and maintained, are safe.
But the South Fork Dam was not properly maintained. During
the more than twenty years that the Pennsylvania Railroad
owned the dam, virtually no maintenance was performed. Leaks
occurred, and in 1862, there was a break in the dam. The lake
was only about half full at the time, and no major flooding or
damage occurred. But some people in Johnstown began to
wonder whether a more significant break might occur in the
future and what would happen to the town if it did.

Shortly thereafter, the wooden tower from which the
sluice pipes were controlled burned down. It was not rebuilt.
Eventually the pipes and valves were dismantled and sold for
scrap. There was now no way of preventing the waters of Lake
Conemaugh from overflowing or breaking the dam completely.

Conditions would have to be just right for this to happen, but as Murphy's Law tells us, whatever can go wrong eventually will.

We move ahead to 1879. A group of wealthy speculators led by Henry Clay Frick purchased the dam and Lake Conemaugh as the site of their South Fork Fishing and Hunting Club, meant to be a private retreat for wealthy industrialists and financiers. Among the members were Andrew Carnegie, Andrew Mellon, and Philander Knox.

During the construction of the industrialists' retreat, the dam was lowered and the top widened so that a carriage road could be built on it. A fish trap was installed in the dam's lone spillway. The discharge pipes were not replaced, and repairs to leaks in the dam were done haphazardly or not at all. A consulting engineer was called in and wrote a scathing report predicting that unless systematic repairs were undertaken, the dam would eventually break, with possibly catastrophic results. A representative of the South Fork Fishing and Hunting Club dismissed the report with barely disguised disdain, asserting that the people of Johnstown were in no danger from the club's activities. How wrong he was would soon be demonstrated in almost biblical fashion.

On May 30, 1889, the worst storm in living memory hit the Johnstown area. Perhaps ten inches of rain fell within a twenty-four-hour period. Streams and creeks were converted into raging torrents, and the Conemaugh River overflowed its banks.

On the morning of May 31, the waters of Lake Conemaugh were poised to spill over the top of the dam. The spillway was clogged by debris that had collected in the fish trap. Desperate attempts were made to unclog the spillway, then to dig a new one, but without success. Workers also tried to shore up the dam itself, but the pressure of the water was too great. Twice telegrams were sent to Johnstown warning of the dam's imminent collapse, but the town itself was already flooded, with many people trapped inside their homes by the rising water.

Shortly after three p.m., the South Fork Dam broke.

Twenty million gallons of water hurtled toward Johnstown, fourteen miles away. Building momentum as it traveled, the water picked up trees, houses, livestock, and other debris before crashing into the town.

Just under an hour after the dam collapsed, a wall of water sixty feet high hit Johnstown. Many homes and businesses were completely destroyed, and 2,209 of the townspeople were killed. It was the worst flood in American history up to that time, with a greater loss of life than any other previous disaster. Property damage was estimated at $17 million, the equivalent of about half a billion of today's dollars.

The members of the South Fork Fishing and Hunting Club survived the disaster. The titans of industry had neglected to perform basic maintenance and repairs to their property, and Murphy's Law had done the rest. The people of Johnstown paid a terrible price for the robber barons' negligence.

Sinking of the Indianapolis

The USS Indianapolis was a heavy cruiser launched in 1931. It was one of two Portland-class cruisers in the US Navy, designed to serve as a fleet flagship. It displaced nearly ten thousand tons and had a crew of 950 officers and men, which increased to some 1,200 sailors in wartime.

As a heavy cruiser, the Indianapolis was not equipped with sonar because heavy cruisers were not meant to sail alone through submarine-infested waters. Like battleships and aircraft carriers, heavy cruisers were to be escorted in wartime by smaller warships such as destroyers, frigates, and light cruisers, which did carry sonar and other antisubmarine devices such as depth charges.

The Indianapolis was the favorite ship of President Franklin Delano Roosevelt (a former assistant secretary of the Navy), who spent twenty-eight days aboard her during a goodwill cruise to three Latin American countries in 1936. Roosevelt sailed on the Indianapolis on two other occasions as well.

The Indianapolis served as the flagship of Scouting Force 1 until 1941. She was conducting exercises in the Pacific when the Japanese attacked Pearl Harbor on December 7, 1941. She was part of the naval task force that searched for but couldn't find the Japanese aircraft carriers that carried out the attack. In 1943, she became the flagship of the 5th Fleet commanded by Vice Admiral Raymond A. Spruance. In 1943–44, she fought with distinction in the battles of Tarawa and Kwajalein, the conquest of the Caroline and Mariana Islands, and the Battle of the Philippine Sea. In early 1945, the

Indianapolis was part of a task force that attacked the Japanese coast. She then participated in the battles for Iwo Jima and Okinawa. She won ten battle stars during the war.

During the battle for Okinawa, the Indianapolis was struck by a Japanese bomb, causing severe damage. She was well riveted and well built , however, and was able to sail under her own power across the Pacific to California for repairs. It was here in July 1945, as the war in the Pacific approached its climax, that she received fateful orders.

On July 15, 1945, Captain Charles McVay, the commanding officer of the Indianapolis, was called to a meeting at US Naval Headquarters in San Francisco. McVay was told only that his ship would receive a secret cargo that was to be delivered to the island of Tinian in the Marianas. Already on July 12, he had been told to prepare his ship, which was still undergoing refit, to sail within four days' time. On the 12th, he was told nothing more than that the mission the Indianapolis would carry out was secret.

On July 16, the secret cargo was delivered: two nondescript containers, one of steel and the other of lead. The materials inside had been shipped to San Francisco from Los Alamos, New Mexico, home of the top-secret Manhattan Project. The steel container held components for the firing mechanisms of Little Boy and Fat Man, the atomic bombs that were to be dropped on Hiroshima and Nagasaki, Japan. The lead container held the uranium 235 that would provide the explosive power of Little Boy, the Hiroshima bomb.

The Indianapolis set sail that very day, ironically within hours of the first successful atomic bomb test conducted at Alamogordo, New Mexico. According to some accounts, Captain McVay was told that if his ship were sunk, his first priority would be to save his secret cargo, not the crew. As it turned out, his ship reached Tinian without incident, delivering its deadly cargo on July 26.

With its secret mission completed, Indianapolis sailed to Guam, where she received orders to proceed west 1,500 miles to Leyte Gulf in the Philippines, where she would conduct gunnery practice and other training before joining US naval forces preparing for the invasion of the Japanese home islands.

It was at Guam that Murphy's Law began to kick in, eventually dooming the Indianapolis and most of her crew. A series of incredible oversights and blunders were committed that would end in a horrible death for nearly three-quarters of the men aboard.

Captain McVay, a distinguished and much-decorated officer, requested a destroyer escort for the voyage to the Philippines. His request was denied on the grounds that the war had moved so far to the north, the danger of encountering Japanese surface ships or submarines was insignificant. This was quite true as far as surface ships were concerned, but in fact there were two Japanese submarines patrolling the waters that the Indianapolis would have to cross. Astonishingly, the US Navy was aware as a result of communication intercepts that the Japanese subs were there. And yet no escort was provided.

The Indianapolis sailed on July 28 and was due to reach the Philippines on the 31st. But she didn't turn up that day. It was assumed both on Guam and at Leyte that she had arrived as scheduled. The operations officer at Leyte, a Lieutenant Gibson, who was responsible for tracking the Indianapolis, took no action and did not even inform his superiors when the ship failed to arrive as scheduled. Even more incredibly, three US naval stations picked up distress calls from the ship yet failed to respond to them. One station believed, for no discernible reason, that the message was a Japanese trick. The commanding officers at the other two stations were either asleep or intoxicated when the SOS came in. Nothing was done. Meanwhile, the crew of the Indianapolis was undergoing tortures worthy of hell.

Just after midnight on July 30, the Indianapolis crossed paths with the Japanese submarine I-58. As the big ship approached, the Japanese sub unleashed a flurry of torpedoes. The Indianapolis was hit and sank within twelve minutes.

Despite the swift sinking, only about 300 of the almost 1,200 mean aboard went down with the ship. This was because the watch was being changed; most of the crew was up and about when the torpedoes struck. Almost 900 men went into the water. Barely one-third of those men would survive.

July 31 passed, then August 1, and still the Navy took no action to determine the whereabouts of the ship. The men in the water suffered from hypothermia and saltwater poisoning. Some began to hallucinate and go mad. And then there were the sharks.

As morning dawned on the 30th, sharks began to appear. They picked off sailors one by one, killing and then consuming them. This went on for three days until on the morning of August 2, aviators spotted the survivors bobbing in the sea. Ships were directed to the area, and slightly more than three hundred men were rescued.

The loss of life was the greatest due to the sinking of a single ship in the history of the US Navy. The ship's captain, McVay, was court-martialed, the only officer in the history of the Navy to be tried for losing his ship. Found guilty, his punishment was remitted by the chief of naval operations, Admiral Chester Nimitz. The conviction itself was a gross miscarriage of justice, and McVay was finally exonerated by a Congressional resolution passed in 2000. But too late—Captain

McVay, haunted by the sinking and his scapegoat status, committed suicide in 1968.

Texas City Disaster

The worst industrial accident in US history occurred on April 16, 1947, in Texas City, Texas. Texas City is a port on Galveston Bay, built in the 1890s. During World War II, it became a major oil refining and petrochemical center, with a large Monsanto plant.

With the war's end in 1945, Texas City became a transshipment point for ammonium nitrate fertilizer. Ammonium nitrate is a chemical compound found in nature but also produced synthetically in countries with advanced petrochemical industries. It has a secondary use as a major component of ANFO, a widely used industrial explosive. Its explosive power has also led to its being used in improvised explosive devices (IEDs), such as the bomb that destroyed the Murrah Federal Building in Oklahoma City on April 19, 1995.

In 1947, ammonium nitrate fertilizer produced in the Midwest was being shipped via Texas City to farmers in Western Europe. In mid-April, the SS Grandcamp, a Liberty ship mothballed after the war and then given to the French, was docked at Texas City prior to sailing for Europe. Its cargo consisted primarily of some 2,200 tons of ammonium nitrate. It was also carrying small arms ammunition, machinery, tons of peanuts and leaf tobacco, and bales of sisal twine.

Berthed about six hundred feet from the Grandcamp was a second ship, the SS Highflyer, which held 961 tons of ammonium nitrate and about 2,000 tons of sulfur. Additional ammonium nitrate was stored in warehouses nearby. The Monsanto chemical plant was just yards from where the Grandcamp was berthed, and several oil refining and storage facilities were about a mile away.

That in certain circumstances ammonium nitrate could cause powerful explosions was known in 1947. Major industrial accidents had occurred at Oppau, Germany, in 1921 and in Belgium in 1942. Both the US Army's Bureau of Ordnance, which oversaw the production of ammonium nitrate fertilizer, and the Coast Guard, which had the power to regulate the loading of dangerous materials at US ports, knew of the potential danger. The Grandcamp had arrived from the Port of Houston, which did not allow ammonium nitrate to be loaded on ships there. But at Texas City in 1947, Murphy's Law was at work.

The Coast Guard port official at nearby Galveston (there was no officer at Texas City) claimed after the disaster that he didn't know ammonium nitrate was being transshipped through Texas City. The Coast Guard itself was underfunded in the immediate postwar period and for that reason was not fully up to the task of regulating the arrival and loading of dangerous materials at US ports.

Perhaps even more astonishing is the fact that no one in Texas City was aware of the potential dangers—not the dockworkers, their supervisors, or the executives of the railway company that brought the ammonium nitrate in from the Midwest. Not even the port's own insurance underwriters knew that ammonium nitrate could go off like a bomb under certain conditions.

What are those conditions? Ammonium nitrate is an oxidizer, which simply means that it supports combustion. When heated, ammonium nitrate begins to break down. This creates further heat and, eventually, fire. If there is additional fuel present, and particularly if the burning fuel is in a confined space, the temperature can become high enough to cause a powerful explosion. This is what happened at Texas City on April 16, 1947.

The tragedy began to unfold that morning when stevedores discovered a smoldering fire in one of the Grandcamp's holds, where bags of ammonium nitrate were stored. It's uncertain how the fire started, but it quite likely was the result of the careless disposal of a cigarette.

Some water and a fire extinguisher were applied to the fire without result. The stevedores then grabbed a fire hose but were told by a supervisor not to turn it on because the water would damage the cargo. The supervisor ordered that steam be piped in from the engine room in the belief that this would smother the fire. From this particular order, the disaster flowed. "Steaming the hold," as this procedure is called, was in fact the worst possible response to a fire of this kind.

The hatch and ventilators were closed and the steam turned on. The temperature inside the hold began to increase, and the cargo began to melt. A chemical chain reaction was underway.

The ammonium nitrate began to break down, giving off nitrous oxide. This created further heat inside the confined space. Now the paper bags in which the ammonium nitrate was packaged began to burn. The fertilizer particles were coated with wax (to prevent moisture damage), which added more fuel to the fire. At this point the hatch cover blew off. Orange and reddish-brown smoke began pouring from the hold. The sight drew onlookers to the docks. It was a case of fatal curiosity. Soon fire crews from both Texas City and the nearby petrochemical plants arrived on the scene. But they were too late, brave men rushing to their death

The colorful smoke pouring from the hold was nitrogen oxide, the chemical compound given off by nitroglycerine just before it explodes. The inside of the hold was now over eight hundred degrees Fahrenheit, almost hot enough to cause the ammonium nitrate to go off like a bomb. Flames were shooting out of the hold. It had been barely an hour since the stevedores had first discovered the small fire. A few more minutes passed, and then over 2,000 tons of ammonium nitrate exploded.

The explosion was heard 150 miles away. The shock wave was felt some 250 miles from the site. The ship and the nearby Monsanto plant were obliterated, with heavy debris flying through the air like shrapnel. Almost one thousand buildings in Texas City were flattened. Two small planes flying thousands of feet above the city were blown out of the sky.

Later in the day, fires caused the Highflyer's cargo of ammonium nitrate to explode, causing more death and destruction. According to the official estimate, a total of almost six hundred people lost their lives, but the toll may have been even higher. Some two thousand people were injured.

Whatever could go wrong did go wrong in Texas City that day, and the consequences were among the worst in history.

Apollo 13

Apollo 13, America's third manned moon mission, never made it to the moon. The three astronauts aboard— mission commander Jim Lovell, Fred Haise, and Jack Swigert—almost didn't make it back to Earth.

America's National Aeronautics and Space Administration (NASA), a rational, science-based organization, had no qualms about this mission being the thirteenth of the Apollo program. NASA's leadership was not about to bow to superstition and skip over that numeral (as is often done when numbering the floors of buildings) in the name of luck. Yet two days after launch, on April 13, 1970, a malfunction occurred that seemed to indicate that thirteen was a very unlucky number indeed.

On that Monday the 13th (at least it wasn't a Friday), one of the two oxygen tanks that provided both power for the spacecraft and air for the astronauts to breathe exploded, knocking a panel off Apollo 13 and damaging the one remaining oxygen tank as well. The mission was two hundred thousand miles from home when the accident occurred. Over the next four days, brilliant improvisation and the steady nerves of the crew allowed the crippled spacecraft to execute a circumlunar return to Earth using the moon's gravity to help power the flight back to the blue planet.

What had caused the accident? The oxygen tanks were built to NASA specifications by Beech Aircraft Corporation, a subcontractor for North American Aviation, the main contractor for the Apollo program. Tests at the factory revealed minor flaws, which were corrected. Delivery to North American began in 1967.

During 1968, the tank that exploded on Apollo 13 was installed in the service module for Apollo 10. Meanwhile, unmanned Apollo missions had revealed a design flaw in the pumps for the oxygen tanks. As a result, the tank in question had to be removed from the Apollo 10 service module so that it could undergo modification.

During this process, a technician failed to remove one of the bolts that held the tank shelf assembly in place. As a crane lifted the shelf assembly, the bolt still in place caused the shelf to catch and then fall about two inches back into place. The bolt was then unfastened and the assembly removed.

No one gave much thought to this small glitch. The technicians and engineers at NASA were unaware that the interior of the oxygen tank had been damaged—a fill tube had come loose. In 1969, the tank in question was installed in the future Apollo 13.

Tests done a month before launch, in March 1970, revealed that after pressurization, the tank could not be emptied in the normal fashion. Normally, oxygen gas was fed into the tank in order to force supercooled liquid oxygen out. But in this case the gas was simply hissing back out while the liquid oxygen remained in the tank. The loose fill tube was of course the cause of the problem. It would have been prudent to simply replace the malfunctioning tank. This, however, could have delayed the scheduled launch of Apollo 13. And so technicians emptied the tank by using the tank heater to boil off the liquid oxygen inside.

This created a new problem. Originally the tanks' heaters were designed to run on twenty-eight volts, but later this was changed to sixty-five volts. The change was made at Beech Aircraft, except for one small omission: someone forgot to change the heater thermostat switches from twenty-eight to sixty-five volts.

This meant that when technicians were boiling off the liquid oxygen in Apollo 13's oxygen tank number two, the thermostat was unable to cut the flow of sixty-five-volt current to the heater. The heat inside the tank just kept rising, to the point that it burned much of the insulation off the wiring inside the tank. A technician monitoring the operation believed the temperature inside the tank was eighty degrees Fahrenheit (sufficient to boil off liquid oxygen, the temperature of which is minus 297 degrees) whereas it had actually risen to about one thousand degrees.

A few days before launch, managers discussed the odd behavior of tank number two. No definite conclusions were reached, and it was decided to proceed with the launch.

On day three of the mission, the heater for tank two was turned on. The current flowing into the tank caused a spark, which set alight the remaining insulation. In the oxygen-laden environment inside the tank, an explosion was inevitable. And the drama of Apollo 13's brush with death began.

Thankfully Apollo 13 had a happy ending when on April 17, 1970, the damaged spacecraft came down safely in the Pacific. A series of trivial mistakes and omissions caused by human error had brought the mission within a whisker of disaster. At the same time, human intelligence and improvisation had prevented the worst from happening. We might therefore say that Murphy's Law was "amended" by NASA Mission Control and the gutsy crew of Apollo 13.

Nuclear Errors

An even more expensive and potentially more deadly accident occurred on March 28, 1979, at the Three Mile Island nuclear power plant south of Harrisburg, Pennsylvania. On that day, about half of the nuclear fuel in the reactor core of TMI's Unit 2 melted down.

A presidential commission later concluded that the reactor came within half an hour of total meltdown. A total meltdown would have either caused the fuel to melt through the reactor containment vessel into the ground below (the "China Syndrome") or, even worse, created a gigantic steam explosion that would have spewed radiation across populated areas for miles around.

What happened on March 28? The core of a nuclear reactor, where the nuclear fuel is located, is hot. Very hot. The core requires constant cooling. Three Mile Island is a pressurized water reactor, which means that water is pumped past the reactor core under high pressure to keep the core from overheating and the nuclear fuel from melting. The heat is carried away from the reactor and is then used to create steam, which in turn is used to generate electricity.

In the early morning of March 28, 1979, technicians were performing routine maintenance on a part of Unit 2's steam-making equipment. This could be done safely even though the reactor was in operation because valves were employed to isolate the area the men were working on from the high temperatures and pressures that would otherwise be present.

In simple terms, the men were trying to unclog a filter (technically a condensate polisher) in the steam-making apparatus. As they struggled to accomplish this, they failed to notice a small amount of water seeping back into a compressed air line.

Shortly thereafter, the water entered the control line for all the plant's condensate polishers. In response, all the coolant valves shut down automatically. Lacking water, the feedwater and condensate pumps ceased operation. Auxiliary pumps should have activated automatically, but the valves on these had been closed for routine maintenance, a clear violation of safety rules when the reactor was in operation. Meanwhile, steam was no longer flowing to the power-generating turbines, which also shut down.

Since the steam generators were no longer receiving water, heat and pressure increased in the reactor's coolant system. This triggered an automatic emergency shutdown of the reactor, which halted the nuclear chain reaction in the core. Nevertheless, the temperature and pressure continued to rise dangerously. To relieve the pressure caused by heated and expanding water, the pilot-operated relief valve (PORV) opened, allowing steam and water to escape. But now the final straw was placed upon the camel's back. Unbeknownst to the plant's operators, the PORV remained stuck open due to a mechanical flaw. Water continued to escape from the coolant system, which would eventually, and inevitably, lead to the worst possible scenario—core meltdown.

The plant's operators did not know that the PORV had failed to close; an indicator light led them to believe it had. This false signal was to delay a proper response to the unfolding accident until it was almost too late.

The instruments in TMI-2's control room indicated that pressure was falling and the water level rising in the coolant system, a puzzling and contradictory signal. Finally an operator discerned that there had to be a leak. He asked for and received permission to close a valve that would in effect override the PORV if the latter was still open. The draining of coolant from the core stopped. Half the core had already been exposed, and a partial meltdown had occurred. But the worst—complete core meltdown—had been averted with only minutes to spare.

Not so lucky were the operators of the Chernobyl nuclear plant in Ukraine. The date was April 26, 1986. The Soviet Union was still in existence though soon to take its well-deserved place on the trash heap of history.

As it struggled to keep pace with the West during the Cold War, the USSR, a less wealthy and technologically sophisticated society, often cut corners on safety, even in areas where safety ought to have been paramount. This was true even of its nuclear plants. The nuclear chickens came home to roost in Chernobyl on that April day.

The Chernobyl plant (officially known as the V. I. Lenin Chernobyl Power Station) was a so-called RBMK model, a design based on a military facility that produced plutonium for nuclear weapons. Remarkably, the RBMK design did not include a containment building around the reactor, which meant that in the event of a meltdown or explosion, radioactive material would be sure to escape into the environment. And so it happened.

In the early morning hours of April 26, the operators at Chernobyl were running a routine test on Reactor 4. The reactor was in the process of being shut down so that annual maintenance could be performed. The operators made a series of errors, including turning off the emergency core cooling system as part of the test. For reasons that have not been clarified to this day, an emergency shutdown of the reactor was initiated. A power surge followed, and control rods being inserted into the reactor (a standard part of the shutdown process) jammed. The pressure inside the reactor increased dramatically, fuel elements ruptured, and a massive steam explosion occurred, followed seconds later by a second even bigger explosion. The roof of the reactor building was blown off, and radiation from the destroyed reactor core began pouring into the environment.

Two people died as a result of the explosion; almost thirty more died later from radiation poisoning. A vast dead zone surrounding the town of Chernobyl was created; tens of thousands of people had to be permanently relocated.

Poor design, poorly trained personnel, and a lack of safety culture and best practices—all these contributed to the disaster at Chernobyl. Murphy's Law at work again.

Bhopal

Texas City was the worst industrial accident in US history. The worst industrial accident in world history occurred on December 2–3, 1984, in Bhopal, India.

Union Carbide India Limited (UCIL), a subsidiary of the US chemical company Union Carbide (which today is itself a subsidiary of Dow Chemical), operated a pesticide plant in

Bhopal. As chance would have it, 1984 marked the fiftieth anniversary of UCIL's founding. The plant in question had been in operation since 1969.

The Bhopal plant produced the insecticide Sevin, the components of which include the dangerous chemical methyl isocyanate (MIC). Methyl isocyanate is made by combining monomethylamine with phosgene. The latter substance was the chief ingredient in the deadly "green cross gas" of World War I. Originally, the MIC used at the Bhopal facility was shipped there from a Union Carbide plant in the United States. Starting in 1980, however, Bhopal began producing its own MIC.

The Bhopal facility included three large underground storage tanks for MIC. Each could hold fifteen thousand gallons of the chemical. Union Carbide safety guidelines stated that the tanks should never be more than 50 percent full. The tanks were pressurized with nitrogen gas, which allowed MIC to be pumped out as needed.

In late October, one of the tanks lost pressure, making it impossible to pump out the MIC inside. MIC production was halted. Simultaneously, parts of the plant were shut down for maintenance, including the vent gas scrubber tower, a tower or stack used for breaking down and rendering harmless any MIC that did not meet quality standards. Also shut down was the flare tower, which could burn off escaping MIC gas.

The plant had experienced several small-scale leaks and accidents during the early 1980s, mostly due to lax safety procedures and inadequate training. So it was perhaps not surprising that in late November, Sevin production was resumed, using MIC stored in the underground tanks despite the fact that parts of the operation were either malfunctioning or shut down for maintenance and repairs.

Here's a partial list of the known safety breaches at Bhopal as Sevin production resumed at the end of November 1984:

> Vent gas scrubber tower shut down for maintenance

> Flare tower shut down for repairs (a corroded pipe needed to be replaced)

> Cooling system for the MIC storage tanks (designed to keep impurities out and prevent dangerous reactions caused by high temperature interacting with the chemical) shut down; employees had actually drained the refrigerant for use elsewhere in the plant

> Pressure system for the MIC storage tanks deteriorating and in need of repair

> No maintenance supervisor on site (position unfilled)

On the night of December 2, workers began cleaning out some of the pipes connected to the MIC storage tanks. Somehow over one hundred gallons of water got into one of the storage tanks, initiating a dangerous chemical reaction.

Pressure inside the tank began to increase, and gas began to escape. Operators tried to bring the vent gas scrubber back online, but it wouldn't respond. The flare tower and refrigeration system were out of action. The last hope was to neutralize the gas with water from fire hoses. But the gas was escaping from a tower one hundred feet high, and the plant's hoses couldn't shoot water that far. Disaster was therefore inevitable.

The prevailing winds carried the gas cloud over Bhopal. The result was similar to Ypres and Verdun: thousands choking and eventually suffocating to death as the gas attacked their throats and lungs. Immediate deaths totaled over 2,200. Thousands more suffered to varying degrees from gas exposure. A ghastly toll by any measure.

Union Carbide maintains to this day that a disgruntled employee deliberately caused the tragedy through sabotage. No objective account takes this argument seriously, however. Strong evidence for the sabotage theory is lacking. Bhopal was in fact an accident waiting to happen—a very gruesome example of Murphy's Law in action.

The Challenger Disaster

The United States is the most technologically sophisticated and advanced society in human history. The US government, working together with private industry and academia, has carried through to completion such vast and complex undertakings as the Manhattan Project to build the atomic bomb and the Apollo program to land a man on the moon.

As an encore to the Apollo program, NASA created the space shuttle program, known officially as the Space Transportation System (STS). The shuttle project began in 1972, the same year as the last manned mission to the moon. Spaceflights began in 1981 with the successful launch and return of the shuttle Columbia. Challenger was the second shuttle delivered to NASA (in all, five shuttles were built).

Although the shuttle was a great technical feat, returning from space and landing like an airplane, it was sent into space by a combination of its three liquid fuel engines and two giant solid fuel rocket boosters. The shuttle crew, like previous astronauts, was in effect sitting on a bomb that was powerful

enough to blast them free of Earth's gravity and into space. The
rocket boosters were essential to providing enough thrust to
escape Earth's atmosphere. They provided over 80 percent of
the total thrust at takeoff. The boosters, however, would also
prove to be lethal on January 28, 1986, when Challenger was
launched on what was to be its tenth mission.

The rocket boosters were designed and built by the
Morton Thiokol Corporation in Utah. They were (and are) one
of the most powerful rockets ever to fly. They were a cutting-
edge technology of the time. And yet they also incorporated a
component right out of the early machine age.

The rocket boosters were enormous. Each weighed
about two hundred thousand pounds empty and was 149 feet in
length, or half a football field. Because of their great size and
the need to transport them from Utah to Cape Canaveral,
Florida, they were built in four segments, which were then
assembled by workers at the Kennedy Space Center. The
segments were joined together by steel pins. To prevent any
burning fuel from escaping during takeoff and flight, the joints
were sealed with heat-resistant putty. Finally, two rubber O-
rings were placed over the joints as a final precautionary seal.

The O-rings were basically rubber gaskets, a technology
developed in the nineteenth century. Marrying such a basic
technology with a rocket designed to blast people into space
was to prove dangerous and, eventually, fatal.

The effectiveness of the O-ring seal was in question
from the start. Tests showed that the stresses involved in takeoff
created gaps in the seal that allowed combustion gases to erode
the O-rings. Engineers at the Marshall Space Flight Center in
Alabama declared that Thiokol's joint design was flawed, but
their warnings failed to reach Thiokol senior management, and

the joints were unchanged when the first shuttle flight took off on April 12, 1981.

After only two shuttle flights, it was apparent that the O-rings were being damaged in flight. At last, NASA and Thiokol began working on a redesign of the joint.

Meanwhile the shuttle program was experiencing other problems. The shuttle had originally been sold to its customers, particularly the military (which wanted to use it to put spy satellites in space), as a convenient and ready-to-hand means of reaching space. It had been hoped that weekly missions would be launched. However, the complexity of the shuttle system and other circumstances such as bad weather led to delays. By 1986, the shuttle was going aloft only about once every two months.

The shuttle's failure to perform up to expectations led NASA to take serious risks. Flights continued even while the original O-ring problem remained unsolved. Now, in January 1986, as Challenger prepared to blast off into space, weather intervened to finally bring about disaster.

The O-rings were susceptible to failure in low temperatures. Quite simply, cold would harden the rubber, making it less flexible and thus less capable of forming a seal if a gap was created in a joint by the high stresses created during liftoff. According to Thiokol engineers, the O-rings could fail at temperatures below forty degrees Fahrenheit. No launch had ever taken place with the temperature below fifty-four degrees.

An unusually cold weather front hit Cape Canaveral in late January. As takeoff approached on the morning of the 28th, the temperature was hovering around the freezing mark. Thiokol engineers urged NASA to postpone the launch, but NASA managers ignored their warnings. NASA was under even more pressure to get this particular flight off the ground because the shuttle crew included high school teacher Christa

McAuliffe, America's first teacher in space. This PR stunt meant that an unusually large audience was tuned in for the launch. Scrubbing would be just another embarrassment for the program, already troubled by its failure to live up to the expectations of politicians and taxpayers that the shuttle would make space travel routine and easy.

NASA insisted on launching as scheduled, and Thiokol management concurred, overriding its own engineers' warnings. At 11:38 a.m. on the 28th, the great rocket engines roared to life. Liftoff took place without an apparent hitch. But a gap opened in one of the solid rocket booster's joints, allowing hot gas to escape. This damaged the O-rings. Had the O-rings not hardened so much from the cold, they could have been flexible enough to recover and form a seal, as had happened during previous launches. The slowed response of the O-rings allowed a plume of flame to escape from the solid rocket booster (SRB). Fire spread from the SRB to the external fuel tank, and seventy-three seconds after liftoff, spectators on the ground and watching on TV witnessed a fireball in the sky and the breakup of the spacecraft.

The crew cabin was blown clear of the rest of the spacecraft, and the crew was almost certainly alive and probably conscious as well. However, nothing could have saved them from the impact on the surface of the Atlantic Ocean at a speed of over two hundred miles per hour. There were, needless to say, no survivors.

Design flaws, groupthink, and putting PR ahead of safety placed the shuttle and its astronauts in jeopardy from day one. On January 28, 1986, the crew of the shuttle Challenger paid the price for other people's negligence and hubris.

13

MILITARY MISCOMMUNICATION

*The race is not always won by the swift nor the battle to the
strong, but that is the way to bet.*

– Damon Runyon (attributed)

The Valley of Death

In another chapter I mentioned the fact that during the
nineteenth century, Russia and the Ottoman Empire (present-
day Turkey) engaged in a series of wars. For the most part
Russia was victorious, but in one of these wars, the Crimean
War of 1853–1856, Turkey got the better of their longtime
opponent. The fact that Britain and France fought alongside
Turkey in the Crimean conflict was the main reason Russia
suffered defeat. The most well-known incident of the war, at
least for people from English-speaking countries, is the British
disaster known as the Charge of the Light Brigade, which
occurred during the Battle of Balaclava on October 25, 1854.
Here a blunder of miscommunication occurred that caused a
major military debacle.

The war itself began over the protection of Christians in
Palestine, then under Turkish rule. Russia, an Orthodox power,
and France, a Roman Catholic one, vied for the leading role in
guarding Christian rights in the Holy Land and for the prestige

that this would bring. A series of diplomatic insults and missteps eventually led to Russia declaring war on Turkey.

Britain and France were fearful that a Russian victory would increase Russia's power and decide the so-called Eastern Question (i.e., the future of the Ottoman Empire as a whole) in Russia's favor. They therefore came to Turkey's aid and declared war on Russia in March 1854.

After some desultory fighting in the Balkans, it appeared that the war might simply end through lack of interest. But war fever was running high in Britain and France, and it was decided to mount a joint expedition to the Crimea in order to capture the great fortress and naval base of Sevastopol.

The British and French landed in the Crimea in September 1854. They defeated the Russians at the battle of Alma and then laid siege to Sevastopol. The British forces had the double duty of holding their portion of the siege lines and guarding the allied armies' eastern flank at Balaclava. On October 25, the Russians attacked the British here, hoping to break the siege.

The Russian attack made initial gains. Several redoubts manned by Turkish troops on high ground were successfully stormed and prisoners and cannon captured. The main British force was still facing Sevastopol, with only the cavalry division under Lord Lucan between the Russians and the British base at Balaclava.

The British commander in chief, Lord Raglan, arrived at the scene and ordered his cavalry to support the faltering Turks. Russian cavalry struck first, attempting to break through to Balaclava, but were repulsed by infantry of the 93rd Highlanders—the famous "Thin Red Line." Then the British Heavy Brigade, consisting of eight squadrons of dragoons under

General Scarlett, charged the Russian cavalry and drove it from the field.

While this was going on, the Light Brigade under Lord Cardigan stood by observing, though they were only a few hundred yards away. Here we have the first miscommunication, or possible miscommunication, that occurred during the battle. Cardigan claimed that the commander of the Cavalry Division, the Earl of Lucan, had ordered him to remain on the defensive. Lucan countered that while he had indeed ordered Cardigan to adopt a defensive posture, he had clearly indicated that Cardigan could and should take advantage of any opportunity to strike the enemy. Had the Light Brigade joined the charge of the Heavy Brigade, a success would have turned into a complete victory.

Lord Raglan, wishing to recapture the ground lost earlier, issued the following order to the Cavalry Division: "Cavalry to advance and take advantage of any opportunity to recover the Heights. They will be supported by infantry which have been ordered. Advance on two fronts."

This order was unclear and ambiguous. Lucan took it to mean that he should wait and attack only after supporting infantry were brought up. In fact, Raglan wanted him to attack at once. The Russians could be seen dragging away some British cannon that had been captured from the Turks. Raglan dispatched a second order to Lucan, ordering the cavalry to pursue the Russians at once and prevent them from carrying off the guns. A staff officer was sent to convey the order to Lucan.

Unfortunately, from his position in a valley, Lord Lucan could not see the guns being carried off by the Russians. When he received the order to attack, Lucan asked the staff officer what was he to attack? What guns?

With a wave of his arm to the east, the staff officer replied, "There is your enemy, my lord! There are the guns!"

To Lucan and his staff, it appeared the officer was waving toward the Russian batteries at the other end of the valley, opposite his cavalry. Without further discussion, he rode over to Lord Cardigan and the Light Brigade. He ordered Cardigan to assault the Russian position at the end of the valley approximately a mile away.

Cardigan was astonished. His forces would be charging into a valley with Russian batteries on three sides, supported by infantry. He brought this to the attention of Lucan, his superior.

"I know it," Lucan replied. "But Lord Raglan will have it. We have no choice but to obey."

And so, the Charge of the Light Brigade began. The staff officer who had conveyed the order to attack, a Captain Nolan, participated in the charge and was the first man killed. He rode out in front of the brigade—some say to force the pace while others claimed that he realized the mistake that had been made and was trying to stop the charge. In any case, his death ended the last possibility of averting disaster. The charge proceeded.

It was magnificent, but it was not war. Almost half of the 670 men in the Light Brigade were killed or wounded. The survivors actually reached the Russian lines at the end of the valley and drove the Russian gunners from their cannon, but as with Pickett's men at Gettysburg, they had suffered too heavily to conquer.

Lord Lucan held back the Heavy Brigade, not wanting it to suffer similarly. Ironically, had the Heavy Brigade been sent in as well, the combined forces might have been enough to defeat the Russians.

The Charge of the Light Brigade was both a tactical blunder and tactically insignificant. The battle ended in a minor British victory anyway. The chance for a decisive success was missed earlier in the battle when the Light Brigade failed to join the Heavy Brigade's charge against the Russian cavalry. However, the siege of Sevastopol continued, the allies eventually took the fortress, and peace was eventually made on essentially the allies' terms.

At Balaclava, simple miscommunication all but destroyed an elite unit. The blunders of Lord Raglan and his messenger, Captain Nolan, led to disaster for the Light Brigade.

Hitler Saves Britain

Although the tide of war in Europe definitely turned against Nazi Germany with the Allied victories at El Alamein and Stalingrad in late 1942, Hitler's best chances to win a complete victory in World War II occurred in 1940 and 1941. Had Hitler been able to conquer either the British Isles or the Soviet Union, any chance of defeating him would have been very slim indeed. There were three particularly dangerous moments in 1940–1941 when Hitler came within a hairsbreadth of complete victory.

Hitler's first opportunity came at Dunkirk in 1940. He held back the German Panzers outside the French port for two days, probably because he believed the Luftwaffe could prevent any evacuation of the trapped British Expeditionary Force. When he changed his mind and ordered his armored divisions to resume their advance, the British had recovered sufficiently to prevent a breakthrough. Over the next several days, the Royal Navy and British civilian sailors ran the gauntlet of the English Channel under constant air attack to evacuate the beleaguered British troops.

When the port was finally taken, the 330,000 British soldiers were gone, having escaped to their home island to fight again. Had the BEF been annihilated or captured at Dunkirk, German paratroopers could have easily landed in southern England. Then the German Navy, covered by the Luftwaffe, would undoubtedly have risked a landing on the British coast. A successful landing would have doomed Britain to defeat and occupation.

The third opportunity for a total German victory occurred before Moscow in late 1941. German troops advanced to the very outskirts of the city—a reconnaissance battalion actually glimpsed the spires of the Kremlin before the Russian forces, aided by the early arrival of "General Winter," saved the Russian capital from capture.

Between these two decisive events was a third and equally critical moment in which the fate of civilization hung in the balance. Once again Hitler made a decision that actually saved his most determined enemy, Churchill's Britain, from defeat. While his halting of the Panzers before Dunkirk had proved to be a mistake, it was a decision taken coolly and rationally. It was not a blunder in the strictest sense of that term. Now Britain would again be saved by Hitler changing tactics when his forces were on the brink of victory. This mistake, however, was triggered by a blunder that no one could have foreseen or prevented—a tiny blunder that triggered a chain of events ending in disaster for the Nazi dictator, dashing his hopes of dominating first Europe and then the world.

German air attacks on Britain began even before the fall of France. But the Battle of Britain proper began on August 13, 1940, dubbed "Eagle Day" by the Germans. The Luftwaffe was tasked with defeating the Royal Air Force and gaining air supremacy over Britain, paving the way for a landing and the occupation of the British Isles.

German tactics were to attack Britain's fighter airfields and radar stations, which would force British Fighter Command to commit its well-trained but numerically inferior forces (when the battle opened, Britain had about one thousand frontline pilots for its Spitfire and Hurricane fighters). If Fighter Command could be defeated, then the Germans would be able to bomb targets throughout Britain with impunity, making a successful invasion of the island virtually a foregone conclusion.

The campaign opened unpromisingly. Bad weather and ferocious resistance by the RAF prevented the Luftwaffe from delivering any decisive blows. But then the German air force hit its stride. In the two-week period between August 24 and September 6, it consistently pounded the airfields and radar stations of southern England, knocking some of them out. Repairs could not be performed quickly enough under the daily and effective attacks the Luftwaffe was delivering, and by early September, Fighter Command was contemplating the possibility of a withdrawal from its forward deployment areas in southern England. Such a move would have been the equivalent of an admission of impending defeat.

Worse, during this period, nearly one-quarter of Britain's trained pilots were either killed or wounded. Losses among this precious cadre, barely one thousand strong when the battle began, could not be made good quickly. British aircraft losses during these two terrible weeks actually exceeded those of the Luftwaffe even though the latter was the attacking force. The German fighters, which had the double duty of protecting the German bombers and engaging the RAF's fighters, were winning the Battle of Britain.

The British were now staring defeat in the face. But they were about to be saved by a tiny blunder committed a few days earlier—a blunder that would lead to a turning of the tide and the salvation of their beleaguered island.

On August 24, the very day on which Britain's two terrible weeks began, a German aircraft accidentally dropped a few bombs on a residential area of London. Hitler had specifically ordered that civilian targets in London were not to be bombed. The docks of the East End were legitimate military targets, however, and the Luftwaffe did attack them. On August 24, for reasons that remain unknown, one German plane failed to release its bombs over the docks.

Perhaps it was a communications foul-up or a navigational error, or perhaps the pilot, having missed the docks, simply wished to unload his bombs before returning to base. In any case, a few bombs fell on central London, and a handful of British civilians were killed and injured. It was not a terror attack or retaliation for British raids on German cities (since May 1940, the British had carried out a few small air raids on towns in western Germany) but a blunder, pure and simple.

Despite the insignificant amount of damage done by the stray Luftwaffe bomber, the pugnacious British prime minister

Winston Churchill ordered immediate retaliation. A small force of British bombers raided Berlin on the night of August 25–26, causing almost no damage. On the night of August 28–29, the British sent a further eighty-one bombers to the German capital. Some damage was done, and a handful of Berliners were killed. The raid embarrassed Reich Marshal Hermann Goering, the commander in chief of the Luftwaffe, who had bragged that no British bomber would ever reach Berlin.

Hitler was not embarrassed but enraged. German prestige demanded a crushing response. On September 4, with the RAF reeling under the Luftwaffe's daily attacks, the Führer ordered a change in tactics. London would now become the Luftwaffe's main target.

The massive bombing of London began on September 7, 1940. Over the next week, London suffered a series of daylight attacks, with great damage and loss of life. But by concentrating on the British capital and neglecting the ravaged fighter airfields and radar stations, the Luftwaffe gave Fighter Command breathing space. Repairs could now be made, and the infrastructure of Britain's fighter defense was saved from imminent collapse. At the same time, Fighter Command was not compelled to commit its forces against every wave of attacking German aircraft; it could husband its resources of men and planes even though doing so left London exposed to the fury of the German onslaught.

September 15, 1940 was the decisive day in the Battle of Britain. The Luftwaffe mounted its biggest daylight attack of the war, seeking to finally crush the RAF and the morale of the British people. But the eight days' grace Fighter Command had been given provided the margin of victory. On this day, British pilots shot down fifty-six German planes against a loss of only twenty-six. The RAF was now master of the daylight skies over southern England. Britain would survive and fight on to eventually become the "unsinkable aircraft carrier" from which Allied bombers would mount their massive attacks on German cities.

The Germans now switched tactics again, turning to night bombing of London and other British cities. But this could not decide the war in Germany's favor. The failure to crush the RAF had prevented Germany from conquering Britain. Hitler's rash decision to bomb London in retaliation for minor British raids on Berlin had snatched defeat from the jaws of victory. And what was the origin of this monumental mistake on Hitler's part? A German pilot had accidentally dropped a few bombs on London. This small blunder set off a chain of events that ended, improbably, in the salvation of Britain. For Nazi Germany, of course, Hitler's decision proved to be disastrous.

"Never in the field of human conflict was so much owed by so many to so few," said Winston Churchill in tribute to the fighter pilots who saved Britain in the summer of 1940. But if not for that small blunder committed by a German pilot, Churchill's words might not have proved true.

Surprise at Pearl

No event in American history, with the exception of the assassination of President John F. Kennedy, is more controversial than Pearl Harbor. How could the Japanese stage a surprise attack on the US Pacific Fleet given that the United States had broken Japan's Purple code, used for diplomatic communications, and achieved a partial break of the Imperial Japanese Navy's JN-25 code? Could the fog of war concept be extrapolated to explain a failure of communication occurring just before war broke out? Did incompetence play a role? Was it pure bad luck that led to disaster? Or was there malfeasance and dereliction of duty involved?

US–Japan relations, so friendly today, were fraught with suspicion and tension from the time Commodore Perry "opened up" Japan in 1854 until the outbreak of war between the two countries in 1941. Once Japan modernized along Western lines after the abolition of the shogunate in 1867, and particularly after the Japanese victories in wars against China (1894–1895) and Russia (1904–1905), the two powers began jockeying for influence in the Pacific and East Asia.

Although Japan was one of the Allied powers in World War I, it felt humiliated by American policies in the postwar period. For example, under the Washington Naval Treaty of 1922, Japan was compelled to accept inferiority in naval strength as measured by battleships (the prime instrument of naval power at the time, though soon to be replaced by the aircraft carrier). The United States also pointedly refused to accept the concept of racial equality, first in the Versailles Treaty of 1919 and then in its 1924 Immigration Act.

China was an even bigger sticking point. Japan sought to dominate that sleeping giant while America advocated the Open Door policy under which all nations would compete on equal terms for the Chinese market. In addition, influential Americans believed that the United States should be a mentor to China, as evidenced by the widespread American missionary activity in that country. This somewhat patronizing attitude toward a much older civilization was widespread in American circles at least until Mao Zedong and the Communists took power in the late 1940s. In any case, prior to Pearl Harbor, the Japanese resented what they perceived as American interference in their own backyard. The worldwide economic depression of the 1930s only exacerbated the tense relationship between the two major Pacific powers.

The United States had begun breaking Japan's secret codes as far back as the early 1920s. The so-called Black

Chamber organization, funded by the US Army and the State Department, broke Japan's diplomatic code during the negotiations for the Washington Naval Treaty. The US Navy had considerable success breaking Japan's early Red and Blue naval codes.

In 1929, Secretary of State Henry Stimson put an end to the highly successful Black Chamber program, basing his decision on the idea that "gentlemen don't read each other's mail." Remarkably, and in stark contrast to what would happen today, there was no real opposition or bureaucratic infighting as a result of this antiquated and indeed foolish policy enunciated by Stimson. Secretary Stimson compounded his error when he announced the Stimson Doctrine in 1932. This called upon the Japanese to withdraw from the Chinese province of Manchuria, which they had occupied in the previous year. How abandoning the effort to break Japan's codes could be reconciled with demands that it withdraw from Manchuria was never explained by Stimson, who during World War II served as Franklin Roosevelt's Secretary of War.

Fortunately, US code-breaking efforts were resumed by the Army's Signal Intelligence Service (SIS) in 1930. By 1940, the United States had broken Japan's new diplomatic code (Purple) and had achieved some success in breaking the JN-25 naval code. Just how much of JN-25 had been compromised at the time of Pearl Harbor remains unknown to this day; most accounts say only a very partial break had been achieved by December 7, 1941.

Not satisfied with the occupation of Manchuria, Japan attacked China directly in July 1937. A long, bloody, and atrocity-filled war ensued, with the Chinese driven from their coastal areas and major cities. The Japanese, however, were unable to completely defeat the Chinese and bring the war to an end. China became a morass from which the Japanese were neither able nor willing to extricate themselves.

The administration of Franklin Roosevelt was distracted by domestic problems stemming from the Great Depression and furthermore recognized the overwhelming danger presented by Nazi Germany, so it did little in response to Japanese aggression beyond issuing protests and providing some limited aid to China. But after the outbreak of war in Europe in 1939 and particularly after the fall of France in 1940, tensions heightened, and the possibility of conflict grew increasingly likely until war finally came in December 1941.

The Japanese saw the collapse of France and the Netherlands, both major colonial powers in Asia, and the British preoccupation with surviving Hitler's onslaught as a golden opportunity.

Japan is a nation with virtually no natural resources. As a modern industrial state and a military power, Imperial Japan required access to oil and various metals, none of which existed in its home territory. Most of Japan's needs were met by purchase from the United States, a situation that from the Japanese point of view was humiliating. Moreover, there was a danger that at some point America would impose economic sanctions or completely embargo commodities such as iron, steel, and oil. (To us today, it may seem remarkable that US sanctions were not immediately imposed in response to Japan's aggression in China. But we must remember that any lessening of US economic activity and trade in the face of the Great Depression would have been a risky move for any president to make. Additionally, in the 1930s the American citizenry had no appetite for involvement in foreign wars.)

After France fell, the Japanese occupied northern Indochina (a French colony) and signed an alliance with Nazi

Germany and Fascist Italy—the so-called Tripartite Pact. In the summer of 1941, Japan occupied southern Indochina, an obvious springboard for attacks on Singapore (Britain's "Gibraltar in the East") and the resource-rich Dutch East Indies. When Germany attacked Russia in June 1941, the Japanese debated whether to join in that war or move south against British, Dutch, and American territories. The southern plan was decided upon in a conference presided over by Emperor Hirohito in July. The questions of how and when to move now became the focus of planning.

Meanwhile, American pressure on Japan began to increase. Although he was preoccupied with the Nazi danger and the struggle to maintain the supply lifeline for Britain in the Atlantic, Roosevelt could not ignore Japan's increasingly aggressive moves in the Pacific.

Economic sanctions now began to be imposed—first an embargo on scrap iron and high-octane aviation fuel, then a total embargo on oil shipments to Japan. The latter move in particular made war all but inevitable. Without American oil, the Japanese war machine would eventually grind to a halt.

At the same time, an accommodation with Japan was something the United States would have welcomed so that it could turn its full attention to Europe. American contingency planning was from the beginning grounded in the principle of "Europe first." With Hitler's armies nearing Moscow and U-boats infesting the Atlantic, the last thing America needed was a major war in the Pacific. Nevertheless, American terms for a détente included Japan's withdrawal from China, something the Japanese viewed as utterly incompatible with their country's honor. In November Japan sent a special envoy to Washington for talks with Secretary of State Cordell Hull. The Japanese government and high command set a deadline of late November for an agreement; if none was reached by then, Japan would attack the USA.

The Japanese had concluded that a move south could be undertaken only if the US Pacific Fleet based at Pearl Harbor, Hawaii, was destroyed in a surprise attack by their formidable carrier forces. Planning for such an attack, which would be followed by the occupation of the Philippines, Guam, Wake Island, Singapore, Burma, and the Dutch East Indies, had been underway for months. Ironically, in early 1941, FDR had ordered the Pacific Fleet shifted from its base at San Diego to Hawaii in order to deter the Japanese from embarking on any aggressive moves in the Pacific.

On November 20, the Japanese negotiators offered to refrain from further aggression in Asia and the Pacific in return for a free hand in China and an end to the American embargo on strategic materials. Six days later, Secretary Hull made a counterproposal that still included America's long-standing insistence on Japanese withdrawal from China. The Washington negotiations were going nowhere as neither side would budge

Pearl Harbor, December 7, 1941

from its position on the key issue of China. The inexorable countdown to war now began.

On November 26, the very day that Hull handed his counterproposal to the Japanese negotiators, Admiral Isoroku Yamamoto, the commander in chief of the Japanese Combined Fleet, ordered his carrier forces to sail from Japanese waters to carry out the surprise attack on Pearl Harbor. Strict radio silence was to be maintained. A westerly weather front would, it was hoped, hide the task force (an armada consisting of six carriers and accompanying battleships, cruisers, destroyers, submarines, and supply ships) from any aerial reconnaissance. The attack was to begin in the early morning of Sunday, December 7, 1941. At the same time, Japan's formal declaration of war would be handed to Secretary Hull in Washington, DC.

As the Japanese forces steamed eastward toward Hawaii, what was going on in the minds of American political and military leaders in Washington and the Army and Navy commanders in Hawaii? Did they believe hostilities were imminent? Did they have any forewarning of the Japanese attack?

Since 1941, there has been a persistent view among a minority of scholars and other observers that Roosevelt and his advisors were aware of the impending Japanese attack, its timing, and its location, and allowed it to go forward in the belief that it would finally bring America into the war against the Axis powers. This reasoning goes on to posit that the apparent sneak attack would inflame American opinion to such an extent that the nation would throw itself wholeheartedly into defeating not only Japan but Germany as well.

It's not part of the purpose of this essay to ponder the question of possible foreknowledge on the part of the Roosevelt administration. It should be said that a solid majority of scholars reject the notion of a Pearl Harbor conspiracy. Readers interested in exploring the question further should consult, for the pro-conspiracy arguments, Robert Stinnett's Day of Deceit.[48] The majority anti-conspiracy view is ably summed up by David Kennedy in his Freedom from Fear.[49]

What is known for certain is that it became clear to American authorities in the final days before hostilities broke out that an attack somewhere was indeed imminent. But where? Possible targets included the Philippines, Singapore, and locations in the Dutch East Indies. But no one seems to have expected that the Japanese would be so bold as to strike Hawaii[50]

On November 27, the War Department issued a "war warning" to all US overseas commands, including Hawaii. This was based on the Japanese conduct of the negotiations with Secretary Hull and specifically on messages sent in the compromised Purple code. But there was still no hint of where the Japanese would strike. Then, about noon on December 7 in Washington, D.C. (with dawn just breaking in Hawaii), Army Chief of Staff George C. Marshall was handed a fresh decrypt of a Purple message instructing the Japanese negotiators to break off the talks that very day at 1:00 p.m.

In the 1920s, US Army aviator Colonel Billy Mitchell had prophesied a Japanese attack on Pearl Harbor, and US Navy war games conducted in the 1930s had confirmed the practicability of such a strike. But no reference to these warnings seems to have been made in the months and weeks prior to the December 1941 attack.

Marshall was alarmed by the specificity of the timing, which seemed to indicate that a declaration of war was coming. He immediately composed a message warning all US Army commands and had it dispatched by radio. However, weather conditions made it impossible to radio the message to one particular command—Hawaii. It was necessary to send the message via Western Union instead. The message reached Hawaii when the Japanese planes were already in the air and in fact was not delivered (by dispatch rider) to General Walter C. Short, the Army commander in Hawaii, until after the Japanese attack was over. In any case, Short's conduct since the war warning of November 27 had all but guaranteed Japanese success. His lack of preparation (and that of his naval counterpart, Admiral Husband E. Kimmel) for a possible Japanese attack was later judged to have amounted to dereliction of duty. Still, there was one final opportunity, on the morning of December 7, to alert US forces in Hawaii before the Japanese struck. But a small blunder occurred that guaranteed the morning of December 7 would end in disaster.

The Japanese carriers launched the first wave of 183 planes at about 6:00 a.m. Hawaii time. As the planes approached the island of Oahu, they were picked up by the US Army radar station at Opana Point. Two privates on duty as radar operators reported the incoming target to their superior, Lieutenant Kermit Tyler. But the radar operators, who were still in training, failed to mention the large size of the target. Lieutenant Tyler assumed that the radar returns were in fact those of a flight of six B-17s that he knew to be flying toward Oahu on practically the same course. As a result, no further investigation of the target was made.

What a stroke of bad luck! Had the radar station personnel determined that a large body of planes was heading for Pearl Harbor, there might have been just enough time to issue a warning and get US flyers into the air to intercept the incoming Japanese. But it was not to be. The attack waves proceeded to the target unopposed, and disaster ensued. Over 2,400 Americans were killed and more than 1,100 wounded. Damage to Pearl Harbor and to the ships there was extensive.

Of course, the disaster could have been much worse. The precious aircraft carriers of the Pacific Fleet were not at Pearl that morning. The Japanese neglected to attack the dry docks, maintenance facilities, and fuel depots, the destruction of which could have prolonged the war by up to two years, according to no less an authority than Admiral Chester Nimitz (commander in chief of the Pacific Fleet, 1942–1945).

Moreover, if the Japanese attack had failed, Hitler might not have declared war on the United States and as a result might have gone on to defeat Russia and Britain while America concentrated on fighting Japan in the Pacific. The "what-ifs" only multiply the more one investigates the possibilities of a different outcome at Pearl Harbor. The tiny blunder that guaranteed disaster on December 7, 1941, might well have been for the world at large a blessing in disguise.

Friendly Fire

Death in war caused by friendly fire is by no means infrequent. Studies have attributed nearly 50 percent of the casualties in some conflicts to friendly fire. Civilians in particular often view friendly fire deaths as especially tragic, but such losses are inevitable in modern warfare. Friendly fire deaths are known to have occurred even in ancient times, but modern weaponry—the repeating rifle, the machine gun, and heavy ordnance of all types—has caused casualty rates from friendly fire to skyrocket. Modern means of communication are by no means a guarantee against mix-ups leading to friendly fire casualties. Most readers will recall the death of US Army Ranger and former NFL star Pat Tillman, who was shot and killed by friendly fire in Afghanistan in 2004. Below, I examine two particularly gruesome events, both of which occurred in the European theater during World War II.

July 1943 near Gela in Sicily: The first Allied invasion of Nazi-dominated Europe began on July 10, 1943, when US forces led by General George S. Patton landed in Sicily. As part of the invasion, US paratroopers made their first-ever combat landings near the Sicilian town of Gela. The initial parachute drop on July 10 took place without a hitch. A second drop on July 11, however, did not come off as hoped. This particular operation began on the evening of the 11th when 144 C-47 and C-53 transport planes carrying some two thousand men of the 504th Parachute Infantry Regiment (part of the 82nd Airborne Division) took off from airfields in Tunisia.

As the transports crossed the coast of Sicily, US naval and ground forces opened fire. American soldiers and sailors were shooting at their comrades-in-arms, on American airmen and paratroopers! What had caused this terrible mix-up?

Plans for the airborne landings had been worked out by General Matthew B. Ridgway, the commander of the 82nd, and his staff in collaboration with General Patton's staff. To avert the danger of friendly fire from US naval and ground forces, a specific route was to be designated for the transports as they flew into the drop zone. On the morning of July 11, Patton and Ridgway conferred about the danger of friendly antiaircraft fire being directed against the transports. After the conference, Patton sent out an order to his subordinate commanders telling them to alert their forces concerning the timing and location of the coming airdrop. Curiously, the order also indicated that Patton's subordinates should advise naval commanders of the coming drop. Communication on short notice across service lines in the heat of battle is a recipe for trouble—for miscommunication that can put operations and lives in jeopardy.

As it happened, or at least so it appears (subsequent investigations reached no firm conclusion), the details about the operation did not reach some of the army and naval units that were locked in combat with German and Italian forces. Indeed, July 11 had been a tough day on the beaches, with numerous German air raids against both the landed troops and the naval forces providing support. The drop was planned to take place at night. Darkness is inherently a double-edged sword—providing cover on the one hand but capable of promoting confusion and misidentification on the other. And, as ill luck would have it, the C-47s and C-53s bore a superficial resemblance to the German Junker-52 aircraft.

About two hours before the planes were to arrive over the Sicily battlefield, Patton sent out another order warning his troops of the imminent drop. But the fog of war hung heavy in the air above Gela. At first all went well. The first wave of transports proceeded to the drop zone without incident, successfully discharging the paratroopers on board. But as the second wave of planes crossed the coastline, a lone machine gun on the beach opened up. As often happens in war, trigger-happiness spread like wildfire. Almost all the antiaircraft guns ashore and on the ships began firing on the transports.

Losses were considerable. Over twenty planes were shot down and over two hundred men killed, wounded, or reported missing. One C-47 that managed to return to base was found to have more than one thousand bullet holes in its fuselage. It's a wonder that the casualties were not higher. Even so, the fiasco was the worst friendly fire incident suffered by the US armed forces up to that time.

No one was ever held responsible for the disaster. Eisenhower was furious with Patton and reportedly considered relieving him and making General Omar Bradley the overall commander of US forces in Sicily. Patton claimed that the staff of the Mediterranean theater commander, the British general Harold Alexander, had failed to provide him with the specific air route the transports would follow until almost the last minute, although he had been asking for the information for a full week. Whatever the exact truth may be, it's clear that miscommunication produced the disaster.

Patton of course remained in command in Sicily, and his forces and the British swept the Germans from the island in a lightning five-week campaign. While in Sicily he committed the not-so-small blunder of slapping a soldier that he believed was malingering. The incident eventually cost him the command of the 7th Army and left him for some months in limbo until he returned to win fame in the Normandy campaign, to which we now turn.

July 1944 in Normandy, France: A year has passed since the disaster at Gela. Operation Overlord, the Allied invasion of Western Europe, began on June 6, 1944 ("D-Day") with the Allied landing in Normandy. After securing a lodgment, the Allied forces became bogged down in the bocage country— heavy undergrowth that impeded the movement of troops and vehicles, even tanks. In addition, the German forces opposing our troops put up strong resistance despite their inferior numbers and firepower, particularly in the air.

The US commander of the invasion forces, Lieutenant General Omar Bradley, came up with a plan to break out of the bocage country. Code-named Cobra, the operation would begin with a massive artillery bombardment and the carpet-bombing of a less than ten-square-mile area near the town of Saint-Lô by more than 2,500 medium and heavy bombers. After all this metal had been laid down on the German positions, US armor and infantry would punch through into open country and head for Paris and the Seine basin, the prelude to a war-winning push toward the Rhine and the heart of Germany.

The plan worked spectacularly. The German line was broken. In the following days, hundreds of thousands of German troops were killed, wounded, or captured at the battle of the Falaise pocket, and a month after Cobra began, Paris was liberated. Yet on the first day there was a disaster that cost the lives of over one hundred American soldiers, including a three-star general. More than five hundred other Americans were wounded.

What happened and why? As mentioned, the plan called for an unprecedented preliminary bombardment, including an air bombardment by thousands of US bombers, some two thousand of them four-engine B-17s. Carpet-bombing was not normally employed on the battlefield, mainly because with so much ordnance going off so close to friendly forces, the danger of friendly fire casualties was vastly increased. In the planning for the operation, Bradley and his staff attempted to ensure the safety of the frontline troops by having them pull back from their forward positions during the bombardment, and by having a line of red smoke laid down behind which no bombs were to be dropped. But miscommunication would ensure that these precautions were for naught.

Meeting with British and American air commanders during the planning stages of Cobra, Bradley asked that the bombers make their runs parallel to the American lines. This would help to prevent any friendly fire damage to his forces. On leaving the meeting, Bradley believed that this was the tactical pattern that had been agreed upon. However, when Cobra began, the air forces conducted their bombing runs perpendicular to the American lines; i.e., they flew toward the Germans rather than across the field of fire that the Germans could put up against them.

Flying toward the German lines was a tactically sound procedure. A course that ran parallel to the lines meant exposing the aircraft to longer and more concentrated German fire. It would almost be equivalent to a ground army offering its flank to the enemy. Nevertheless, Bradley thought he had obtained agreement for the flyers to do just this. Was there miscommunication during the planning stages, or did the Allied air forces simply disregard the tactical plan Bradley and his staff had devised? To this day that question remains unanswered.

In any case, the results were catastrophic, at least for the US ground troops dug in near the area to be carpet-bombed. The offensive was originally scheduled to begin on July 24. Bad weather caused a last-minute postponement of the operation. Nevertheless, the attack went off at half-cock anyway with some 350 bombers striking the target because—military miscommunication once again—some of the flyers didn't get the word in time and proceeded with the mission. The limited bombing that day caused about 150 friendly fire casualties, including twenty-five deaths.

Apparently, no lessons were learned from the events of the 24th. On the 25th, the full force of Allied airpower was turned upon the Germans at Saint-Lô—and upon some of the American troops facing them as well.

As the attack opened, red smoke laid down by American artillery to mark the no-bomb zone began blowing back toward the American lines. Once again, the bombers, this time in full force, made their runs perpendicular rather than parallel to the German lines. The unlucky winds, combined with the sheer impossibility of carrying out such a truly massive bombardment with flawless precision, led to tragedy. Over five hundred American infantrymen became casualties; over one hundred of these were killed (accounts vary; some say 111 men were killed; others list as many as 136 dead). Among the dead was three-star general Lesley J. McNair, who was in a trench observing the action. He became the highest-ranking American soldier ever to die in battle.

Cobra was the worst friendly fire incident in US military history. The operation itself was a smashing success. On July 26, American forces broke through the German lines and began to race for Paris. It was the beginning of the end for Nazi Germany.

American casualties during the Normandy campaign were heavy. The Germans, despite their numerical and material inferiority, fought well right up until and even during Operation Cobra. But on July 24–25, 1944, at Saint-Lô, Americans proved to be their own worst enemy.

B-17 dropping bombs

14

---•◦•---

THE USS MAINE
AND THE WAR WITH SPAIN

Why assume a conspiracy when simple incompetence is the answer?

- An old saying from law enforcement

On February 15, 1898, the US battleship Maine blew up and sank in the harbor of Havana, Cuba. The sinking helped touch off a war between the United States and Spain (how odd it seems today to think of war between these two countries), which in turn resulted in the creation of an American overseas empire in the Caribbean and the Pacific. In 1890, according to Frederick Jackson Turner, the American frontier had closed—or to put it another way, the conquest of the continental United States had been completed. The year 1898 was a fateful one in which America joined the great European powers in the rush for territorial acquisitions in what later became known as the Third World. The age of imperialism was at its height, and the United States now took its place alongside Great Britain, France, Germany, Russia, and Japan as one of the world's imperial powers.

No warship has had a more curious history than the USS Maine. Laid down in the late 1880s, she was commissioned only in 1895 and was already outdated by that time (it was only under President Theodore Roosevelt that the United States created a true blue-water navy). Incredible as it may seem, the construction of the Maine was in response to the earlier acquisition by Brazil and Argentina of ships built in Europe. For a time in the late nineteenth century, the United States was not the number one naval power in the waters of the Western Hemisphere. The chief admiral of the US Navy during this period complained that the American navy "was too slow to run and too weak to fight."

As just mentioned, the Maine represented 1880s warship design. Advances in naval technology and tactics had rendered her all but obsolete compared to the battleships and fast cruisers being constructed in Europe during the 1890s. Nevertheless, she was still useful for power projection in the waters of the Western Hemisphere. It was in this role that she found herself anchored in Havana Harbor on February 15, 1898.

At the time, Cuba was in revolt against its colonial master, Spain. Spain had controlled Cuba since the sixteenth century. Beginning in the 1860s, the Cubans had periodically risen against the Spaniards. What proved to be the final revolt began in 1895. The Cubans actually hoped to gain independence before the United States took over the island. The US had coveted Cuba since the early days of the Republic. When in the 1880s Secretary of State James G. Blaine made known his belief that Cuba (and indeed all of Central and South America) should be acquired by the United States, he was merely echoing the expressed beliefs of men such as Thomas Jefferson and Alexander Hamilton.

In 1897, President William McKinley offered to buy Cuba from Spain for $300 million, but Spain refused. At the same time, the "yellow press" in the United States, particularly William Randolph Hearst's New York Journal and Joseph Pulitzer's New York World, were exaggerating the viciousness of the fighting in Cuba and Spanish atrocities against the rebels. These press reports inflamed American opinion. Probably a majority of Americans already supported the idea of taking Cuba from Spain, although there were also many people who were antiwar and anti-imperialist.

In January 1898, the Maine was sent to Cuba to show the flag and "protect US interests." It was at anchor in Havana Harbor for three weeks. Then, at about 9:40 p.m. on February 15, a massive explosion destroyed the fore part of the ship. The front third of the Maine was practically obliterated, and more than two-thirds of the 355 officers and men on board were killed. The captain, Charles Dwight Sigsbee, and most of his officers survived, simply because the officers' quarters were in the aft part of the ship.

The investigation into the explosion revealed that several tons of powder charges for the Maine's guns had detonated. But what had caused the charges to explode? That has remained a matter of controversy to this day. The initial Navy Board of Inquiry in 1898 concluded that because some witnesses heard two explosions and a portion of the ship's keel was bent inward, an underwater mine had caused the explosion. An investigation conducted by the Spanish Navy concluded that spontaneous combustion inside the ship's coal bunker had provided the spark that caused the powder charges in the forward magazines to blow up. The Spanish investigators pointed out, quite correctly, that (1) no dead fish were found in the harbor, as would be expected from an explosion in the water; and (2) the waters were calm on the night of February 15, meaning that an electrically detonated mine rather than a drifting contact mine would have to have been used—yet no cables were found.

Further supporting the Spanish conclusion is the fact that the Maine used bituminous coal as fuel. Bituminous coal is known to give off gases, particularly methane, which may cause spontaneous combustion. Nevertheless, the US Navy stuck to its mine theory, reaffirming its original conclusion at a second board of inquiry held in 1911.

However, a third Navy investigation, conducted in the 1970s at the behest of the legendary Admiral Hyman G. Rickover (the "Father of the Nuclear Navy"), endorsed the original Spanish conclusion from 1898. Two private investigations, one conducted at the behest of National Geographic magazine in the late 1990s and the other by the Discovery Channel in the early 2000s, came to opposing conclusions: the former favored the mine theory while the latter agreed with the Rickover investigation's conclusion that a coal bunker fire caused the explosion. The exact cause of the Maine tragedy remains a matter of controversy, which will probably never be resolved to everyone's satisfaction.

While I cannot claim to be an expert on the technical matters involved, common sense leads me to believe that the Maine's destruction was accidental and not deliberate. If the explosion was caused by a mine, what human agency would have been behind the act? There are three possibilities.

The Spaniards

The US government, undertaking a "false-flag" operation in order to precipitate a war and the US takeover of Spain's colonial empire It stretches credulity to believe that Spain, a second-class power barely able to cope with the Cuban insurrectionists, would want to provoke a war with the United States, a rising power only ninety miles from Cuba's shores, and certain, moreover, to prevail in any war fought between the two countries in the Caribbean. As for the Cuban revolutionaries, they did not possess either the means or the motive to carry out such an act. They had no mines and no technical expertise in deploying one successfully against a warship. In any case, they were desperately hoping to win independence on their own before any US intervention, which they rightly feared would mean exchanging a Spanish master for an American one. Provoking US intervention was not a goal of the Cuban revolutionaries.

The concept of a false-flag operation carried out by the United States and entailing the murder of hundreds of US sailors is a product of Cold War and post–Cold War thinking. We now know that at the height of the Cold War, the CIA and even the Joint Chiefs of Staff were willing to contemplate the deliberate killing of American citizens in order to advance US interests—the Operation Northwoods documents from 1962, released only in the 1990s, make this sad fact all too plain. However, such fantastic and diabolical notions were not in the minds of the political, military, and naval authorities of 1890s America. There is, simply put, not a scintilla of real evidence supporting a false flag theory for the destruction of the Maine.

Given these facts, we are all but forced to conclude that an accidental explosion on the Maine helped precipitate the Spanish-American War and all of its consequences— consequences that have reverberated down the years and still affect the America of today.

The tragedy of the Maine was of course a godsend for those Americans desiring to go to war with Spain and for their mouthpiece, the yellow press. In the wake of the sinking, the Hearst and Pulitzer papers engaged in an orgy of propaganda designed to provoke war. The papers resorted to speculation, distortion, and outright lies in order to create a war fever in the United States.

Coverage was intense and unrelenting, with multiple pages devoted to the sinking day after day. The famous war cry, "Remember the Maine, to hell with Spain!" was a product of the yellow press's coverage of the Maine's sinking.

The sinking of the Maine did not provoke an immediate declaration of war on Spain by the United States. During March and April of 1898, political and popular pressure to "liberate" Cuba grew stronger, with some prominent figures switching from an antiwar to a pro-war stance. A joint resolution of Congress demanding Cuban independence was passed and signed by President William McKinley on April 20. The US began a naval blockade of Cuba on the following day, and on April 25, Congress formally declared that a state of war existed with Spain.

A "splendid little war" of ten weeks' duration followed, resulting in a sweeping American victory. Cuba was invaded and conquered by US forces, and Spain's other colonial possessions in the Caribbean and the Pacific—Puerto Rico, the Philippines, and the island of Guam—were taken as well. America became an imperial power with overseas possessions like the European empires that already controlled much of the rest of the earth.

Whether war would have broken out absent the sinking of the Maine is a question that cannot be definitively answered. Surely the sinking of the ship and the blame placed upon the Spaniards for it did much to inflame American opinion and push the country down the road to war.

The theme of this book is that tiny blunders can lead to great disasters. In the case of the Maine, we must ask what tiny blunder occurred and what disaster followed from it.

If we maintain the opinion that the explosion on the Maine was accidental, then who blundered and how? The ship's design did not sufficiently isolate the coal bunkers from the ammunition magazines, nor did it allow for sufficient ventilation. The use of volatile bituminous coal as fuel could also be seen as a blunder. A number of similar fires using bituminous coal had been reported aboard American warships, which almost led to the ships being lost. Thus forewarned, should the Navy have foreseen the danger and taken preventative action?

Prior to this, the Navy had used anthracite coal to fuel its ships, and the properties of anthracite were such that the danger of self-ignition was negligible.[51] We can perhaps conclude that miscalculations regarding the ship's design—including small details such as adding windows and using fans for ventilation—was the crux of the problem. There was also a gap between the coal bulkheads and the powder bulkheads, which allowed fire to spread between the two areas. These slippages in the planning of certain key specifics led to the tragedy of February 15, 1898, which was certainly a disaster for the US Navy and above all for the men who perished on board the ship. But perhaps there is something deeper we should examine as well.

Was sending the Maine to Havana a blunder in and of itself? The ship sat for three weeks in Havana Harbor, accomplishing nothing other than showing the flag. When tragedy struck, the circumstances were such that the ship became a cause célèbre, helping to fuel passions that led to America's first imperial adventure outside the continental United States. The Spanish-American War was in some respects the forerunner of future, less successful American interventions in places such as Vietnam and Iraq. Some would say that the American presence in Cuba after 1898 contributed to the eventual rise of communism on the island, which in turn almost led to nuclear war in 1962. However, that is a stretch.

On the other hand, US intervention did assist the Cuban people in throwing off the yoke of Spanish domination. If we had to do it all over again, what course of action should have been chosen? We would do well to ponder that question rather than dismiss it out of hand.

USS Maine

SIDEBAR

———◦———

MILITARY PUNISHMENT

MUTINY, DESERTION, AND RANK INSUBORDINATION: THE CHALLENGE FACING EVERY COMMANDER

In his book *My Life in the Mountains and on the Plains*, David Meriwether opens a window for modern readers into nineteenth-century military punishment at its very worst. The story, which took place in the late 1830s, was part of the grim reality of the western frontier. To celebrate the holiday season, a senior army officer was having a number of his troopers flogged for various infractions. In the middle of the ordeal, one of the bloody and suffering "celebrants" called out to the commander, "This is a fine Christmas present, Colonel." From the commander's perspective, the trooper seemed to exhibit an absence of remorse. [52]

As retaliation for this act of insubordination, the commander ordered the post surgeon to cut the man's ears off. That night, in a final act of disobedience, the disfigured soldier wrapped himself in chains and threw himself in the river to drown. His bloated and mutilated body was found in the river the next morning.

In a spiteful salute to his superior officer, the soldier had given a final testament to the pain and hardship of military life.[53] One has to wonder if his family ever knew what became of him, or if they even cared. Would they have been proud or ashamed of his unbending and implacable defiance?

But what would cause a commander to take such sadistic action against his own men, men whose loyalty and cooperation he badly needed when facing hostile Native Americans? Before too harsh a judgment is passed on the severity of his actions, we should consider the dilemma of the combat commander leading a unit in the field against such an elusive enemy. He has a large number of armed and dangerous men who outnumber him and his fellow officers by perhaps as much as thirty to one—men who in many cases want to escape the military and avoid combat altogether.[54] Many of them at various times may be considering desertion or even mutiny.

There was always the challenge of a relatively small number of officers maintaining some semblance of discipline in a turbulent situation. Men were being asked to risk their lives under the force of law and commitment to duty, with perhaps a glimmer of inspiration. But conventional law enforcement was not close at hand, and duty is sometimes an intangible concept.

Exceptional leaders such as Joshua Chamberlain at Little Round Top or Julius Caesar at Alesia could inspire men to turn around and face the enemy rather than refusing to advance. But not all leaders are so charismatic or persuasive.[55] In fact, at least one Union general, Brigadier General James H. Ledie at the Battle of the Crater, became a deserter himself.

Some observers suggest that mutiny is a natural inclination in the majority of military units and a reality that all commanders must deal with. A considerable number of mutinies did in fact take place. And for every one that did transpire, there were many other unruly situations that came dangerously close.

Recent History

Until approximately 2014, it was very difficult to get Iraqi soldiers to even show up for everyday noncombat duty. It was nightmarishly more difficult to persuade them to stand firm in their ranks when facing a determined enemy such as ISIL. They would often throw down their weapons and "bug out" when there was serious fighting to be done. If US air support was unavailable because of sandstorms or other technical problems, the troops on the ground would often disintegrate under pressure.

Through US and allied support, the current situation has been greatly improved. The elite Special Operations Forces, also called the Golden Division, have been far more successful in the last two years in scoring major victories against their fanatical enemy. In just a brief period of time, they have gone from being known as "the Dirty Division" to the saviors of the nation.[56] Songs are written about their victories, and children throw them candy in admiration. In February 2016, Ramadi was retaken. And in July of 2017, they were successful in driving ISIL from the city of Mosul. The Golden Division has brought discipline and pride back to the Iraqi Army.

It has not always been pretty however. Along with their glory on the battlefield they have acquired a reputation for extreme brutality. Of course the reputation of their terrorist enemy is far worse.

Vietnam

Our Army that now remains in Vietnam is in a state approaching collapse, with individual units avoiding or having refused combat, murdering their officers, drug-ridden, and dispirited where not near-mutinous.

-Colonel Robert D. Heini, *Armed Forces Journal,* 1971

Our nation owes a great debt to economist Milton Friedman, not just for his Nobel Prize–winning advice and counsel on economic matters but also for persuading Richard Nixon to sponsor the creation of the all-volunteer army. Mr. Friedman pointed out to then–President Nixon that volunteer soldiers "would fight longer, harder and better" than men who were forced against their will into military service.

Flogging, a common military punishment

One conspicuous example of the value of this voluntary principle is the contrast between our combat military forces in the Vietnam War and the one that we have today in Iraq and Afghanistan. The very unpopular war in Vietnam produced many attempts at assassination or "fraggings," as they were sometimes called. Draftees, angry and embittered would throw hand grenades into the quarters of officers and NCO's at night as a act of extreme defiance.

This brutal form of insurrection was responsible for the deaths of dozens, hundreds, or by one report even two thousand officers and NCOs. There were many nonfatal causalities as well.

Military experts say that such activity is rare in today's all-volunteer army. The military personnel who serve in Afghanistan and Iraq have volunteered to be there to one extent or the other. The military situation that forces men against their will into combat had many negative consequences. Tragic lessons were learned the hard way. Hopefully with bitter wisdom, the system of forced participation will remain a thing of the past.

Ancient Times

The struggle to maintain discipline and control over fighting men has been a thorny issue for thousands of years. When Roman units did not perform well in the field, their commanders would sometimes go through a decimation process. The tribunes and centurions would go down the line and have every tenth soldier hacked to death by the men around him. It is hard for the twenty-first-century mind to grasp the experience. However, it is said that the process strengthened the morale of the rank and file.

American and European History

Christopher Columbus had his problems as well. Early in their voyage to the New World, Columbus's men had sabotaged the rudder of one of the ships. They wished to stop the voyage before it really began. The damage caused a delay but did not halt the overall mission.

Even greater problems took place near the end of the voyage. The disgruntled sailors in the small fleet were convinced they were facing impending doom. They insisted that Columbus turn the three ships around and return home to Spain. They had come so far across the broad Atlantic and the Sargasso Sea that they were losing hope of even surviving let alone finding great fortune.

On October 10, 1492, Columbus entered into a bargain with his sailors: The small fleet would be allowed to sail on for three more days. If they did not sight land within that time, they would then return home to Spain. Luckily, on the now famous 12th of October—Columbus Day—the land of the New World came into view.

It is hard to know who was more sadistic in dealing with the native people of the Americas, the newly arrived Europeans or native chieftains. The Aztecs killed large numbers of their own people in ceremonies of human sacrifice—tens of thousands, in fact. Ostensibly it was done to please the gods, but its practical purpose was to keep the populace intimidated and obedient. Under the guise of devoted worship, this was the Aztec way of enforcing discipline and avoiding insurrection.

Columbus, for his part, would cut off one hand of native workers who were not bringing in the assigned amount of gold from the mines. If the worker did not improve his performance, he would then be crucified. Union organizers and collective bargaining were still many years into the future.

The Lewis and Clark expedition also faced disciplinary problems even though their force was entirely voluntary. Their experience might have been typical of many military units around the world. Early in the expedition, a certain private flew into an emotional outburst in which he verbally abused his commanders in a very confrontational manner—an act of rank insubordination. He might have been under the negative influence of another member of the expedition. The young man was tried by court-martial, sentenced to forty lashes, and then "discarded"—that is to say, given over to the French as a deckhand on their riverboats plying the Mississippi.

Captain Kidd dealt with a confrontational sailor named William Moore by hitting him in the head with a leaden bucket and crushing his skull. The captain was later court-marshaled by an admiralty court in England. The murder of William Moore was one of the charges of which he was convicted. This was part of the reason, however justified or unjustified, that Captain Kidd was put to death by hanging. His body was framed in a gibbet and hung from a gallows at Tilbury Point. This was done as a warning to those who would not adhere to British law. Whether Captain Kidd was treated fairly or not is still the subject of considerable debate.

General Robert E. Lee of Old Virginia was a leader who was adored by his troops and is an icon of Southern tradition. Historians regard him as one of the best military leaders in American history. Nevertheless, this outstanding leader faced the crippling problem of men leaving the army to go home and harvest the crops in order to support their families. This was especially true in the last few weeks of the Civil War, when rations grew short and victory seemed more and more unlikely.

General Lee had forty-nine men executed for desertion during his tenure as commander of the Army of Northern Virginia. He informed Confederate president Jefferson Davis that unless desertions could be brought under control, "I fear the army can not be kept together." Until the last few weeks of the war, Lee had encouraged leniency in dealing with desertion, but desperation bred extreme measures even on the part of this consummate Southern gentleman.

Beginning in April 1865, Lee determined that failure to enact stricter measures upon those who fled the army "encourages others to hope for like impunity." He therefore called for heavier measures, even to include capital punishment. Most of these executions by firing squad took place in the last few days of the war. They were done so with the pronouncement, "So perish those who would betray their country in its hour of need and peril."[57]

George Washington also faced the challenge of having his army disintegrate in front of him and handled the problem with both severity and a carefully orchestrated bluff. He ordered a mass execution of deserters in a very public ceremony, but in the end, after much dark pageantry and the rolling of drums, only two were actually hung.

Desertion was a major problem in the cavalry units on the western frontier. Generals Custer and Mackenzie both had to deal with this ongoing challenge. Deserters were constantly being run down and returned to justice.

The Korean War was in some ways a low point for the US Army. A female reporter for the *New York Times* wrote in an article covering the war that she saw American soldiers throw down their weapons and run to the rear in the face of the Red Army onslaught. The American units had grown soft and undisciplined in peacetime Japan, where they had been stationed for years before the Korean conflict began. When the call to arms came, the Eighth Army, which included the First Cavalry and the Second Infantry divisions, were poorly equipped and unready to face the T-34 tanks and the mass attacks of the Chinese and North Koreans.

Scuttlebutt has it that these units left behind their dead
and wounded, which had to be retrieved in some cases by the
United States Marine Corps. It is not a part of any official
record, but the rumored story in the US Army is that the First
Cavalry Division fell into disgrace -"lost its colors" -in Korea
because of its poor performance and was not allowed to return
home as an identified unit. It was deactivated, an act amounting
to quiet disgrace. In 1965, when army units were transferred
from Ft. Benning, Georgia, to Vietnam, it was reactivated, and
these units were designated as the First Air Cavalry Division.
Because of its outstanding record in Southeast Asia, the Cav
then "regained its colors" and was allowed to return home to
Fort Hood, Texas, with full military honors. None of this is part
of any official record. It may or may not be true and belongs in
the category of barroom lore.

In World War I, after suffering huge casualties on the
Aisne (the Nivelle Offensive of 1917), the French army
mutinied and refused to engage in further attacks. Enormous
sacrifices had been made. The men were desperate. Meetings
were held with officers and compromises finally worked out.

The mutinies in the Russian Army in World War I
became a part of the revolution that helped bring the Bolsheviks
to power. It was a successful uprising in the sense that the
insurrectionists won, and the officers and the ruling class were
vanquished.

We should also mention the great mutiny of the British
Fleet in 1797 at Spithead and Nore. It led to better conditions
for some but also the execution of many of the leaders of the
revolt. And of course there was the mutiny on the Bounty.
Some say Fletcher Christian made it back to England near the
end of his life. Some even go so far as to say he was the model
for Samuel Taylor Coleridge's "The Rime of the Ancient
Mariner," although that may be a fanciful interpretation.

Hollywood has largely avoided this thorny issue altogether. Audiences much prefer to see heroic action by their men at arms, which make them feel good about themselves and about their country. Dissension in their military is conflicting and embarrassing. Kirk Douglas's movie Paths of Glory and Oliver Stone's Platoon are among the few exceptions to directly deal with this sensitive issue.

In summary, all armies and navies face the difficult task of forcing men into battle, often bitterly and against their will. These men are by definition armed and dangerous. The situation is often tense, difficult, and explosive. The officers, with the authority of the nation behind them, normally win the struggle. However, as we have seen, the mutineers sometimes prevail.

Captain Kidd

Jared Knott

PORTRAIT GALLERY

Robert E. Lee
Chapter 16
*Most people don't realize how close
the South came to winning the war.*

General Matthew Ridgeway
Chapter 7 and Sidebar page 393
*Without Matthew Ridgeway, there
would be no South Korea. North Korea
would have prevailed.*

Henning Von Tresckow
Chapter 3
*A man of great character. One of the
leaders in the German general's plot to
assassinate Hitler.*

General Dwight D. Eisenhower
Sidebar page 393
*Behind the famous grin, a man known for his
short and explosive temper. He was very
unforgiving of subordinates who disappointed
him.*

Benito Mussolini
Sidebar page 393
A man who failed his own people.

Major Patrick Ferguson
Chapter 21 page 263
The man who could have killed George
Washington.

Napoleon Bonaparte
Chapter 7
*The population of France is much
smaller today as a result of Napoleon's
conquests and defeats.*

Kaiser Wilhelm
Chapter 21
*World War I : A war that could have
been avoided for the good of humanity.*

Edward Norton Lorenz
Author's Introduction
Mathematician who coined the term "butterfly effect"

James McCord
Chapter 29
Undercover agent: The war that was lost by a single piece of tape turned the wrong direction.

Lyndon Baines Johnson
Chapter 27
Almost withdrew from politics at an early age.

Richard Nixon
Chapter 29
One of our greatest presidents – almost.

Inga Arvad
Chapter 2
Caught the eye of many powerful men.

Theresa LePore
Chapter 2
The design flaw that started a war.

Queen Ann Boleyn
Chapter 2
Did King Henry VIII's head injury lead to her death?

Lady Bird Johnson
Chapter 27 page 345
Saved the career of LBJ.

Maxwell Taylor
Sidebar: One Man's Stand Against Groupthink
*The most dangerous undercover misson of
World War II.*

Atul Gawande
Conclusion
*His book has saved thousands of lives and
continues to save many more lives than any other
book in history.*

B299 Crash
Conclusion
*A famous airplane crash that cost the lives of two men but
saved the lives of many thousands.*

Joseph Goebbels
Sidebar: One Man's Stand Against Groupthink

The face of evil. He and his wife committed suicide and murdered their six children as well. "I will jump into my grave a happy man knowing that millions of Jews have preceded me."

General George S. Patton
Conclusion

His fall from a polo pony in Hawaii in 1936 caused World War II to last six months longer. Patton was the U.S. General that Hitler feared the most.

Andrew "Stonewall" Jackson
Chapter 15
His eccentric military genius was the South's most consistent and dependable military asset.

Sam Houston
Chapter 7
His biggest secret was that he knew the Mexican army's biggest weakness.

228

Adolf Hitler

Did he miss an obvious chance to win
the war because of his overriding thirst
for vengeance?

Joachim von Ribbentrop

Germany's WWII foreign minister – along
with Hitler's top generals - advised the
dictator against declaring war on the United
States.

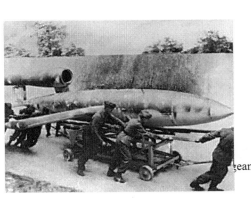

V-1 Rocket

Over 9,000 were dropped on
London, killing thousands of
civilians.

V-2 Rocket

1st Rocket to reach outer space. Over
3,000 dropped on London.

After the war, Eisenhower said that if the V-1s and V-2s had been directed at
Plymouth and the other embarkation points, the D-Day invasion would have to
have been postponed.

Chapter 2 and 24

THE CIVIL WAR

15

THE MUSKET BALL
THAT CHANGED HISTORY

I have lost my right arm.

> - Robert E. Lee, upon hearing about the death of
> Stonewall Jackson

Thomas Jonathan "Stonewall" Jackson was probably one of the two greatest tacticians in US military history, the other being General George S. Patton. The similarities between the two soldiers are striking. Both men were West Pointers. Both saw their first action in Mexico. Both were devout Christians (though Jackson was extremely pious while Patton used salty language and had at least one extramarital affair). And each died on active duty and at the height of his fame.

For Patton, death came after his mission—leading the Third Army to victory in Europe—was completed. Jackson, on the other hand, died in the midst of the Civil War. He had played a key role in most of the Confederate victories during the first two years of the war, culminating in the Battle of Chancellorsville. Chancellorsville was perhaps Stonewall Jackson's finest hour. It was also, of course, his final hour. And in a sense it was the Confederacy's final hour also. After Chancellorsville and the disappearance of Jackson from the scene, the Confederates never won another great victory.

Like Patton, Jackson struggled academically at West Point. A native Virginian, he was left an orphan at age seven. Because he lived with various relatives, his schooling was patchy and incomplete ; to a great degree he was self-taught.

Jackson gained admission to the Point only after the prospective cadet nominated for his congressional district withdrew. He made up for his lack of formal schooling through application and a determination to succeed, graduating seventeenth in his class of fifty-nine. The year was 1846.

As a second lieutenant serving in the artillery, Jackson found himself posted immediately to service in the war that had just broken out against Mexico. He served with distinction at the siege of Vera Cruz and the battles of Chapultepec and Mexico City. By the time the war ended in 1848, he had been promoted to first lieutenant. It was in Mexico that Jackson first met then-captain Robert E. Lee. Only fifteen years later, the two men were to form the greatest partnership in US military history, together masterminding a series of victories that for tactical skill were unsurpassed by any won by other generals before or since.

In 1851 Jackson accepted a teaching position at the Virginia Military Institute (where half a century later George S. Patton would be a cadet). An admirer of Napoleon as a military commander and an ardent student of the Corsican's campaigns, in his lectures Jackson (like Napoleon) stressed the importance of artillery in preparing the way for successful infantry assaults. Mobility and masking one's intentions were also high on Jackson's list of principles of war. Some of his teaching is still part of VMI's curriculum today.

Jackson was not, however, popular with his students. He lacked humor and the ability to present his teaching in an accessible fashion. Instead he memorized his lectures and then recited them back to his students, eschewing gestures, anecdotes, or other tricks of the trade that can enliven an academic presentation. He was nicknamed "Tom Fool," and at one point a group of alumni attempted to have him dismissed from his faculty position.

Nevertheless, on the battlefield of Chancellorsville, Jackson, surrounded by officers who had been students or colleagues at VMI, was heard to say, "The institute will be heard from today." Needless to say, Stonewall Jackson, like George S. Patton, is revered at VMI and by those who have studied or taught there.

Jackson, a Presbyterian, was very devout. He strictly observed the Sabbath and frequently read and quoted the Bible. Although he himself owned slaves, he was said to have been kind and respectful to them, to the extent that this was possible for people caught up in an inherently cruel institution. He is also said to have been respectful to free blacks that he encountered. He was twice married. His first wife died in childbirth; his second survived him.

At the outbreak of the Civil War in 1861, Colonel Thomas Jackson was given command at Harper's Ferry (now Harpers Ferry) in what is today West Virginia. Here he assembled and trained what would become known as the Stonewall Brigade, a body of troops formed from several Virginia regiments. The brigade proved its mettle on July 21, 1861, during the first Battle of Bull Run (or first Manassas). In this battle, the first major engagement of the war, the Union forces gained an early advantage. At a critical juncture, when the Confederate troops began to break and flee the battlefield, Jackson and his brigade stood fast, causing their comrades to gain faith and stand firm.

"Rally yonder by the Virginians. There stands Jackson like a stonewall." Thus said General Bee to give courage and direction to his men. The tide of battle turned, and the Union forces were routed. The stand by Jackson and his brigade was therefore the origin of the name "Stonewall" by which both were known from that day forward.

In the spring of 1862, Jackson cleared the Shenandoah Valley of Union forces in a brilliant campaign. During the Peninsula Campaign that followed, Jackson did not particularly shine, but then even Napoleon couldn't repeat Austerlitz every time he took the field. During the next ten months, Jackson established himself as the most capable field commander in the Confederate Army and indeed one of the ablest ever to put on a uniform.

Although remembered primarily for his audacious offensives and flanking maneuvers, Jackson's defensive successes deserve mention. In August 1862, after completely outmaneuvering Union general John Pope's Army of Virginia, Jackson assumed the defensive and held off the numerically superior Union forces until General James Longstreet arrived with fresh troops to complete the victory (Second Battle of Manassas).

The Army of Northern Virginia, commanded by General Robert E. Lee, followed up this victory by invading the North. Jackson retook Harper's Ferry and then joined Lee at Sharpsburg, Maryland.

The battle of Antietam was fought on September 17, 1862—the bloodiest single day in American military history. Tactically the battle was a draw, but the outnumbered Confederates escaped defeat because of the stubborn resistance offered by Jackson's troops on the Northern (left) flank of the Confederate line. After retreating into Virginia, the

Confederates won another great victory at Fredericksburg—a defensive success in which the attacking Union forces suffered three times as many casualties as the Confederates. Jackson's corps once again bore the brunt of a fierce but unsuccessful Union assault. The opposing forces then went into winter quarters.

The spring campaign of 1863 opened with the Confederacy in the ascendant. The Southern generals and soldiers had again and again shown themselves to be superior to their Union opponents on the battlefield—if not in courage, then in battle smarts and resourcefulness. In the first big battle of the spring, Chancellorsville, the South won its greatest victory so far. But it also lost its most capable field commander, a blow from which it would never recover.

The spring campaign opened with yet another Federal attempt to advance on the Confederate capital, Richmond. President Lincoln and his new commander, General Joseph Hooker, were more concerned with beating Lee's army than taking the capital, but they knew that if they marched on Richmond, Lee would certainly give battle rather than let Union forces occupy the town.

On the last day of April, Hooker's Army of the Potomac executed a flawless crossing of the Rappahannock River. Although heavily outnumbered, Lee decided to attack Hooker immediately on the thickly wooded ground near Chancellorsville, a little over fifty miles north of Richmond as the crow flies.

The first day's battle was inconclusive. Hooker now chose to dig in and let Lee attack him. The plan was for a Fredericksburg in reverse: Lee, Hooker believed, would launch a frontal attack and suffer the consequences, just as the Army of the Potomac had at Fredericksburg. Given Lee's inferiority in numbers—both men and artillery—it was a plan that should have worked. But Hooker hadn't counted on the qualities of imagination, improvisation, and boldness embodied by Lee and Jackson.

Lee and Jackson conferred on the evening of May 1. They came up with a bold plan to outflank the Union forces. Jackson would take about thirty thousand men, more than half of the available Confederate troops, and march west in order to get around and then attack Hooker's right flank, which was not anchored on any natural feature such as a river or mountain range but instead was "in the air." A flanking march over difficult, heavily wooded terrain would be no mean feat. But the battle-hardened Southern troops proved up to the task.

It took Jackson's forces most of the next day to complete their maneuver. Although the marching Confederates were spotted and Hooker issued orders warning his right wing to be prepared for an attack, the less-than-energetic Union commander on the right, Major General Oliver O. Howard, took no steps to protect his flank. This was an unforgivable lapse.

In the late afternoon of May 2, Jackson's men emerged from the forest, shouting the rebel war cry. The Union right, taken completely by surprise, was routed. Only nightfall saved the Union Army from a catastrophic defeat on the scale of a Cannae or Austerlitz. Fierce fighting continued on May 3 and 4, ending in a complete though costly victory for Lee (by the end of the battle, his losses in killed, wounded, and missing exceeded one-fifth of his force). But the victors suffered an even heavier blow during the battle: on the night of May 2, Stonewall Jackson was mortally wounded by what we today would call friendly fire.

Friendly fire is far more common than civilians realize. As discussed earlier even with today's advanced technology, the "fog of war" sometimes creates enough confusion to cause soldiers to shoot at their own side. And so it happened with Stonewall Jackson.

As the fighting died down temporarily on the night of May 2, Jackson and his staff rode back toward his headquarters. Confederate pickets mistook them for Union cavalry and opened fire. The first volley apparently missed Jackson. His staff desperately tried to identify themselves. Suspicious of their efforts at friendly communication, a confederate major thinking it was a ruse cried out "It is a Union Trick." A second volley rang out. Jackson was hit by three musket balls. One caused a minor wound to his right hand. The other two struck him in the left arm with what proved to be fatal consequences.

Jackson's arm was badly mangled, and he had lost a lot of blood. A young staff surgeon determined (correctly) that the wounded arm required amputation. The general was operated on under chloroform, and the procedure was a success. Remarkably, infection did not set in, and the general's wounds began to heal. It appeared as if he would survive to fight again. But then he developed pneumonia.

That the onset of the disease was caused by a general weakening resulting from his wounds is likely. In any case, there were no antibiotics in those days, no wonder cure. Stonewall Jackson's condition continued to worsen until he died on May 10, 1863.

Robert E. Lee was devastated by the loss of his principal lieutenant. "General Jackson has lost his left arm, and I have lost my right arm," he is quoted as saying after being told that Jackson had been wounded. The truth of his words was revealed as the war proceeded and the Confederate star went into eclipse.

What might have happened at Gettysburg had Jackson been present? The decisive battle of the war was fought with the ablest tactician on either side unavailable to help Lee. Would a desperate frontal assault such as Pickett's Charge have been Lee's choice on the final day had his ablest commander been available?

Thomas "Stonewall" Jackson

We can never know. But some historians believe that Gettysburg was lost earlier, on the very first day, when the Confederates failed to seize Cemetery Hill. Lee's orders on that day were not particularly crisp, and the Confederate general to whom they were issued, Richard Ewell, chose not to take the important height. Jackson, many believe, would have acted more aggressively and stormed Cemetery Hill.

One thing is not in dispute. After Stonewall Jackson's death, the South never again won a smashing victory along the lines of First and Second Manassas, Fredericksburg, or Chancellorsville. The odds were always stacked against the South. But the loss of Stonewall Jackson made those odds insurmountable.

A night ride during the confusion of battle. A volley fired mistakenly yet finding, tragically, its mark. A brilliant commander cut down while the scales of war were still finely balanced. A tiny blunder leading to a major disaster for one side. Thus, history was changed.

16

ANTIETAM CREEK: HOW THE SOUTH ALMOST WON THE WAR

Shelby Foote, the famous southern writer, was never very sanguine regarding the South's prospects of ever prevailing in the Civil War. Mr. Foote, who acquired a large following after being featured in Ken Burns' 1990 documentary on the Civil War, famously said, "The North fought the war with one hand tied behind their back. If there had been more southern victories, and I mean a lot more, I think that the North would have just taken that other arm out from behind their back. I don't think that the South had any chance to win that war."[58]

Those who agree with Mr. Foote point to the overwhelming numerical advantage the North possessed versus their more rural Southern counterparts. An unbiased, straightforward accounting of the military and industrial assets of one region versus the other might leave some observers wondering what made the South think it ever had a chance of winning the war in the first place.

Nearly twenty-one million people lived in twenty-three Northern states versus nine million in the eleven Southern states—and that number included 3.5 million slaves. (However, in the first year of the war, the South had an army equal in size to that of the North.) Proportionately speaking, the Confederacy was making a much larger commitment to the conflict. This might have reflected the deeper passion for the war that ran through the people of the South.[59]

The North also benefited from an immense overbalance in the area of industrial capacity. The numbers again paint a bleak picture for the chances of a Confederate victory. The South had only one-ninth the industrial capacity of the Union. But the numbers regarding war related production are even more telling regarding the Northern advantage. In 1860, the Union manufactured 97 percent of the country's firearms, 96 percent of its railroad locomotives, 94 percent of its cloth, 93 percent of its pig iron, and 90 percent of it boots and shoes.[60] The North had twice the density of railroads per square mile. There was not a single rifle works or cannon factory in any of the eleven Southern states.

But for all that was arrayed against them, Southerners did have the tactical advantage of fighting a defensive war on their home territory. The South also had the edge when it came to experienced military leadership (Many Southern families encouraged their sons to pursue a career in the army, and six out of the seven military schools in the United States were located in the South.)

But in spite of all the material disadvantages stacked against the Confederacy and the conventional wisdom that they had no hope of winning, this last advantage, as will be seen, *came very close to making all the difference.*

One of the most conspicuous examples of this superiority in military leadership came in the form of an 1829 graduate from the United States Military Academy who went by the name of Robert E. Lee. While a cadet at West Point, Lee earned the nickname "the Marble Model" for being the only cadet in the history of that institution to graduate with zero demerits: a perfect record.

When Lee was given command of the Army of Northern Virginia in June of 1862, the situation was grim to the point of desperation. Lee faced what seemed like an unstoppable tide of Union victories that were on the verge of overwhelming the Confederacy cause.

In the previous four months, the North had gained control of one hundred thousand square miles of Confederate territory in western Virginia, Tennessee, the Mississippi Valley, and other areas. An even more ominous threat to Southern survival was the advance of Union troops, whom at this point were only five miles away from Richmond. The fall of the Southern capital to General McClellan's Union forces would have been a disheartening setback—so damaging a blow that it might have led to the collapse of the Southern government altogether.

But it was at this point that General Lee introduced himself to the world with a series of stunning victories over the Union Army of the Potomac. His list of successes in that brief period is nothing less than astonishing. First came the Seven Days Battles (June 25–July 1), in which Union forces were pushed back from Richmond. Then came the Battle of Cedar Mountain (August 9), the Battle of Second Manassas (August 29-30), and then Chantilly (August 29–30).

Lee believed that in spite of these encouraging tactical successes, the South could not win the ongoing war of attrition. With the Union blockade of its ports, the Confederacy would eventually be starved into submission.

Lee felt that the only viable course of action was to invade the North and achieve victories so convincing that the European nations, specifically Britain and France, would extend

formal recognition to the Southern states. This might in turn
lead to the breaking of the blockade, which would force Lincoln
into a negotiated peace—the equivalent of a Southern victory. A
successful invasion, in addition to demoralizing the North,
might persuade the British and French governments to grant the
South the formal recognition it so badly needed. The hope and
possibility of ultimate success was therefore very real.

In early September 1862, Lee crossed the Potomac at a
ford thirty-five miles north of Washington with an army of
thirty-nine thousand men. His purpose was to stun the North
with yet another victory and bring the war to an early
conclusion. There was a feeling among the Southern troops that
with "Marse Robert" as their leader, the South might win the
war after all.

This developing situation is well summarized by noted
historian James M. McPherson in the book *What If?:* "Two of
Lee's hallmarks as a commander were his uncanny ability to
judge an opponent's qualities and his willingness to take great
risks."

Lee's plan for invading the North did indeed involve
great risks and was predicated on the perceived weakness of the
leadership of his major opponent. Lee explained the purpose
and plan of his campaign to Brigadier General John G. Walker,
commander of one of the columns that were to converge on
Harper's Ferry.

After capturing the garrison and its supplies, the army
would re-concentrate near Hagerstown. "A few days rest will be
of great service to our men," Lee said. "I hope to get shoes and
clothing for the most needy. But best of all it will be that the
short delay will enable us to get up our stragglers."

These stragglers had not been able to keep up with the
army because of exhaustion, hunger, and lack of shoes. Lee

believed that there were between eight and ten thousand stragglers who could be brought up to rejoin his army. This number proved to be correct.[61]

Lee then intended to tear up the Baltimore and Ohio Railroad and then move to Harrisburg and destroy the Pennsylvania Railroad Bridge over the Susquehanna, thus severing the Union's two east–west links. "After that," Lee concluded, "I can turn my attention to Philadelphia, Baltimore or Washington as may seem best for our interests."

Walker expressed astonishment at the breathtaking boldness of this plan, which would leave the Union army at his rear.

"Are you acquainted with General McClellan?" Lee responded. "He is an able general but a very cautious one. His army is in a very demoralized and chaotic condition and will not be prepared for offensive operations—or he will not think it so—for three or four weeks. Before that time, I plan to be on the Susquehanna."

At the same time of Lee's invasion of Maryland, important events interconnected with his overall strategy were unfolding on the other side of the Atlantic. In the time period leading up to Lee's invasion of the North, the economies of Britain and France were undergoing a cotton famine. They were desperately short of the Southern cotton needed to spin and weave cloth for their critically important textile industry.

The war was putting a tight squeeze on the European economy. Both nations were eager to end the Northern blockade of the South, and recognition of the Confederacy as a separate nation was under serious consideration.

With the string of Southern victories already achieved by General Lee, one more major success might bring an irreversible turning of the tide in favor of the South. The war had reached a critical moment. Everything depended on the success of Lee's invasion of the North.

General Lee had undertaken a great gamble, placing his entire army in wager. The world's leaders awaited the turning of the cards that would determine the fate of two nations. However, what might have been a striking success was fumbled away in a strange twist of fate. Maybe it was the hand of God moving in mysterious ways or maybe just a quirk of human frailty. The strange story unfolds as follows:

In the early morning hours of September 13, 1862, a small group of Union soldiers chose to rest in a field near Frederick, Maryland. As it happened, Confederate forces had camped there a few days earlier. Lying on the ground of the former Confederate encampment, they found a thick envelope containing official-looking documents wrapped around three cigars. The documents were signed by R. H. Chilton, Assistant Adjutant Gen., and at the bottom were the words "By Command of Robert E. Lee." To their surprise, they had found a copy of Lee's Special Order 191. The order had been carelessly dropped by a Southern officer.

The soldiers recognized the importance of the documents and showed them to their captain, who in turn sent them up the chain of command until they reached General McClellan. The authenticity of the documents was verified by a Union staff officer, Colonel Samuel Pitman, who had worked with Chilton before the war. The officer recognized the adjutant's handwriting.

McClellan therefore had a complete picture of Lee's bold and risky plan laid out before him. The Southern army was divided into five separate columns in a wide array that stretched for thirty miles from one end to the other.

McClellan knew immediately that he had the opportunity for a masterstroke. He wired President Lincoln: "I have all the Rebel plans and will catch them in their own trap." With understandable delight, he told General John Gobbon, "Here is a paper by which if I am unable to whip Bobby Lee, I will be sent home."

Softening McClellan's advantage somewhat was the fact that a spy informed Lee that his orders had been discovered. His plan for the invasion of the North had been compromised. Upon hearing the news, Lee began concentrating his far-flung units before complete disaster could strike his army.

Had McClellan moved quickly, he could have attacked Lee's divided army and destroyed it one section at a time. Instead, after a quick start on the morning of September 14, he again became overly cautious. He did not launch the full attack until the 17th, by which time Lee's army was mostly reunited along Antietam Creek. The ensuing battle was the bloodiest single day in American history with twenty-three thousand casualties. But Lee's forces survived the battle and were able to retreat across the Potomac into Virginia. The Union won a narrow but bloody victory on points, but a great opportunity had been lost.

Many have speculated that except for the lost order, Lee's plan as outlined to General Walker would have succeeded. The Army of Northern Virginia would have been on the Susquehanna and in a position to threaten Northern cities. Shocking as it seems to modern observers, the South might very well have won the War Between the States. And sadly, history would have been turned on its head.

The Confederacy came within an ace of winning the war. And that ace took the form of Order 191, which was wrapped around three cigars stuffed in an envelope and dropped in a Maryland cornfield.

General McClellan

Dead at Antietam

MISTAKES OF FIRE
AND BRIMSTONE

17

ALFRED NOBEL AND THE ACCIDENTAL INVENTION OF DYNAMITE

People around the world recognize the name Alfred Nobel as that of the father of the Nobel Peace Prize and the prizes awarded annually in literature, physics, chemistry, medicine, and economics. Nobel was the quintessential Renaissance man who had a genuine and abiding interest in each of these areas. As an inventor, however, he is primarily remembered, for his development of explosives for use in mining and the construction of roads and rail lines. To his later embarrassment his explosives were also used for military purposes.

The story of how Nobel came to establish the Peace Prize is especially revealing of the complex character of this man for all seasons. It passes all the tests for inclusion in this chronicle of blunders and their unforeseen repercussions because it was a tragic accident with nitroglycerine that killed his brother and spurred him on to complete the work they had started together. And it was by another mishap that Nobel discovered how to stabilize nitroglycerine. As a result of this mistake, he became the inventor of dynamite, which became invaluable in the field of heavy construction, such as tunnel building. However, it had deadly consequences when it was used by the arms industry in the production of powerful weapons. Finally, as will be seen it was because of a case of mistaken identity that Nobel was faced with a foreshadowing of his legacy as a "merchant of death." And it was because of this premature obituary that he started engaging in the soul-searching that brought him to the idea of the creation of the Nobel Peace Prize.

Nobel's father, Immanuel Nobel, was an inventor-entrepreneur who patented the concept of plywood and worked on early versions of underwater mines that were used to protect harbors. Although Alfred was born into poverty in Stockholm in 1833, his father's inventions brought increasing opportunity and financial security to the family. When the family moved to St. Petersburg, Russia, in 1842, the young Alfred benefited from the best education available to the upper class at the time.

Alfred was drawn to chemistry and had his father's inventor genes. He would eventually be granted 355 patents for everything from gas meters to detonator caps to artificial silk. It is said that as a child he escaped from being in time-out in an upstairs bedroom by making a parachute from an umbrella and ropes.

In addition to being a natural-born inventor, Alfred was also of a poetic bent and drawn to the study of literature. So, perhaps to persuade him to follow a more practical career, Immanuel sent his son at age sixteen to Paris, where he studied with the Italian chemist Ascanio Sobrero, the inventor of nitroglycerine. The next year, 1850, Alfred was sent to the United States to apprentice with the Swedish-American inventor John Ericsson, who would go on to build the ironclad ship Monitor of Civil War fame.

In 1852, Alfred returned to St. Petersburg to help with the family business, which was booming as a result of the increased orders for armaments in the lead up to the Crimean

War (1853–1856). There he continued to work on the problem of how to stabilize nitroglycerine so that it could be handled safely in mining and construction operations.After the war ended, Alfred and one of his brothers, Emil, returned to Stockholm, while his other two other brothers, Robert and Ludvig, remained in St. Petersburg to try to salvage the family business, which was teetering on the brink of bankruptcy now that the war was over and orders had declined substantially.

In Stockholm, Alfred and Emil pursued the family goal of finding a way to stabilize nitroglycerine. In 1864, after several smaller accidents, an explosion killed Emil and several workers. After that, as if to ensure that his brother's life had not been lost in vain, Alfred was more determined than ever to find a way to stabilize the volatile substance. That discovery was to be made by accident, one that might have killed him but instead culminated in a "eureka moment."

While in the process of transporting a quantity of nitroglycerin, one of the cans became damaged. Some of the explosive liquid leaked out into the bed of crushed sedimentary rock called kieselguhr in which the container had been set for stability. Nobel found that the resulting puttylike substance retained the explosive power of nitroglycerin but was far less volatile. His testing showed that this new stabilized compound could now be safely transported by wagon and formed into explosive charges. Nobel patented his new product in 1867 under the name dynamite.

Nobel's involvement in the armaments industry intensified in the last decades of his life—as, paradoxically, did his interest in world peace. He elaborated on his views regarding war and peace in an ongoing correspondence with the Austrian peace activist, the Countess Bertha von Suttner. Even as early as their first meeting in Paris (1876), Nobel had tried to justify the advancement of more powerful weapons. He argued from a perspective familiar to those of us who grew up during the Cold War, when MAD (mutual assured destruction) was the doctrine that assumed the nuclear arsenals of the Soviet Union and the United States would cancel each other out. World leaders would understand that the devastation of a nuclear attack would make it unthinkable to use when your adversary could respond in kind. In correspondence with the countess in 1891, Nobel tried to reconcile a commitment to world peace with his activities in the arms industry. He wrote, "Perhaps my factories will put an end to war sooner than your congresses: on the day that two army corps can mutually annihilate each other in a second, all civilized nations will surely recoil with horror and disband their troops."

Nobel was never able to fully face up to the consequences of his invention's destructive capacity. However, another blunder, this one by a journalist, would serve as a wake-up call that inspired Nobel to create the Peace Prize that would become his enduring legacy.

In 1888, when his brother Ludvig died, a French newspaper mistook him for Alfred and published a scathing obituary, "LE MARCHAND DE LA MORT EST MORT" ("The merchant of death is dead"). The obituary further characterized Alfred as a man "who became rich by finding ways to kill more people faster than ever before." Nobel was horrified by this premature obituary. He resolved to rectify this horrific image and leave the world with a more benign legacy. So this part of the story, at least, can be classified as one of those mistakes that led to a rich and positive outcome.

In 1896, one year before his death, Nobel drastically revised his will, devoting most of his vast fortune to the creation of the Nobel Prizes, including the Peace Prize. Because of the existence of this prestigious prize, the work of many great Nobel Laureates has been supported and acknowledged before

the whole world. Jane Addams, Albert Schweitzer, Mother Teresa, Martin Luther King Jr., Nelson Mandela, and Jimmy Carter are among the people who have received the Nobel Peace Prize. Organizations as diverse as the UN, the Red Cross, the European Union, and the Grameen Bank have also been acknowledged in this way for their work for world peace.

Albert Einstein addressed the issue of the scientist's social responsibility in a speech he delivered only months after two atom bombs had been dropped on Japan. He pointed to the parallels between their predicament and that of Nobel. Einstein said, "Alfred Nobel invented an explosive more powerful than any then known—an exceedingly effective means of destruction. To atone for this 'accomplishment' and to relieve his conscience, he instituted his award for the promotion of peace."

Nobel's legacies—dynamite and the Nobel prizes—are still with us. But if not for a can of nitroglycerine that leaked into the right kind of crushed rock, Nobel might never have created dynamite. And if not for a premature obituary published in a Paris newspaper, he might never have been moved to create the Peace Prize that has played such a positive role since his actual death. These tiny blunders have had great and lasting consequences.

Emil Adolf von Behring, the first recipient of the Nobel Peace Prize. He is most known for his work in developing a serum to help cure diphtheria.

18

THE GREAT CHICAGO FIRE

"Where has this fire gone to?"

The answer was swift and apt: "She has gone to hell and gone."

Residents noticed that a freakish wind whipped the flames into great walls of fire more than 100 feet high, a meteorological phenomenon called "convection whirls"—masses of overheated air rising from the flames and began spinning violently upon contact with cooler surrounding air.

"The wind, blowing like a hurricane, howling like myriads of evil spirits," one witness later wrote, "drove the flames before it with a force and fierceness which could never be described."

- Karen Abbot

According to the 1870 US Census, Chicago was well on its way to surpassing St. Louis as the metropolis of the American Midwest. Before the nineteenth century ended, it would become the second-largest city in the United States, surpassed only by New York City. Its population had tripled between 1850 and 1860, and then tripled again in the next decade. But in 1871, Chicago suffered a great disaster—a fire of epic proportions.

The Great Chicago Fire burned for three days, from Sunday, October 8, to Tuesday, October 10. It destroyed some two thousand acres of the city, killed three hundred Chicagoans, and left one hundred thousand more homeless. Contemporaries compared it to the burning of Moscow during the Napoleonic Wars. Only heaven-sent rains finally quenched the blaze on the 10th.

Conditions were ripe for disaster in Chicago during the fall of 1871. Many of the city's buildings were constructed of wood. Fire codes and firefighting techniques were of course not as advanced as they are today. Perhaps the most critical factor was the terrible drought that was affecting the city and the upper Midwest as a whole. We could say that Murphy's Law was looming over Chicago in the autumn of 1871, casting a dark shadow that would suddenly be transformed into a burst of terrible, fiery light.

The fire broke out on the West Side of the city, in a barn on DeKoven Street. The barn belonged to an Irish immigrant family name O'Leary. Who or what started the fire remains a mystery to this day.

There's no evidence for deliberate arson. Most likely an accident started the blaze, but spontaneous combustion cannot be ruled out. There's even an extraterrestrial explanation for the origin of the fire. Of course, those who know their folklore will recall that the fire was attributed to Mrs. O'Leary's cow kicking over a lantern, which set the straw ablaze. The ensuing fire consumed first the barn, then the neighboring houses, and finally much of the city. Let's briefly examine the theories about the fire's origin.

Milk Thieves and Neighbors

The fire began around 9:00 p.m. on October 8. As it happened, there was a party going on in a nearby house on the O'Learys' street. According to some accounts, a man (possibly drunk) left the party and entered the barn, whereupon he decided to steal some milk. While milking Mrs. O'Leary's cow, either he or the cow knocked over the lantern. There is, however, no solid evidence supporting this story. The O'Learys' neighbor across the street, a one-legged man named Daniel Sullivan, was the first person to report that fire had broken out in the barn. Suspicion fell upon him simply because he had made the report. But no evidence whatsoever points to him as the arsonist.

Mrs. O'Leary. Catherine O'Leary and her husband, Patrick, were hardworking Irish immigrants with five children. Catherine sold milk from the family's five cows door to door in her neighborhood, while Patrick worked as a laborer. According to Catherine, on the night of the fire, she went to bed between eight o'clock and eight-thirty. She was awakened by her husband shouting that the barn was on fire. She emerged onto the street to see neighbors desperately battling the blaze as it spread from house to house. There is no real reason to doubt her account.

After the fire, the Chicago Board of Police and Fire Commissioners conducted an exhaustive inquiry into the fire, coming up with no evidence against Mrs. O'Leary (they were in fact unable to establish any cause for the fire). Why then did Mrs. O'Leary and her cow go down in history (or at least in folklore) as the villains of the piece? Enter the yellow press.

American journalism in the nineteenth century, and particularly the daily newspapers of the time, often displayed a disregard for the truth. Standards were low, and ethics frequently gave way to the pursuit of readers and profits. At the same time, ethnic prejudices were often openly displayed, even reveled in. One of the ethnic groups most often targeted in the 1870s was the Irish. Mrs. O'Leary and her husband were, of course, Irish. When reporters descended upon DeKoven Street in the wake of the fire, some children told them that the blaze had been caused by a cow kicking over a lantern. Rather than take this children's story with a proper grain of salt or undertake a proper investigation, the reporters fixed on Mrs. O'Leary as the cause of the disaster. The fact that the wind had caused the blaze to blow away from the O'Leary house, thereby miraculously saving it from destruction, further whetted the journalistic appetite for sensationalism, slander, and lies.

Mrs. O'Leary was tried and convicted in the court of public opinion by a merciless pack of journalists eager to fix blame for the fire upon a member of a detested ethnic group. She was portrayed as a bitter old hag (she was in fact only forty-four years old) who resented her lack of social status and had sworn to have revenge upon a city that had refused to embrace her. There was not a scintilla of truth in the florid accounts produced by the Chicago newspapers, but the slander stuck. Mrs. O'Leary entered the folklore of the city and the nation as the woman who, accidentally or intentionally, burned down Chicago. The following ditty was still being sung by Chicago schoolchildren decades after the event:

> Late one night, when we were all in bed,
>
> Mrs. O'Leary lit a lantern in the shed.
>
> Her cow kicked it over, then winked her eye and said:
>
> "There'll be a hot time in the old town tonight!"

Catherine O'Leary, alone and embittered, died in the 1890s. Only in 1997 did the city of Chicago get around to admitting publicly that she had had nothing to do with the great fire.

Spontaneous combustion or a cinder. Spontaneous combustion of hay or straw is a well-known phenomenon and may possibly have occurred in Chicago in 1871. Typically hay and straw ignite spontaneously due to bacterial fermentation. The exceedingly dry conditions at the time, however, perhaps indicate that the straw in the barn was set alight by a stray cinder, possibly from a chimney. Winds were strong on October 8, and certainly many fireplaces would have been lit on an autumn night in Chicago, which is definitely a northern city. An accident of this kind seems the most likely origin of the fire.

To repeat, there is no evidence pointing to any person (or cow) accidentally or deliberately starting a fire in the O'Leary's barn.

The extraterrestrial explanation. A fascinating possibility is that the fire was sparked by a visitor from outer space. The Chicago fire was in fact only one of several huge conflagrations that took place simultaneously in Illinois, Wisconsin, and Michigan. By a curious coincidence, the Great Peshtigo Fire in Wisconsin (considered by many to be the greatest natural disaster in American history—a wildfire that killed possibly as many as 2,500 people) and huge fires in Michigan coincided with the Chicago fire. It has been speculated that the breakup of the comet Biela caused a meteor shower that ignited the blazes. However, scientists are skeptical because meteorites reach the earth's surface in a cold state. However, we don't yet know everything there is to know about what falls from the sky, so the jury is still out on this theory. I don't dismiss it, although it seems to me more likely that a

terrestrial cinder or spark carried on the wind was what brought
Chicago to grief.

We've already touched upon some of the Murphy's Law
aspects of the Great Chicago Fire. I should add that the fire
brigade was initially misdirected and therefore arrived late at
the scene; this probably doomed any slim chance that the fire
could have been contained. If we step back and look at the city
of Chicago in early October 1871, we see a crowded town built
largely of wood, with primitive firefighting equipment and
many sources of sparks or cinders that could get a fire going.
Add to this a massive drought that rendered all sorts of tinder
ready to burn and you have a disaster waiting to happen. When
disaster did strike, human error ensured that the worst would
occur. Whatever could go wrong did go wrong in Chicago on
October 8, 1871.

19

THE FORGOTTEN FIRE
THAT SUNK A GREAT SHIP

The sinking of the RMS Titanic may have been caused by an enormous fire on board, not by hitting an iceberg in the North Atlantic, [as] experts have claimed.

- Senan Molony

Perhaps the most famous example of Murphy's Law run amok is the fate of the White Star liner RMS Titanic. The Titanic was a technological wonder of its time. A huge ocean liner, Titanic was just a few inches short of 883 feet in length (almost three football fields!). She was over one hundred feet tall from the bottom of her keel to the top of her bridge (175 feet to the top of her funnels) and weighed a whopping forty-six thousand tons. There were ten decks. She was the largest ship afloat when she entered service in 1912 and could carry over 3,500 passengers and crew. While at sea, she burned over eight hundred tons of coal per day. Even by today's standards, these numbers are pretty staggering.

Construction of the ship began in 1909. It reportedly cost $7,500,000 to build the Titanic—about $180,000,000 in today's money. At completion in 1912, Titanic and her sister ship Olympic were the biggest passenger liners ever built (though soon to be surpassed in size by three German liners launched in the following year).

Titanic was perhaps the most luxurious ship of her time, though some have said that the White Star liner Oceanic, launched in 1899, was even more well-appointed. No expense had been spared in her construction and no convenience or luxury overlooked. The ship's first-class accommodations contained for dining and other refreshments restaurants, cafés, tea gardens, and dining salons.

Passengers could seek recreation in the gymnasium, squash court, or heated pool, after which they could relax in the Turkish bath. The ship had a barbershop and a library, as well as reading, writing, and smoking rooms, a post office, and even a kennel (how many dogs were on the ship is unknown, but two were saved when it sank). The opulence found in first class was epitomized by the famous Grand Staircase, encased by a glass dome. There were enclosed decks on which passengers could promenade or sit and gaze at the sea.

The comfort of second-class passengers was also assured, although they of course enjoyed somewhat less luxurious surroundings. For example, dinner in second class consisted of three courses (soup, main course, and dessert), whereas dinners in first class typically contained ten courses, each served with a different wine.

The lowest passenger level was third class or steerage. These passengers were mostly immigrants traveling to America or Canada in search of a better life. Their accommodations were in no way comparable to those in first or even second class. Flying coach today probably approximates the conditions in third class on the Titanic, with the difference that today a trip across the Atlantic takes only six or seven hours rather than the six or seven days that a ship like the Titanic needed to reach its destination.

The Titanic was built in Belfast by the firm Harland and Wolff. It incorporated some though not all of the best shipbuilding technology of the time. In fact several flaws in the ship's design contributed to the ensuing disaster. First and foremost was her rudder, which was considerably smaller than the rudder of other, smaller liners such as Cunard's Lusitania. A smaller rudder meant a less maneuverable ship, and maneuverability is at a premium when one is sailing in waters containing icebergs.

The steel used for the Titanic's hull was of inferior quality. Specifically, its sulfur content was high, making it brittle in cold temperatures and liable under such conditions to break rather than bend in a collision.

The hull might have been further weakened by a fire in one of the coal bunkers that was burning before the ship sailed and possibly continued to burn while Titanic crossed the Atlantic. Bunker fires of this type were fairly common on passenger ships of the time, caused by the physical properties of coal and the manner in which it was stored. A documentary by Irish journalist Senan Molony, broadcast on the Smithsonian Channel in January 2017, asserted that the fire created a chain of events that led to the sinking of the ship. Molony's theory has not yet been accepted by many experts.

The lower portion of the Titanic was divided into sixteen watertight compartments. The ship could survive the flooding of up to four of these compartments. However, the compartments were not truly watertight. In fact, the tops of the compartments were open, and the bulkheads extended only a little above the waterline. If the ship were damaged and began to list or dip, water could overflow from one compartment into another.

Worst of all perhaps was the fact that the Titanic carried only twenty lifeboats with a capacity of not quite 1,200 people. It was felt that too many lifeboats would crowd the decks, interfering with the passengers' enjoyment of their journey. And so many lifeboats might lead some passengers to believe that the ship was unsafe. How unsafe was soon to be revealed!

The Titanic was capable of carrying over 3,500 passengers and crew. If an accident befell her while at sea, what would happen to the people left on board after the lifeboats had all been launched? Unless rescue craft could reach the scene before she sank, those still on board would be doomed to die. Water temperatures in the North Atlantic quickly produce hypothermia, followed by death. Anyone unlucky enough to be in the water would survive only a very short time.

The flaws outlined above were to contribute mightily to the tragedy of the Titanic. It is generally believed that the builders of the Titanic described her as an unsinkable ship. This has been disputed. Some researchers and historians claim that the term "practically unsinkable" was used. Be that as it may, it seems clear that complacency reigned and that no person of importance in maritime affairs was the least bit concerned about the safety of the ship.

Sea trials were held on April 2, 1912, immediately after construction was completed, and they were uneventful. The ship then sailed from Belfast to the British port of Southampton. Passengers began boarding the Titanic on the morning of Wednesday, April 10. They included some of the richest and most prominent people in the world—for example, American millionaire John Jacob Astor IV and his near-contemporary, the businessman Benjamin Guggenheim. Many other people who were prominent and even famous in 1912 (though largely unremembered today) were also aboard the ship.

The Titanic left Southampton at noon on April 10. Stops were made at Cherbourg, France, and Queenstown (now Cobh) in Ireland to pick up additional passengers. As she set out across the Atlantic, bound for New York, Titanic was carrying over 2,220 passengers and crew (the precise number is uncertain as some people who booked passage didn't make it to the ship, and some passengers who boarded at Southampton are believed to have left the ship at Cherbourg or Queenstown).

For the first four days, the ship's journey was uneventful. As she approached the Grand Banks off Newfoundland, Titanic received warnings from other ships in the area that she would be encountering floating ice. Despite this, she continued ahead at nearly full speed—a procedure that would prove fatal to many on board, including the captain, Edward Smith.

Captain Smith was a highly experienced merchant captain. By 1912, he had been commanding ships of the White Star line for some twenty-five years. He was captain of the Titanic's sister ship Olympic on her maiden voyage in 1911. On another voyage later that year, Olympic collided with the British cruiser Hawke, an accident for which a Royal Navy board of inquiry held Olympic and her captain responsible. Despite this mishap, Smith was given the job of guiding Titanic on her maiden voyage to New York.

To proceed at full speed into waters infested with drifting ice seems sheer madness, but amazingly, it was nothing unusual for the time. Priority was given to arriving at the destination on time, and lookouts were relied on to provide sufficient warning so that ships could take evasive action if necessary. Given what we know today about the maneuverability (or lack of same) of this gigantic ship, equipped as it was with a too-small rudder, we can only shake our heads at the foolhardiness displayed. Had the captain simply ordered the ship to proceed more slowly, the worst might very well have been averted. But it was not to be.

Shortly after 11:30 p.m. on April 14, a lookout spotted an iceberg ahead. The first officer, William Murdoch, who was on the bridge, ordered a change of course to avoid the looming ice giant. But to no avail. The starboard side of the Titanic scraped the berg, tearing holes (recall the poor-quality steel mentioned earlier) along the waterline. Five of the ship's "watertight" compartments were breached, which made it inevitable that the ship would sink. The bow dipped, and water overflowed into more compartments, hastening the demise of the ship.

In his quarters, Captain Smith felt the collision and immediately came to the bridge. He called for Thomas Andrews, the naval architect who had built the Titanic, who was aboard for the maiden voyage. The two men went below to examine the damage. Finding five compartments flooded, Andrews gave Smith the melancholy news that the great ship was doomed to sink. Water was pouring into the ship at a rate much faster than it could be pumped out. Nothing remained but to try to save as many of the people aboard as possible.

Just minutes after midnight, Captain Smith ordered that the lifeboats be readied and the passengers brought on deck. Many passengers were asleep and had to be wakened. They then had to dress and put on their lifebelts before proceeding to what they hoped would be the safety of the lifeboats.

But of course, there were only enough lifeboats to accommodate about half of the people on board. The rule of "women and children first" was largely followed, particularly in first and second class. Panic was largely absent because most passengers and even many of the crew did not know the ship was sinking.

Captain Smith did not perform well in this, the crisis of his career. He seems to have been overwhelmed by the enormous tragedy unfolding before his eyes. He failed to direct or communicate clearly with his crew, making the evacuation of the passengers a somewhat haphazard affair. He never actually gave the order to abandon ship.

Many lifeboats reached the water with empty seats because there were no further women and children close by when the boat was lowered. Several hundred additional passengers could have been saved if all the lifeboats had been filled to capacity. After John Jacob Astor placed his wife on a lifeboat, he was turned back even though the boat was being lowered with twenty seats empty. Some passengers refused to enter the lifeboats, preferring the perceived safety of remaining on board the "unsinkable" ship. In all, only slightly more than seven hundred passengers made it into a lifeboat, leaving some fifteen hundred on board to die.

The ship's wireless operators began sending out distress calls almost immediately after the collision with the iceberg. The first SOS ever sent using the relatively new marconigram technology was from the Titanic. Unfortunately, most ships in the vicinity were hours away. One exception was the British steamship SS Californian. The Californian had sent one of the iceberg warnings to the Titanic; she had also, prudently, come to a full stop for the night in order to avoid the ice danger.

Baffling as it may seem, the Californian's captain did not respond to the distress rockets being fired from the sinking liner. These were quite visible to the men on the British steamer, which was probably only about ten miles away. The Californian's wireless operator had turned off the wireless set and gone to bed just minutes before Titanic struck the iceberg, so Titanic's distress call was not picked up by the Californian. The Californian's captain merely ordered that an attempt be made to contact the other ship by Morse lamp. When Titanic did not reply, the captain washed his hands of the matter. He went to bed. Even the following morning, after learning of the sinking, the captain at first sailed his ship away from the scene of the tragedy. Only later that morning did he reverse course and head back toward the Titanic's position, arriving just after the last survivors had been picked up by other ships. The callous behavior of the Californian's captain has been the subject of much controversy but has never been adequately explained to this day.

There was a brief period of false hope on the Titanic, at least for most of the passengers and crew who were not aware that the ship was fated to sink. For a time, the ship seemed

stable in the water, her bow only slightly dipped. About 1:30 a.m. on April 15, the condition of the ship worsened, and at 2:20 a.m., Titanic's bow slipped underwater. Simultaneously the stern rose high into the air. People who had been huddling together on deck fell into the sea. The ship broke in two and was swallowed by the Atlantic.

Captain Smith went down stoically with his ship, as did its builder, Thomas Andrews. Not so the chairman and managing director of the White Star Line, J. Bruce Ismay, who was also aboard for the maiden voyage. Ismay found a seat on the last lifeboat after helping other passengers to secure seats. He was roundly criticized in the press and elsewhere for not going down with the ship. In fairness, however, it seems clear that he would have accomplished nothing by dying other than adding to the sad total of over 1,500 fatalities.

Some passengers behaved nobly in death. Benjamin Guggenheim helped other passengers to safety, then dressed as if for dinner and was last seen sitting in a deck chair, calmly smoking a cigar. Some wives refused to part from their husbands, preferring death to separation.

Ironically, J. P. Morgan, who owned the White Star Line and therefore the Titanic, had been scheduled to travel on the ship but had cancelled at the last moment. Violet Jessop, a stewardess who survived the sinking, went on to become a nurse on the Titanic's sister ship Britannic during World War I. She again survived when the Britannic was sunk, probably by a German U-boat or mine, in 1916. Of course, the greatest irony of all is that nearly five hundred passengers on the Titanic perished because lifeboats were lowered with seats still empty.

Reportedly some people had premonitions of the disaster, although I have been unable to confirm that anyone predicted beforehand that the Titanic would sink. An American writer, Morgan Robertson, published a novella, Futility, or the Wreck of the Titan, in 1898. It told the story of a huge passenger liner hitting an iceberg while crossing the North Atlantic during the month of April. In the story, huge loss of life occurs because the liner did not have enough lifeboats. Pretty eerie. The superstitious reader will also be interested to learn that thirteen honeymooning couples were aboard the Titanic when it sank.

In truth, the Titanic was the victim of Murphy 's Law. Design flaws, lack of lifeboats, and a captain's decision to sail at full speed through what's known as "Iceberg Alley" all set the stage for disaster. Any one of these things could have led to the worst. As it turned out, they all contributed to the tragedy. What can go wrong most likely will.

The "Unsinkable" Molly Brown

20

THE HINDENBURG:
THE FIERY END TO AN ERA

It's smoke, and it's in flames now; and the frame is crashing to the ground, not quite to the mooring mast. Oh, the humanity!

- Herbert Morrison

The Hindenburg disaster of May 6, 1937 ended the era of the airship as a major means of transportation. It is perhaps hard for most of us to imagine that a mere eighty years ago, people thought of the airship as the standard vehicle for crossing the Atlantic by air. The development of large and powerful propeller-driven airplanes, then jets—not to mention the fact that the space age began a mere twenty years after the crash of the Hindenburg, and that we today are on the verge of tourist trips by rocket into outer space—makes the airship era seem both quaint and far distant in time. But in fact there are people still living today who once thought of the airship as the way to travel long distances by air.

The Hindenburg (named after Paul von Hindenburg, the World War I German field marshal who went on to become president of Germany) was what is known as a rigid airship, that is, one containing a rigid metallic structure into which are fitted gas bags or cells filled with hydrogen or helium. (A nonrigid airship is just a big gas-filled bag with a gondola attached, as in the classic Goodyear Blimp.) Almost all airships achieve lift by being filled with the lighter-than-air elements hydrogen or helium; since the 1970s a few have used hot air instead. An airship also has an internal combustion engine or electric motor to provide power for flying the craft.

People had been ascending into the sky in hot air balloons since the eighteenth century. Then in the nineteenth century, German and French engineers developed powered airships. Count Ferdinand von Zeppelin built his first airship just before the beginning of the twentieth century. The first zeppelin took flight on July 2, 1900.

Count von Zeppelin was born in 1838. He joined the army of the German state of Württemberg in the 1850s, fought on the Prussian side in the war of 1866 against Austria, and fought in the Franco-Prussian War of 1870–1871. He also served as a military observer with the Army of the Potomac during the American Civil War. He eventually reached the rank of lieutenant general but was forced to retire from the army after mishandling his forces during maneuvers in the year 1890.

Von Zeppelin had a background in science and already in the 1870s had shown an interest in the airship as a means of transportation and for military purposes. After leaving the army, he focused almost all his time, wealth, and attention on constructing an airship that would surpass those developed in France. After ten years of effort, he had achieved his goal. The Luftschiff Zeppelin, the first rigid airship to fly, made its maiden flight over Lake Constance on the German–Swiss border.

Count von Zeppelin spent the next several years further refining and improving his airship design. At this time, zeppelins were viewed mainly as a military weapon, an instrument that could negate British naval superiority through bombing and, if necessary, conduct raids against London and

Paris. When World War I broke out in 1914, the zeppelins had their chance.

The results were pretty unimpressive. A few zeppelin raids on London caused terror and damage to property, but they were in no way decisive to the war's outcome. With time the British learned how to cope with the raids. The superiority of the single-seater fighter aircraft was demonstrated in 1916 when for the first time a British flyer shot down a zeppelin over the British capital.

Count von Zeppelin died on March 8, 1917. He was spared witnessing both Germany's defeat in World War I and the disaster that befell the last of the zeppelins twenty years later.

The airship had shown itself to be far from a war-winning weapon, but after the guns fell silent, its peacetime potential still seemed enormous. In the early 1920s, airships represented the only means of conveying passengers and cargo by air over very long distances. When Charles Lindbergh crossed the Atlantic in the Spirit of St. Louis in 1927, airplanes were still too small to make transatlantic passenger or cargo flights. The airship ruled the skies so far as long-distance travel was concerned. Airships were also faster than passenger liners such as the Queen Mary, though their carrying capacity was smaller.

In the mid-1920s, after restrictions placed by the Treaty of Versailles (1919) were lifted, the Zeppelin Company began constructing airships for passenger and cargo service. Rigid airships were also being constructed at this time in Britain and the United States. The US, however, abandoned the airship after all three of its craft (built by the Navy) were lost in accidents.[62] These losses were rather ironic in that US airships were inflated with helium, a stable, nonflammable gas whereas European airships used highly flammable (and therefore potentially dangerous) hydrogen. Helium is a rare element on Earth. In the 1920s, the main supply was found in Texas, and the United States refused to export the gas for national security reasons.

Britain abandoned airship development after the crash of its R101 in 1930 (forty-eight of fifty-four passengers, including the secretary of state for air, were killed in the crash). As the fateful year of 1937 approached, the hydrogen-filled German zeppelins had by far the best safety record in the world.

Germany's Graf Zeppelin began carrying passengers across the Atlantic between Germany and Lakehurst, New Jersey, in 1928. In 1929, it flew around the world in twenty-three days, starting at Lakehurst and stopping for landings at Friedrichshafen, Tokyo, and Los Angeles. An airplane had already circumnavigated the globe in 1924 but had required 175 days to do so, making seventy-four stops.

When German engineers completed construction of the Hindenburg in 1936, airships still ruled the air. The Hindenburg was bigger than its predecessors and thus able to carry more passengers. It had a very successful 1936 season, making seventeen trips to the United States and Brazil. On May 3, 1937, the Hindenburg departed Frankfurt on its first flight of the season to the United States. It would not return.

The flight was routine (though delayed by headwinds) until Hindenburg attempted to land at Lakehurst on May 6. Thunderstorms in the Lakehurst area caused the captain, Max Pruss, to fly the ship over Manhattan Island and along the Jersey shore while he waited for the weather to clear. Shortly after 7:00 p.m., half a day behind schedule, the Hindenburg finally prepared to land at Lakehurst. The crew dropped mooring lines to personnel on the ground. As these were being connected by the ground crew, some witnesses noticed the fluttering of fabric in front of the airship's upper fin (located at the rear of the ship), a possible indication that gas was leaking.

Suddenly, flames were spotted, though the exact location on the ship where the fire started remains in dispute. In any case, the body of the airship was soon in flames, and it crashed to the ground tail first. Of the ninety-seven people on board, thirty-five were killed and many others badly burned. Some burned to death or died from smoke inhalation while others jumped to their deaths attempting to escape the flames. One member of the ground crew was also killed.

What caused the disaster? To this day the cause is not definitely known. Perhaps the most likely scenario is that static electricity built up on the ship's outer skin and then ignited hydrogen that was leaking from the ship. The fire spread from one gas cell to another, consuming the ship. Another theory is that St. Elmo's fire, which some witnesses claim to have seen playing along the top rear of the ship in the seconds before it burst into flames, provided the deadly spark. Given the weather conditions at the time (thunderstorms earlier in the day), the possibility that St. Elmo's fire was the culprit should not, in my view, be dismissed. Sabotage has even been put forward as a possible cause of the disaster, though no real evidence for this exists.

In truth, the Hindenburg was simply a disaster waiting to happen. Although prior to the accident the Zeppelin Company could point to a perfect safety record, the airship design created by Count von Zeppelin was inherently unsafe. As already mentioned, the airship was basically a giant floating bag filled with highly flammable hydrogen gas. It was probably inevitable that at some point something would happen to ignite the hydrogen. And once ignited, there was no practical way to stop the fire from spreading, with fatal consequences for many if not all of those on board. In other words, it was only a matter of time before Murphy's Law would come into play.

The Hindenburg (May 6, 1937)

The Hindenburg disaster brought the airship era to an abrupt end. No further passenger flights were made. The airplane was by now on the cusp of achieving regular transatlantic passenger flights, though still in far less comfort than the great airships could provide. But in any case, the future belonged to the airplane. The airship was just too likely to suffer the worst possible consequences of Murphy's Law.

WAR AND RUMORS OF WAR

21

A MURDER IN BOSNIA: BEGINNING OF WORLD WAR I

Europe today is a powder keg and the leaders are like men smoking in an arsenal. . . . A single spark will set off an explosion that will consume us all. I cannot tell you when but I can tell you where. Some damned foolish thing in the Balkans will set it off.

- Otto von Bismarck at Congress of Berlin, 1888
(attributed)

Europe in 1914 was indeed a powder keg. The great powers of the day were divided into two opposing blocs: imperial Germany and the Austro-Hungarian Empire on one side, and Britain, France, and tsarist Russia on the other. The rivalries were intense, the potential areas of conflict many. But probably the most dangerous area of all was the Balkans, where Russian and Austro-Hungarian interests were sharply defined and almost impossible to reconcile.

The Balkans comprise the southeast corner of Europe. In 1914, Austria-Hungary lay immediately to the north while Russia bordered the region to the northeast. Austria-Hungary and her ally Germany saw the Balkans as the road to the Middle East—via the Balkans, the Teutonic powers would be able to make direct contact with the Ottoman Empire (present-day Turkey), allowing access to the rich resources (oil, gas, and minerals) that were available there. The German project of building a Berlin-to-Baghdad railway depended upon having an access route through the Balkans.

Austria-Hungary had its own particular concerns about the Balkans. The Austro-Hungarian Empire was a polyglot of peoples held together in large part by the prestige of the Hapsburg dynasty, which had ruled Austria-Hungary for centuries. The Austrians and Hungarians were the dominant peoples in the empire. Their subjects included many Slavic peoples—Czechs, Slovaks, Slovenes, Croats, and Serbs. The Serbs under Hapsburg rule were concentrated in Bosnia, a province Austria-Hungary had acquired from the Ottomans in the nineteenth century and then annexed in 1908.

The Austrian annexation of Bosnia caused a crisis that almost led to war. During the nineteenth century, nationalism and ethnic identity became more and more important throughout the world. The Panslav (or Pan-Slav) movement was one outgrowth of this. Panslavism, which originated in Russia (the largest Slavic country), called for the independence of all Slavic peoples under Russian leadership. Russia also had economic interests of her own in the Balkans. Austria and Russia were bound to be rivals for power and influence there. Tensions between the two powers increased throughout the later nineteenth century and into the twentieth, culminating in the Bosnian crisis of 1908.

The Balkans had once been controlled by the Ottoman Turks. During the nineteenth century, Russia fought a series of wars against Turkey in which the Turks were consistently defeated. As a result, Turkey lost a great deal of territory, particularly in the Balkans. After a resounding Russian victory in a war fought in 1877–1878, the great powers assembled at the Congress of Berlin to parcel out the gains. Russia was deprived of some of the fruits of her victory, including Bosnia, which was placed under Austrian administration.

Bosnia had a Muslim majority, but there was a significant minority of ethnic Serbs who, like the Russians, were Orthodox Christians. Serbia itself, for centuries an Ottoman province, was now an independent kingdom once again and looked to Russia for leadership and support. Both Serbia and Russia chafed at the idea of Catholic Austrians ruling over Orthodox Slavs. When in 1908 Austria-Hungary took advantage of temporary Russian weakness (Russia had just been defeated in war by Japan and had then undergone a revolution, the precursor to the revolutions of 1917) to annex Bosnia, Panslavs in Russia and Serbia were infuriated.

War was avoided in 1908, largely because Russia was too weak to fight Austria-Hungary and Germany. In addition, Britain and France had no interest in getting involved in a war over Bosnia.

Tensions, however, continued to build. Immediately after Austria- Hungary annexed Bosnia, a semisecret National Defense group was formed by leading Serbian officials and generals. Its purpose was to undermine Hapsburg rule in the Slavic territories of Austria-Hungary and then to form a Greater Serbia by combining those territories with the Serbian kingdom. In 1911, young Panslav officers in the Serbian army formed the Black Hand, a secret terrorist organization dedicated to the uniting of all South Slavs in a single state to be called Yugoslavia. The Black Hand received covert support from the Serbian government and the Russian secret service.

The Black Hand was armed, trained, and guided by Serbian army intelligence. In 1913–1914, a plan took shape to assassinate the governor of Bosnia. This, it was hoped, would awaken the Slavs of Austria-Hungary and perhaps provoke a revolution. But before the Black Hand could act, a much bigger target entered the picture.

Archduke Franz Ferdinand was heir to the throne of Austria-Hungary. His uncle, the elderly Emperor Franz Joseph (1830–1916), despised him for marrying a mere countess (Sophie, later Duchess of Hohenberg) rather than a member of one of the ruling families of Europe. Indeed, as a condition of permitting the marriage to take place, Franz Joseph insisted that any children the couple had would be debarred from the throne. Franz Ferdinand, who dearly loved his wife, agreed.

Franz Ferdinand was a man of varied character. He was authoritarian and temperamental yet saw quite clearly that in an age of nationalist fervor, the multiethnic Austro-Hungarian state would have to adapt or die. He had far-reaching plans to grant autonomy to the Slavs and other subject peoples of the empire. He preferred to get along with Serbia and Russia rather than provoke them. Had he lived, the course of European history might have taken a far different turn than it in fact did.

In 1914, Emperor Franz Joseph was eighty-four years old. Almost certainly it would be only a few more years before Franz Ferdinand would come to the throne and begin implementing his projected reforms. Ferdinand was only fifty years old, in the prime of life, and could look forward to a long reign in which the tensions prevailing in Europe could be lessened and peace prolonged, perhaps indefinitely. Such was the hope.

The Black Hand had other ideas. They recognized that Franz Ferdinand represented a major stumbling block on the

road to achieving a Greater Serbia. When in June 1914 they
learned that Franz Ferdinand would make an official visit to
Sarajevo, the Bosnian capital, the terrorists prepared to strike.

The head of Serbian army intelligence provided the
conspirators with weapons. The Serbian prime minister got
wind of the plot but did not attempt to stop it beyond cautioning
the Austrian government that the visit to Sarajevo could prove
dangerous. The Austrians disregarded this veiled warning.
According to most sources, members of the Russian embassy in
Belgrade (the Serbian capital), including the ambassador, were
aware of the plan to kill the archduke yet did nothing. The
Russian ambassador to Serbia died under somewhat mysterious
circumstances just twelve days after the assassination.

Six terrorists, five Serbian nationals, and a Bosnian Serb
were waiting when the archduke and Sophie arrived in Sarajevo
on June 28, 1914. The archduke had been attending army
maneuvers, and now the couple was about to participate in the
opening of a new museum in the center of town.

The date was a special one. June 28 marked the 525th
anniversary of the Battle of Kosovo, a disastrous defeat the
Serbs had suffered at the hands of the Ottoman Turks. It also
happened to be Franz Ferdinand and Sophie's wedding
anniversary.

The couple arrived in Sarajevo by train. The plan was to
travel by car to the Sarajevo town hall for a welcoming
ceremony. A motorcade of six cars was formed, with Franz
Ferdinand and Sophie sitting in the third car. The folding top of
the car was left down, making the couple easy targets. The
assassins were dispersed at various points along the motorcade
route.

As the motorcade passed the first terrorist, who was
armed with a bomb, nothing happened. The man had lost his

nerve. The second terrorist threw his bomb, but it bounced off the folded-down top of the car and exploded underneath the fourth car, wounding several people. The other five cars now proceeded at speed to the town hall, where, incredibly, the planned program was at first continued.

After the reception at the town hall, it was decided to abandon the rest of the itinerary and visit those who had been wounded in the bombing. To this point the archduke and his wife had been quite lucky. But now two blunders occurred that, taken together, proved fatal for the couple and ruinous for the continent of Europe.

Someone proposed that soldiers be brought in to provide security. The governor of Bosnia, a general, vetoed this idea because the only soldiers available were on maneuvers and didn't have the requisite dress uniforms required by protocol! "Do you think Sarajevo is full of assassins?" he reportedly said. Well, it might not have been full of them, but there were still members of the Black Hand at large and prepared to act.

The archduke and his wife reentered the open car, which drove off toward the hospital. Traveling to the hospital required a change in the route originally planned for the motorcade. The first blunder—failing to provide adequate protection for the motorcade—was clearly a major mistake. And yet the archduke and duchess would probably have avoided death but for a tiny blunder that now occurred.

One of the terrorists, a consumptive nineteen-year-old Serbian nobody named Gavrilo Princip had stationed himself outside of Schiller's Delicatessen, an eatery on the original motorcade route. He was armed with a revolver. Given that the motorcade was supposed to travel to the hospital by a different route, Franz Ferdinand and his wife should never have come close to Princip. But now the fatal mistake occurred. The driver in the lead car mistakenly made a turn that put the motorcade back on the original route. As the car approached Schiller's Delicatessen, Princip stepped forward and fired. The first shot pierced the archduke's jugular vein; the second struck the duchess in the stomach. Both bled to death before they could receive medical attention.

The deaths led directly to the most destructive war the world had yet known. Austria-Hungary, with German backing, sent a very sharp ultimatum to Serbia, which included provisions that violated Serbia's sovereignty. Serbia replied in a conciliatory manner, agreeing to all the Austrian demands except the ones that violated its sovereignty, while proposing that those points be submitted to arbitration. But with Franz Ferdinand dead, the hardliners in Austria-Hungary were in control. They wanted to solve the Serbian problem for good—and by force. The Serbian reply was rejected, and Austria-Hungary declared war on Serbia on July 28, 1914.

Serbia's protector, Russia, could not stand by and allow Austria-Hungary to crush a Slavic Orthodox nation. It mobilized against Austria-Hungary. Germany had a formal alliance with Austria-Hungary and France with Russia. By August 3, these four great powers were at war with one another. Britain, after a belated attempt to interest Germany in mediation, threw in its lot with France and Russia, declaring war on Germany on August 4. The European conflagration had begun.

The war shook European civilization to its foundations. Millions of men were killed in four years of brutal fighting. The Russian, German, and Austro-Hungarian empires suffered collapse, and the economic and social progress that had marked the late nineteenth and early twentieth centuries was brought to a halt by the onset of total war. Nor was that all, for the dislocations caused by World War I led directly to a second and even more destructive conflict. Most historians agree that, absent World War I, World War II would not have occurred. A man like Hitler would never have come to power if the political order of prewar Europe had not been overturned by the events of 1914–1918.

The question remains: could World War I have been avoided? Obviously, we can't know for sure, but the best chance for avoiding it was lost when the moderate and reasonable Franz Ferdinand was assassinated. Had he lived, the conflict between Teuton and Slav in the Balkans might have been avoided. And that would have gone a long way toward securing the peace. But it was not to be. A chauffeur made a wrong turn and thereby brought disaster to Europe.

Author's note: It is sometimes said that Princip, the assassin of Franz Ferdinand, emerged from Schiller's Delicatessen, lunch in hand, just as the Archduke passed by. In fact, this tale is a recent invention with no substance.[63]

22

FALLING STARS:
THE DEATHS OF ADMIRALS,
GENERALS, AND PRESIDENTS

Compared to simple soldiers and sailors, generals and admirals are rarely killed in war. But when they do fall, their deaths can sometimes change the outcome of a battle, a campaign, or even a war. The death of a president of the United States, particularly since the US has become a superpower, can have even more profound effects on the course of human history. In this chapter I discuss the deaths and near-deaths of generals, admirals, and presidents, some of whom are among history's most famous (and powerful) leaders. First, we will look at those who died (or not) at the hands of those who deliver death a great distance through stealth and camouflage, the sniper.

The Snipers Who Did and the Snipers Who Didn't

The sniper is a killing specialist par excellence. A master of marksmanship and usually of camouflage as well, he strikes suddenly and as if from nowhere. The sniper's art was brought to perfection by the superefficient marksmen (and occasionally women) of the twentieth and twenty-first centuries. American, British, and Russian snipers are particularly renowned for their deadliness and stealth.

Sniping has been around since the invention of firearms capable of propelling a ball or bullet hundreds or thousands of yards. And in fact, even an archer can be a sniper. The killing of King Richard the Lionhearted, shot by a crossbowman who was behind a castle's walls while the king was within his own army's lines, could be termed a death by sniper. Here, however, we will focus on snipers who made their kills (or not) with a musket or rifle.

By definition, the sniper kills one enemy at a time. He does not have the power to kill hundreds or thousands of people at once in the way modern ordnance can. However, he can produce an effect as great as the most powerful weapon if with one shot he eliminates a leader who possesses the ability to shape events. The death of King Richard is a perfect example of this.

James Stewart, Earl of Moray and regent of Scotland (c. 1531–1570), was the first notable person to be killed by a sniper wielding a firearm. Moray was the half-brother of Mary, Queen of Scots, and became regent of Scotland after her abdication in 1568. Although a capable ruler and leader, as a member of the Protestant party in Scotland, he was bitterly opposed by the Catholic supporters of Mary. While riding through Linlithgow on January 23, 1570, he was shot and killed by one James Hamilton. Hamilton fired a carbine (in this case a short-barreled musket) from an upper-story window. Given the relatively primitive nature of sixteenth-century firearms, one can only say that Hamilton's feat amounted to good shooting. With Stewart's death, the sniper was born.

Two hundred years later, one of the great figures in American history, the indispensable man of the American Revolution, came within range of a sniper. By all odds this man should have died because the sniper in question was perhaps the best marksman of his day. That the leader survived was possibly a miracle, or perhaps just the result of one man's whim. In any case, history was affected in a very profound way. The story is as follows.

The Man Who Could Have Killed George Washington

Major Patrick Ferguson was a British officer of Scottish descent who fought against the Americans in the Revolutionary War. He was born in 1744 in comfortable circumstances and in his teens obtained a commission in the Scots Greys, one of the most famous cavalry regiments in the British Army. He served with them during the Seven Years' War in Europe, after which he transferred to an infantry regiment. Interested in musketry and highly inventive, he developed the Ferguson rifle in the early 1770s. This gun was lighter and more rapid-firing than the standard Brown Bess musket then in use. Based on a French model, it proved too expensive to produce in large quantities and thus never become standard in the king's forces. Nevertheless, it was the first breechloading gun produced in the Anglo-Saxon world (all previous ones being muzzle loaders) and was used in the Revolutionary War and beyond.

Ferguson became an expert marksman, perhaps the best in the British army of his time. In 1777, he was sent to America at the head of a company of sharpshooters whose purpose was to redress the superior marksmanship that the American forces had displayed at Lexington and Concord and Bunker Hill. Ferguson saw his first major action at the Battle of Brandywine on September 11, 1777.

Brandywine Creek is located east of Philadelphia, which in 1777 was the capital of the fledging United States. British forces commanded by General Howe, including Major Ferguson and his sharpshooters, advanced against the American forces under General George Washington. Brandywine was the biggest battle (in terms of numbers engaged) fought during the

War of Independence; it was also the longest, lasting some eleven hours. The Americans were defeated and withdrew to Germantown, allowing the British to occupy Philadelphia. But something even more serious than the loss of the nation's capital nearly occurred before the battle was joined.

On September 7, as Ferguson and three of his sharpshooters were waiting in ambush at the edge of a wood, an American officer dressed like a general and accompanied by a single aide (the latter described by Ferguson as wearing a hussar's uniform) came into view. The two American officers were perhaps reconnoitering; their exact reason for being in that particular location is not definitely known.

Though they were within range of Ferguson and his men, as chance would have it, they never turned to face the concealed snipers. Ferguson, perhaps considering it ungentlemanly to shoot an officer in the back or perhaps simply on a whim, ordered his men to hold fire. The two officers then rode off.[64]

During the battle four days later, Ferguson was wounded by a musket ball in the arm. While being treated, he garnered information from captured American wounded that led him to believe George Washington was the general he had decided to spare. Had Ferguson passed on the opportunity to kill General George Washington, commander in chief of the Continental Army?

Ferguson certainly believed he had. His correspondence, still extant and in the possession of the Public Records Office in London, states as much. And he probably was correct in this belief. Admittedly, he had never met Washington and almost certainly had never seen a portrait or other likeness of the general, so a positive identification would not have been possible.

Furthermore, some historians have raised questions about the fact that only a single officer accompanied the American general. However, Washington was a brave man willing to expose himself to enemy fire when duty required it, so his riding out on reconnaissance without guards would not have been out of character. And the single officer accompanying the general in question actually helps to confirm that Washington was indeed within Ferguson's sights.

As mentioned, Ferguson described the other officer as wearing a hussar's uniform. There were no hussars in the Continental Army. However, shortly before the Battle of Brandywine, Count Pulaski, a Polish nobleman, had joined the American cause and been appointed aide de camp to Washington. Pulaski, a cavalryman, always wore a hussar's uniform. It therefore seems all but certain that the officers Ferguson and his men spotted were General Washington and his new aide de camp, Count Pulaski. There appears to be corroborating evidence for this in the correspondence of another of Washington's aides, Robert Harrison, which states that Washington did indeed conduct a personal reconnaissance on September 7, 1777.[65]

It was lucky sevens for Washington that day and for the American cause. There is perhaps no greater example of the influence a single person can exert on history than that of George Washington in the Revolution. It's difficult to believe that the American army and the United States itself could have held together against the mighty British Empire without Washington's steady hand at the helm of affairs. Those readers who look askance at luck and see greater forces at work will no doubt see the action of Providence in Washington's escape. Perhaps the hand of God had shielded Washington from death at the hands of Major Ferguson.

There can be no doubt that Ferguson or one of his sharpshooters would have delivered a kill shot had he fired. But Major Ferguson held his hand—and thereby changed history. His blunder, if we can call it a blunder, led to a great disaster for the British Empire: the loss of the American colonies.

Ferguson was killed at the Battle of Kings Mountain in 1780. Count Pulaski, who could have confirmed the events of September 7, was killed in action at Savannah in 1779. Washington lived on to become the father of his country.

Timothy Murphy and Brigadier Fraser

The most famous American sniper of the Revolutionary War, and perhaps indeed until the emergence of Chris Kyle (the Navy SEAL and subject of the book *American Sniper*) in the early twenty-first century, was Timothy Murphy of New York. His marksmanship helped turned the tide of the Revolutionary War in the Americans' favor.

Simon Fraser was a Scottish soldier who fought and died on the British side during the Revolutionary War. A soldier from the time he was eighteen, Fraser served with distinction in the French and Indian War, including at the Siege of Louisbourg (1758) and the Battle of Quebec (1759). He returned to Canada in 1776 to take part in the war to recover the American colonies. Promoted to brigadier general, he was given command of the advance guard in General Burgoyne's invasion of New York.

At the battles of Hubbardton and Freeman's Farm, both hard-fought actions, Fraser's troops bested the Americans, though suffering heavy losses. In the latter battle, they first encountered Daniel Morgan's riflemen, a picked unit of sharpshooters that included Timothy Murphy.

The next engagement was fought at Bemis Heights on October 7, 1777. Brigadier Fraser led his troops into battle with his usual boldness and tactical skill. With the outcome still in doubt, Benedict Arnold (the later traitor) is supposed to have ridden up to General Morgan and pointed to Fraser, saying that the British commander was worth a regiment. Thereupon, according to the story, Morgan turned to Murphy and exclaimed, "That gallant officer is General Fraser. I admire him, but it is necessary that he should die. Do your duty."

Murphy is said to have climbed a tree and fired three shots in quick succession. The first missed; the second grazed Brigadier Fraser's horse; the third found its mark, hitting Fraser in the abdomen. He fell, mortally wounded, and died that night. Murphy is then said to have shot and killed Sir Francis Clerke, aide de camp to General Burgoyne. During the battle, Burgoyne himself was nearly killed by Morgan's marksmen.

The death of Brigadier Fraser demoralized the British, who began a retreat that ended with Burgoyne's surrender at Saratoga on October 17, 1777. Exactly a month after Patrick Ferguson had spared George Washington at Brandywine, American sniper Timothy Murphy had killed the ablest British general in the army that was threatening to split the American colonies and turn the war decisively in Britain's favor. The Battle of Saratoga is generally considered to be the turning point of the Revolutionary War. Certainly, it led directly to the conclusion of the alliance between the United States and France (February 6, 1778), which in turn made the decisive American victory at Yorktown possible. Snipers, it's clear, played a major role in deciding a war whose outcome has resonated through history down to our own day.

Note: Whether Timothy Murphy actually killed General Fraser is disputed; some scholars believe the story is a nineteenth-century invention. However, it's virtually certain that Fraser was shot by one of General Morgan's sharpshooters—if not Murphy then another sniper whose name has not come down to us.

The Death of Lord Nelson

Vice Admiral Horatio Nelson (1758–1805), generally considered to be the greatest of all British admirals, is the most famous commander ever killed by a sniper. Nelson entered the navy in 1771, when he was only twelve years old. He first served on a vessel commanded by his uncle, Captain Maurice Suckling. He became an officer in 1777 and served on several ships during the American Revolutionary War. He was promoted to captain in 1781.

After peace broke out in 1783, Nelson's career languished, but the war against revolutionary France, which began in 1793, provided the backdrop against which he ascended to heroic and indeed legendary status. Posted to the Mediterranean, he distinguished himself in the Corsican campaign of 1794, during which he was wounded and lost the sight in his right eye, and at the Battle of Genoa in 1795. He was given his first independent command (of a squadron) in 1796 and in 1797 won fame at the Battle of Cape Saint Vincent when he disobeyed orders and attacked a Spanish fleet, capturing two enemy warships. Later that same year, he lost most of his right arm at the Battle of Santa Cruz de Tenerife. The arm was badly shattered by a musket ball. A surgeon performed an amputation, and amazingly, Nelson immediately resumed command.

His exploits had already made Nelson a hero to the British public. Now, as he neared age forty, he began his ascent to world fame. On August 1, 1798, he annihilated a French fleet at Aboukir Bay—the Battle of the Nile. This doomed Napoleon's expedition to Egypt, itself designed to be just the first step in a march on British India. Nelson was wounded yet again in this battle but again survived.

His next great feat occurred in 1801, when he led a British fleet in a surprise attack on the Danish Fleet at Copenhagen. His victory ended the Northern Confederacy (Russia, Prussia, Sweden, and Denmark), which had opposed Britain's blockade against French trade in the Baltic.

However,all this was but a prelude to the culmination of Nelson's career and life. After a brief period of peace in 1802–1803, Britain and Napoleon's France were once again at war. Napoleon gathered his Grand Army at Boulogne on the English Channel preparatory to invading and finally conquering England. Success depended on the Franco-Spanish fleet under Admiral Villeneuve joining the army at Boulogne and covering the passage of Napoleon's troops.

In the spring of 1805, Villeneuve's fleet broke out from the Mediterranean into the Atlantic. Blockaded by Nelson's forces in the Spanish port of Cadiz, it sallied forth on October 20. At last Nelson would come to grips with the one force that could bring about the defeat of England.

As the battle was about to begin, Nelson sent his famous signal: "England expects that every man will do his duty." Nelson himself was, as usual, careless of his own safety. He was wearing his full uniform, including all of his many medals. He had been warned not to do so because French snipers in the upper rigging of the French ships might identify him and pick him off. "In honor I have won them, and in honor I will die with them," he replied. Apparently, Nelson had had a premonition of death. He said to one of his captains before the action began, "God bless you, Blackwood. I shall never see you again.

And so, it proved true. The battle resulted in one of the most decisive victories in naval history, with two-thirds of the

French and Spanish ships sunk or captured. The victory was even more remarkable in that the British were outnumbered and outgunned. The "Nelson touch" and the courage and fortitude of the English sailors had carried the day.

But, as he had been warned, Nelson was an easy target for French marksmen. As the battle opened, Nelson sailed his flagship, Victory, into the midst of the enemy fleet.

About an hour after the battle began, a sniper aboard the French ship Redoubtable, which was locked in combat with the Victory, fired a musket ball that shattered Nelson's spine. Nelson, who had been wounded numerous times in action, knew this shot was fatal. "They finally succeeded. I am dead," he exclaimed. He actually died about three hours later, with victory assured.

Trafalgar saved England from invasion and definitely established British naval supremacy. But the cost—the loss of Nelson—weighed heavily on Britain and its people. "We have lost more than we have gained," a weeping King George III said on hearing the news of the victory and the death of England's greatest admiral.

As it turned out, Napoleon never again threatened Britain at sea, and indeed British naval supremacy went unchallenged for more than another century. But this could not have been known at the time. Nelson's blunder in wearing his dress uniform and medals had led to a disaster: the death of the one man who had balked the plans of the apparently unbeatable Napoleon. Britain's ultimate victory over Napoleon was by no means assured by Nelson's victory (Wellington and Waterloo came ten years after Trafalgar). The loss of Nelson might have led to disaster for the British Empire.

Abraham Lincoln

We all know that John Wilkes Booth killed President Abraham Lincoln with a pistol shot in Ford's Theatre. Many of us don't know that in the summer of 1864, Lincoln was twice nearly killed by snipers.

In July 1864, Confederate forces under General Jubal A. Early undertook the last Southern invasion of the North. Briefly it appeared that Early might be able to take the Northern capital, Washington, by a coup de main. On July 12, Early's troops were engaged with federal forces at Fort Stevens on the outskirts of Washington. President Lincoln came to Fort Stevens to observe the battle. While he was standing on the parapet, an army surgeon beside him was shot in the thigh by a Confederate sharpshooter. The commander of the fort, General Horatio Wright, ordered the president to remove himself from the line of fire, and the president complied. The battle ended in a Confederate retreat.

It is said that Oliver Wendell Holmes, the future Supreme Court justice, then a young officer in the Union Army, shouted at the president, "Get down, you damn fool!" after the surgeon was shot. As he was leaving the fort, Lincoln said goodbye to Holmes and supposedly added, "I'm glad to see you know how to talk to a civilian." The story is almost certainly apocryphal; the danger to Lincoln, however, was all too real.

A month later, in August, the president once again came within inches of death. He was in the habit of leaving the White House in the evening and traveling to the Old Soldier's Home about three miles away to work and rest. One night in August (the date is uncertain), he rode out from the White House, alone and unprotected. As he was riding along, a shot rang out. His horse bolted, and the president lost his hat. A soldier was sent to retrieve it and found a bullet hole through it. An unknown sniper had taken a shot at the president, missing him by inches.

Twice in two months, Lincoln had come within inches of being killed.[12] Had he died before the 1864 election, chaos might have ensued. The election might have been cancelled and a dictatorship or something like it set up under the forceful secretary of war, Edward Stanton (the vice president under Lincoln, Hannibal Hamlin, was a nonentity).

Or the election might have been held and the Democratic candidate, General George B. McClellan (a former commander of the Union Army), might have won. McClellan ran on a platform calling for the retention of slavery and a negotiated end to the Civil War. Had he won, the South might have achieved independence just when it appeared its cause was lost. So much depended on one man's life, twice nearly ended by snipers who missed by inches!

The actual killing of Lincoln will be discussed in the section on presidents later in the chapter.

Operation Foxley

Another sniper who didn't was involved in the proposed Operation Foxley. This was a British plan to kill Hitler during World War II. Although der Führer never held the rank of general or admiral, I feel that as commander in chief of the German armed forces, he merits inclusion here.

In 1944, the British Secret Operations Executive (SOE) came up with a plan to parachute an expert sniper into Germany, specifically near Hitler's Bavarian mountain retreat, the Berghof. With the help of anti-Nazi Germans, it was hoped the sniper could infiltrate close enough to the Berghof to get a shot at Hitler while he was on his daily walk from his residence to the property's tea house. The British knew of Hitler's routine as a result of information gleaned from a German prisoner who had served in Hitler's personal guard. The plan was accepted and received support at the highest level in Britain, including the endorsement of Prime Minister Winston Churchill.

In any event, the plan was not carried out because the British concluded that Hitler's leadership had become so erratic that killing him might actually help the German cause. Some within SOE also believed that the assassination of Hitler would make him a martyr and spawn a new "stab in the back" legend to explain Germany's latest lost war.

Had the plan been successful, it's possible that Germany would have surrendered in 1944 rather than May 1945. Shortening the war in Europe by six months or more would have saved the lives of hundreds of thousands of soldiers, both Allied and German, while many deaths of Jews and others persecuted by the Nazis would have been prevented. Thousands of German civilians who died in Allied air raids, such as the fire-bombing of Dresden, would have survived as well. But it was not to be.

Obviously, the sniper has from time to time played a major role in history. But perhaps the most significant snipers were those who didn't find their mark—especially Major Patrick Ferguson, the man who could have killed George Washington, and the two unknown snipers who came close to killing Abraham Lincoln. Had Washington died in 1777 or Lincoln in 1864, where might we be today?

The Death of General McPherson

The death of General James Birdseye McPherson (1828–1864) was a significant event in American history. His character and ability were such that, had his life not been cut short, he might very well have gone on to become president of the United States. He was such an outstanding personality that I feel compelled to tell his story here.

McPherson was born in Ohio. He graduated first in his class from West Point in 1853. Among his classmates were Philip Sheridan, who later commanded the Union cavalry in the Army of the Potomac; John Schofield, who fought alongside McPherson in the Atlanta campaign and went on after the Civil War to become commanding general of the American Army; and John Bell Hood, a Confederate general who fought against McPherson and Schofield at the Battle of Atlanta.

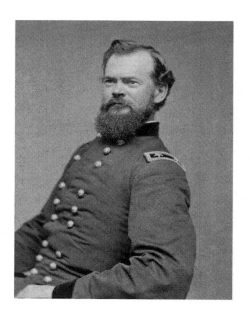

Upon graduation, McPherson joined the Corps of Engineers. He was serving in California when the Civil War broke out. Requesting a transfer back East, he was posted to the staff of General Henry Halleck in the western theater of operations.

As a result of his outstanding ability, McPherson rose rapidly through the ranks. From a mere captain in 1861, he was promoted first to brigadier general and then, in October 1862, to major general. As chief engineer of Ulysses S. Grant's forces in the West, he fought at Forts Henry and Donelson, at Shiloh (where his horse was shot out from under him), and at the Siege of Vicksburg. In late 1862, he was given command of a corps in Grant's Army of the Tennessee.

When in 1864 Grant was made commander of all the Union armies and sent East to confront Robert E. Lee's Army of Northern Virginia, he wrote in a letter to his successor as commander of Union forces in the West, William Tecumseh Sherman, the following: "Thanks to you and McPherson as the men to whom, above all others, I feel indebted for whatever I have had of success."[66]

At this time, McPherson was given command of the Army of the Tennessee. His forces spearheaded Sherman's invasion of Georgia in the spring of 1864. As the campaign opened, McPherson's forces suffered checks at Rocky Face Ridge (May 9) and Resaca (May 13–15). However, many military experts attribute these setbacks to faulty strategy and dispositions on Sherman's part. McPherson suffered a further defeat at Kennesaw Mountain on June 27.

Despite these failures, McPherson doggedly drove his army on toward Atlanta, the objective of the campaign. He was now opposed by Confederate general John Bell Hood, his old West Point classmate. By July 22, 1864, his forces had advanced to the outskirts of Atlanta. Sherman believed that the Confederates were about to evacuate the city, but McPherson correctly discerned that they were preparing to launch a flank attack against the Union forces. While attempting to ride across the battlefield to reach one of the corps under his command, McPherson and some members of his staff encountered a group of Confederate troops (Texans) whose leader, a captain, called upon them to surrender. Refusing to undergo the ignominy of capture, McPherson coolly doffed his cap, checked his horse, and then attempted to ride off. A Confederate sharpshooter's musket rang out, and the general fell dead.

General Hood, his West Point classmate, friend, and the commander of the Confederate forces at the Battle of Atlanta, paid tribute to McPherson:

> I will record the death of my classmate and boyhood friend, General James B. McPherson, the announcement of which caused me sincere sorrow.

> Since we had graduated in 1853 and had each been ordered off on duty in different directions, it has not been our fortune to meet. Neither the years nor the difference of sentiment that had led us to range ourselves on opposite sides in the war had lessened my friendship; indeed, the attachment formed in early youth was strengthened by my admiration and gratitude for his conduct toward our people in the vicinity of Vicksburg. His considerate and kind treatment of them stood in bright contrast to the course pursued by many Federal officers.

Sherman mourned the loss of his subordinate and friend. In his official report he wrote, "The country generally will realize that we have lost not only an able military leader, but a man who had he survived, was qualified to heal the national strife which has been raised by designing and ambitious men."[67] Privately he termed McPherson "as good an officer as I am" but with "a better temper."[68] In his memoirs, U. S. Grant wrote, "In his death the army lost one of its ablest, purest, and best generals."[69]

By blundering into a group of Confederates, McPherson doomed himself to capture or death. His decision to try to escape back to his own lines can also be termed a blunder, though his desire to avoid capture was both understandable and honorable. As already mentioned, some have speculated that had he survived, McPherson, who was only thirty-five when he died, might have gone on to become president of the United States. He had some of the same leadership qualities possessed by Washington and Eisenhower. However, he lacked the blessings of Fortuna[70]; he wasn't lucky.

Atlanta fell to Union forces on July 22, 1864, the day McPherson died. By a curious coincidence, another general and West Point graduate was killed that same day in the same place and in the same way. He was General William H. T. Walker (West Point class of 1836), a divisional commander under General Hood.

Walker, a hero of the Mexican War (1846–1848), was a gallant officer who had fought at Vicksburg and Chickamauga and been wounded several times. At the Battle of Atlanta, his luck ran out. He was shot from his horse by a Union soldier, mirroring the death of McPherson. July 22, 1864, marks the only time in American military history when two generals were killed in action on the same day.

The Killing of Admiral Yamamoto

Admiral Isoroku Yamamoto, the planner of the attack on Pearl Harbor, was probably the most hated man in America during World War II. American wartime propaganda falsely quoted him as saying he would dictate peace to the United States in the White House (presumably, the Japanese would have had to conquer America and occupy Washington, DC, for this to happen).

In fact, Yamamoto was no braggart but a brave and talented officer who, before he became an enemy, was an admirer of the United States. He had visited our country, attended Harvard University, and had many American friends. He enjoyed whisky and poker. He fought us because it was his duty as an officer in the Imperial Japanese Navy to follow the orders of his government when it decided to make war.

Yamamoto was born in 1884 and graduated from the Japanese Naval Academy in Hiroshima in 1904. He served in the Russo-Japanese War of 1904–1905 and was wounded at the Battle of Tsushima, losing two fingers from his left hand.

After World War I, he traveled to the United States, studying English at Harvard from 1919 to 1921. He became a fluent English speaker and an almost unbeatable poker player. He used his poker winnings to travel around the country during the summers. It is said that while on his travels, he took great interest in American industrial development and in particular the Texas oil industry. Certainly, he gained a great respect for America's raw power, which led him in later years to oppose entering into a conflict with the United States.

Yamamoto served as the Japanese naval attaché in Washington from 1925 to 1928. During the 1930s, he became a proponent of naval aviation, seeing it as the wave of the future in naval warfare. At the same time, he opposed the increasing ascendancy of the militarists in Japan. He was against the invasion of China in 1937 and the signing of the Tripartite Pact with Nazi Germany and Fascist Italy in 1940. He was also the officer who apologized to the United States for the Japanese attack on the gunboat Panay, which occurred while the boat was anchored on the Yangtze River in China in 1937. As a result, Yamamoto was constantly threatened with assassination by Japanese ultranationalists, a situation he viewed with philosophical calm. In 1939, he was sent to sea as commander in chief of the Combined Fleet, partly to place him out of reach of potential assassins. He was promoted to full admiral in 1940.

In January 1941, as tensions with the United States increased, Yamamoto undertook planning for a surprise attack on the US naval base at Pearl Harbor, Hawaii, something that another advocate of airpower, US Army colonel Billy Mitchell, had warned against in the 1920s (Mitchell had predicted that the Japanese would eventually attack Pearl Harbor, though with planes flying from island bases rather than aircraft carriers; whether Yamamoto was inspired by Mitchell's warnings is not known for certain). When war with America became inevitable in November 1941, Yamamoto's plans were in place.

The carrier strike force comprising six carriers under Admiral Nagumo plus supporting forces sailed from Japan on November 26. On Sunday, December 7, 1941, America suffered the greatest defeat in its history. Yamamoto's plan had succeeded almost beyond expectations, except for two things:

The aircraft carriers of the US Pacific Fleet were at sea and were not hit during the attack. Yamamoto had called for breaking off diplomatic relations with the United States thirty minutes before the attack began. Due either to a mix-up at the Japanese embassy in Washington, DC, or a deliberate decision on the part of the Japanese government and high command, no such warning was given.

As a result, Pearl Harbor was a sneak attack, and American public opinion was even more infuriated than it would otherwise have been had Japan broken relations and declared war in advance.

Yamamoto had been particularly concerned that the attack would cause America to throw all its resources into a war of revenge that Japan could only lose given America's material superiority. After being told of the success at Pearl Harbor He is quoted as saying, "I fear all we have done is to awaken a sleeping giant and fill him with a terrible resolve." Whether he actually said this at the time is far from certain. However, before the attack, he is known to have told the Japanese government that after victory at Pearl Harbor he would "run wild" in the Pacific for six months or a year but that after that he had no expectation of success.

So, it proved true. Exactly six months after Pearl Harbor, on June 7, 1942, the Battle of Midway ended in the defeat of Admiral Nagumo's carrier force. It was sweet revenge for the Americans, who sank four Japanese carriers, a loss from which the Japanese Navy could never recover. It is universally agreed that Midway doomed Japan to eventual defeat.

Yamamoto's plan for the Midway operation was overly complex. He also divided his forces, sending some units to carry out a diversionary attack on the Aleutian Islands. The Americans enjoyed the added advantage of being able to read the Japanese codes, a matter that I discussed in the section on Pearl Harbor in another chapter. The Americans now took the offensive, landing on Guadalcanal in the Solomon Islands.

Admiral Yamamoto

A series of fierce naval battles were fought during the Guadalcanal campaign, some of which Yamamoto commanded in person. But it was a struggle of attrition that the Japanese could only lose. Japanese forces evacuated Guadalcanal in February 1943. The tide of war had turned against Japan, and Yamamoto was criticized, then and later, for frittering away Japan's remaining naval strength.

However, Yamamoto retained command of the Combined Fleet. To relieve him would have been a great blow to Japanese morale. Nevertheless, his major blunders at Midway and Guadalcanal had done much to lose the war for Japan. Now he committed some small blunders that were to cost him his life.

Fighting continued for some of the other islands in the Solomons chain. In mid-April 1943, Yamamoto planned to make a visit of inspection to Japanese forward bases in the Solomons. On the 14th of that month, US naval intelligence intercepted and decoded a radio message containing the itinerary for Yamamoto's trip. The message was incredibly detailed, giving Yamamoto's arrival and departure times, the type of aircraft he would be using, and the size of the fighter escort.

Admiral Chester Nimitz, commander in chief of the US Pacific Fleet, wanted to have US aircraft ambush and kill Yamamoto. The decision was referred all the way to the White House given the possibility that such a raid could cause the Japanese to believe that their codes had been compromised.

President Roosevelt ordered Secretary of the Navy Frank Knox to "get Yamamoto." The order was transmitted from Chief of Naval Operations Admiral Ernest King to Nimitz, who then instructed Admiral William "Bull" Halsey, commander in the South Pacific, to have the mission, code-named Operation Vengeance, carried out.

On April 18 (the one-year anniversary of the Doolittle Raid on Tokyo), Yamamoto boarded a Mitsubishi G4M bomber, which had been stripped down to serve as a transport plane, at Rabaul in New Britain. He had rejected advice to cancel the inspection from subordinate commanders on the spot who feared an aerial ambush. His choice of aircraft was equally misjudged. The G4M (Betty) had a long range and was fast for a bomber but lacked self-sealing fuel tanks or protective armor.

Because it caught fire so easily, it had several derisive nicknames including the "Flying Cigar," the "One-Shot Lighter," and the "Flying Zippo."

Shortly after 9:30 a.m., Yamamoto's plane was intercepted and attacked by P-38 Lightning fighters of the 347th Fighter Group, which had flown from Henderson Field on Guadalcanal. Yamamoto's escort of six Zero fighters was unable to protect him, and his G4M, true to its reputation, immediately went up in flames. Yamamoto was killed by a machine gun bullet to the head. His plane crashed into the jungle near Bougainville. The Japanese recovered his body, and he was given a state funeral on June 5.

American intelligence had made the attack on Yamamoto possible, but his own small blunders had made his death all but inevitable. Japan's most formidable naval leader had been eliminated and Japanese morale lowered, both disasters of the first order from the Japanese point of view. The final disaster, Japan's complete defeat and unconditional surrender, which Yamamoto had foreseen, followed in 1945.

The Presidents

Because of its frontier heritage, America is a gun-loving society, and an American wielding a gun has more than once changed the course of history. When Aaron Burr killed Alexander Hamilton with a dueling pistol on the Weehawken Heights in 1804, he ended any hopes of a Federalist revival, ensuring that the Democratic-Republican Party, the party of Thomas Jefferson, would dominate American politics for the next half-century and more. But it is the targeting of presidents that has been the principal source of political violence in the United States, proving all too clearly that Mao Zedong's terrible dictum, "Power comes out of the barrel of a gun," is true more often than not.

For no matter how obscure and apparently powerless an assassin is before he commits the act, if he succeeds, then he has wielded, briefly, great power and affected history, sometimes profoundly. Not all would-be assassins of presidents have succeeded, of course, but failure too can sometimes affect the course of events. Recall the two near-misses on Lincoln already discussed. In any case, we will briefly mention, at least in passing, the near-misses and foiled plots directed at American presidents.

Of the forty-five men who have held the American presidency, four have been killed by assassins, and no fewer than twelve others have been targeted, or shot and survived—a shocking total. The first attempted assassination of a president occurred less than fifty years after George Washington became the first man to take the oath of office.

Andrew Jackson

On January 30, 1835, a mentally ill house painter, Richard Lawrence, attempted to shoot Andrew Jackson outside the United States Capitol in Washington, DC. Lawrence had a clear shot at the president (who was leaving the funeral service for a South Carolina congressman), but he had failed to ensure that the two pistols he carried were in working order. Both misfired. Lawrence's tiny blunder saved President Jackson from death. Jackson, although sixty-seven years old and ailing from (among other things) tuberculosis, lived up to his fierce reputation. Old Hickory beat his would-be assassin with a cane, marking the only time in our history in which a president inflicted more damage on an attacker than the attacker did on him. The crowd at the scene, which included Congressman Davy Crockett, then subdued Lawrence.

After a trial at which Lawrence was prosecuted by Francis Scott Key, the US attorney for the District of Columbia (better known today as the author of "The Star-Spangled Banner"), the defendant was found not guilty by reason of insanity. This was possibly the first time insanity was used as a defense in federal court, though it would not be the last time a would-be presidential assassin was found not guilty for this reason. Lawrence was confined to a mental hospital until he died in 1861.

As with other attacks on US presidents, speculation about a conspiracy began almost immediately. Jackson himself believed that his political enemies, and specifically South Carolina senator John C. Calhoun, were behind a plot to have him killed. Calhoun, who had served as Jackson's vice president during his first term (1829–1832), actually made a statement on the floor of the Senate denying any involvement. There is in fact no evidence that Lawrence's attack on Jackson was part of a conspiracy.

Abraham Lincoln

In addition to the two sniper attacks on Lincoln already discussed, his presidency was bookended by two other assassination plots. The first of these, however, might not have been a plot at all but rather an invention of Allan Pinkerton, the founder of the famous Pinkerton Detective Agency.

After his election to the presidency, Lincoln departed Illinois by train for Washington, DC. This was the beginning of a whistle-stop tour during which the president-elect would visit some seventy towns and cities. The final stop before Lincoln's arrival in the nation's capital was Baltimore, the largest city in the slave state of Maryland. Although Maryland would remain in the Union, there was considerable secessionist sentiment there. Baltimore in particular contained many Confederate sympathizers.

Pinkerton, in charge of Lincoln's security, tried to persuade the president-elect to pass through Baltimore without stopping. Lincoln, however, wanted to keep to his itinerary. Pinkerton claimed that a plot existed to stab the president upon his arrival in Baltimore. Supposedly the assassins planned to conceal themselves among the crowd that would greet Lincoln after his train arrived at President Street Station. Lincoln finally agreed to pass through Baltimore incognito, which he did on the night of February 22–23, 1861. Only Mrs. Lincoln and the children were on the train when it arrived in Baltimore on February 23. The president-elect was already in Washington.

According to Pinkerton, his agents had discovered the plot and named one Cipriano Ferrandini, a Corsican immigrant who worked as a barber in Baltimore, as its ringleader. In a book published many years after the war, Pinkerton claimed that while operating undercover, he had met Ferrandini in a Baltimore hotel and that the Corsican spoke of the need to assassinate Lincoln.

Yet, although Ferrandini was publicly known to hold secessionist views, he was never arrested or even questioned about a plot to kill Lincoln. My suspicion is that the story of the conspiracy was invented by Pinkerton in order to inflate his own reputation and that the supposed meeting with Ferrandini never occurred, that it was in fact a mere device designed to sell books. Historians are divided over whether a Baltimore Plot even existed; certainly the "evidence" for it is highly questionable.

Lincoln as president was rather casual about his own safety. He often wandered about Washington with no protection. On the morning of April 14, 1865, the Lincolns decided to see the play *Our American Cousin* and sent a messenger to Ford's Theatre to let the management know that the president and the First Lady would be attending the performance that evening. As it happened, John Wilkes Booth was present and overheard the message when it was delivered. (Adolf Hitler once observed that many assassination attempts were successful because the killers knew in advance where the target would be and when.)

At Ford's Theatre, the president was unprotected because his lone bodyguard chose not to show up on that particular night. Ulysses S. Grant, who was always surrounded by bodyguards, and Mrs. Grant were invited to accompany the Lincolns to Ford's Theatre, but the Grants declined because they were leaving Washington that night to visit their children. And so the stage was set for tragedy.

The death of Lincoln doomed plans for reconciliation between North and South. Whether a milder occupation of the South would have prevented the strong reaction that followed Reconstruction is unknowable. Perhaps the tragedy of Jim Crow was inevitable given the racial attitudes of most white Americans at the time. But certainly, Lincoln's genius, wit, and strong desire for compromise and reconciliation were sorely missed in the postwar period.

James Garfield

James Garfield, a Civil War major general, a nine-term congressman, and a newly elected member of the US Senate, was chosen as the Republican Party's candidate for president in 1880 after one of the most hotly contested nomination fights in American political history, defeating several competitors (among them Ulysses S. Grant, who had already served two terms as president) on the thirty-fifth ballot at the GOP's convention. He was elected president on November 2, 1880.

Four months after beginning his term, on July 2, 1881, Garfield was shot by Charles Guiteau, a Republican who had campaigned for the president and who hoped to benefit by being appointed American consul or ambassador in Paris (the spoils system still reigned in the United States; civil service reform had not yet been instituted).

Garfield was at the Baltimore and Potomac railroad station in Washington, waiting to take a train out of the city. Guiteau, wielding a revolver, shot the president twice, once in the back and once in the arm. The back wound was not necessarily mortal, but in a series of circumstances reminiscent of our chapter on medical mistakes, the president died on September 19, 1881, after lingering for several weeks as a result of his wounds being probed after the shooting by doctors with unsterilized hands. Infection set in, and in an age without antibiotics, this was often fatal. So it proved for President Garfield.

Robert Todd Lincoln, Garfield's secretary of war, who as a young man had witnessed his father die from an assassin's bullet, was at the station to see off the president when Garfield was shot. Although President Lincoln had been shot only sixteen years before, the feeling at the time was that presidents did not require constant protection, and even after Garfield's death, no significant steps were taken to protect presidents from would-be assassins.

The death of Garfield contains another irony that touches upon the subject of this book—his killer, Guiteau, was probably suffering from syphilis, which in turn probably affected the killer's judgment.

William McKinley

We move on to the twentieth century, a particularly dangerous one for American presidents. Very soon after the century opened, the third American president to be felled by an assassin's bullet met his end. This was Republican William McKinley, an Ohio native who had served as an officer in the

Union Army during the Civil War and who had first been elected president in 1896. After winning reelection in 1900, McKinley was shot by anarchist Leon Czolgosz while attending the Pan-American Exposition in Buffalo, New York. The date was September 6, 1901.[71]

Czolgosz, who had turned to anarchism after losing his job in the financial panic of 1893, simply entered a receiving line and shot the president as McKinley was about to shake his hand. As with Lincoln and Garfield, no security was provided for the president, nor did he request any. Despite the example of his two murdered predecessors and despite the fact that anarchists were known to target heads of state (two monarchs, a French president, and the prime minister of Spain had already been killed by anarchists in the twenty years before McKinley was shot), McKinley traveled about Washington and the country without bodyguards.

McKinley, like Garfield, was shot twice. One bullet merely grazed the president, but the other penetrated his stomach and lodged in his body, never to be recovered. Again, like Garfield, McKinley might possibly have survived and gone on to complete his term in office. But once again tiny blunders by medical professionals led to disaster.[72]

A highly qualified surgeon, Dr. Roswell Park, was performing an operation in nearby Niagara Falls. Approached while at the operating table, he replied that he could not leave, even for the president of the United States. Only two weeks later, Dr. Park saved the life of a woman who had suffered an injury almost identical to that of the president by performing an operation that had first been successfully tried by a Swiss surgeon in the 1880s.[73]

The president was left in the hands of less able and less experienced doctors. They performed an abdominal operation but did not find the bullet and did not follow sterile procedures. The doctors sewed up two holes in the president's stomach, closed the surgical incision, and gave the president a painkiller. Dr. Park arrived while the operation was underway but declined to interfere.

At first McKinley seemed to be recovering. The cabinet and Vice President Theodore Roosevelt (who was vacationing in Vermont) had been informed of the shooting by telegraph. Roosevelt and many members of the cabinet rushed to Buffalo but left again on September 9 and 10 when it appeared the president would recover. However, on the 13th, it became apparent that McKinley would die: gangrene had set in, followed by blood poisoning. He passed away in the early morning hours of September 14, five days before the twentieth anniversary of President Garfield's death.

A second disaster was avoided purely by chance. Vice President Roosevelt had started a new vacation in the Adirondack Mountains after it appeared that McKinley was out of danger. Summoned again when it became clear that the president was doomed to die, Roosevelt was racing by carriage over mountain roads in a virtual wilderness, trying to reach a train station. That a serious accident did not occur was due simply to Roosevelt's luck, a luck that we will see come into play again in the next section of this chapter.

Imagine if both president and vice president had died on the same day!

After McKinley's death, the US Congress finally asked the Secret Service to provide ongoing protection for the president.

Theodore Roosevelt

Theodore "Teddy" Roosevelt went on to complete McKinley's second term and win election to one of his own. At the close of his presidency in 1908, he was at the height of his popularity and could easily have won reelection. He chose not to run again, a decision he later regretted. Unhappy with some of the policies of his designated successor, William Howard Taft, and needing an outlet for his almost boundless energy, he sought the Republican nomination for president in 1912. Denied this, he founded and then became the candidate of the Progressive Party, also known as the Bull Moose Party. The 1912 campaign thus became a three-way race pitting Roosevelt against Taft and the Democratic governor of New Jersey, Woodrow Wilson.

On October 14, 1912, Roosevelt was shot in Milwaukee by a German immigrant, John Schrank. Schrank was suffering from the delusion that the ghost of President McKinley had ordered him to kill Roosevelt. He later claimed as well that he was opposed to the idea of a man serving three terms as president. Schrank began following Roosevelt on the campaign trail, eventually getting close enough to shoot him as he emerged from the Gilpatrick Hotel on his way to give a speech at the Milwaukee Auditorium.

Unlike the more primitive pistols Richard Lawrence used to try to kill Andrew Jackson, Schrank's handgun, a .38-caliber Colt revolver, worked all too well. Schrank got off only one shot, but it was aimed directly at Roosevelt's heart. It was lucky that politicians in those days gave long speeches from written texts rather than a teleprompter. Roosevelt's breast pocket contained a folded fifty-page copy of the speech he was planning to deliver as well as a metal glasses case. These slowed the bullet enough so that while it penetrated Roosevelt's chest, it failed to pierce any vital organ such as the lungs or heart.

Roosevelt actually went on to deliver his speech before seeking medical attention. Doctors determined that it would be more dangerous to operate and remove the bullet than to leave it in place, and on this occasion the doctors were right. Like Andrew Jackson, Roosevelt carried a bullet in his chest for the remainder of his life (Jackson had been shot in the chest during a duel in 1806). Roosevelt's assailant, like Jackson's, was judged insane and confined to a mental institution until his death in 1943.

Roosevelt finished second in the presidential contest, garnering more votes than the incumbent Taft. But his candidacy split the Republican vote and gave the White House to the Democrat, Wilson. Had Roosevelt been killed, Taft would almost certainly have won the election. We can only speculate how world history might have been affected had Taft rather than Wilson been in office when World War I broke out in 1914.

Franklin Roosevelt

Twenty years after the 1912 campaign, Theodore Roosevelt's distant cousin, Franklin Delano Roosevelt, was elected president. Shortly after his election, he came close to suffering the same fate as Lincoln, Garfield, and McKinley.

Theodore "Teddy" Roosevelt

On February 15, 1933, an anarchist again struck at the American presidency. While President-Elect Roosevelt was visiting Miami, Italian immigrant and self-professed anarchist Giuseppe Zangara fired five shots from a revolver as Roosevelt was giving an impromptu speech from the back seat of a car.

Zangara was only five feet tall, and he had to stand on a chair in the midst of the crowd that had gathered in order to get the shots off. Onlookers attempted to subdue him after the first shot, but five people in all were wounded by the spray of gunfire. Among them was Chicago mayor Anton Cermak, who later died of his wounds. As he was being rushed to the hospital in Roosevelt's car, Cermak supposedly looked up at the president-elect, who was cradling the wounded mayor in his arms, and said, "I'm glad it was me instead of you." This, however, appears to have been an invention of the sensationalist press; few scholars believe Cermak actually said it. It has been theorized that Cermak was actually Zangara's target, that Chicago mobsters had ordered the mayor's death. But in jail, Zangara maintained that he was indeed targeting the president, in line with his anarchist beliefs.

Repeating another theme that runs through this book, Cermak died on March 6, 1933, from peritonitis brought on by medical mishandling of his wound. His death doomed Zangara, who was immediately charged with murder and then tried, convicted, and executed all within a two-week period (quite a difference from the agonizingly long capital cases of the present day!)

Had Roosevelt been killed, how different might the course of American and world history have been? We can only speculate, but clearly Roosevelt played a huge role in saving democratic capitalism in America during the 1930s and in defeating Nazism and Japanese militarism during the Second World War. It's hard to avoid the conclusion that his death in

1933 would have been a very serious blow to the United States—as bad as or perhaps even worse than death overtaking Washington in 1777 or Lincoln in 1864

John F. Kennedy

We move on thirty years to the fourth US president to be struck down by an assassin's bullet. The circumstances surrounding the Kennedy assassination remain controversial to this day, and it's not likely they will ever be resolved to everyone's satisfaction. The supposed assassin, Lee Harvey Oswald, was not convicted of the murder in a court of law, for he was himself shot and killed by Jack Ruby two days after Kennedy's death. The Warren Commission appointed by President Lyndon Johnson, Kennedy's successor, concluded that Oswald, acting alone, killed Kennedy, and that Ruby, acting alone, killed Oswald.

The assassination of JFK illustrates all too tragically the tiny blunder/great disaster theme that runs throughout this book. First, the tiny blunders.

The route of Kennedy's motorcade was published in the Dallas papers in advance. The route included a hairpin turn that Kennedy's limousine would have to execute just as it approached the kill zone. Such a turn was prohibited by Secret Service rules, but for some reason the risky maneuver was never questioned. Kennedy refused to allow Secret Service agents to stand on the running boards of the limousine because that would have blocked the crowd's view of him. Of course, it would have blocked the assassin's (or assassins') view as well. These were the principal tiny blunders that led to Kennedy's death.

That Kennedy's death was a great disaster is undeniable. The journalist Robert Novak, writing in his 2007 memoir *The Prince of Darkness: 50 Years Reporting in Washington,* stated that the country had never recovered from Kennedy's death. There was and is a great deal of truth to that statement. In concrete terms, Kennedy's decision to withdraw from Vietnam after winning reelection in 1964[74] was reversed by his successor, Johnson, with catastrophic consequences, for the United States became mired in a costly and divisive war that ended, after our withdrawal, in victory for the Communist side.

That Kennedy intended to cut his losses in Vietnam and get out has been well established by scholarship undertaken over the past twenty-five or so years. See, for example, Howard Jones, *Death of a Generation: How the Assassinations of Diem and JFK Prolonged the Vietnam War* (New York: Oxford University Press, 2003), and Major John Newman, *JFK and Vietnam* (New York: Warner Books, 1992).

Gerald Ford

The wave of assassinations and assassination attempts that marked 1960s America continued into the 1970s, but in the latter decade the shooters were less capable, or at least less accurate. Arthur Bremer shot presidential candidate George Wallace in 1972, paralyzing the former Alabama governor for life. Then it was another president's turn to face lead.

Gerald Ford succeeded Richard Nixon as president upon the latter's resignation in 1974. In a less-than-three-week period in September 1975, he twice nearly suffered the fate of John F. Kennedy. First, on September 5, while Ford was visiting Sacramento, California and shaking hands with people in a crowd, Lynette "Squeaky" Fromme, a member of the infamous Manson Family, drew a Colt .45 semiautomatic pistol and fired at point-blank range. Fortunately, Fromme didn't know how to operate an automatic pistol. Although the magazine contained four rounds, there was no bullet in the firing chamber. The gun failed to go off, and Fromme was then quickly subdued by a

Secret Service agent. Seventeen days later, in San Francisco, Sarah Jane Moore, a middle-aged divorcée, took a shot at Ford with a .38-caliber revolver.

Although firing at Ford from about forty feet away, she narrowly missed him with her first shot. She was taking aim again when an ex-Marine, Oliver Sipple, grabbed her arm as she fired. The bullet was wide of the mark, wounding a bystander. Moore was apparently motivated by her radical political views, whereas Fromme is better understood as a mentally unstable. Moore pled guilty at trial and served thirty-two years of a life sentence before being paroled in 2007. Fromme was convicted at trial and served almost thirty-four years of her sentence before being paroled. Curiously, both women escaped briefly and were recaptured.

Even more curious are the tiny blunders committed by both women that undoubtedly saved Ford's life. We have already mentioned Squeaky Fromme's ineptitude with a gun. Moore's failure to kill Ford is an even more bizarre story. Moore had come onto the Secret Service's radar earlier in 1975, but after investigation she was ruled out as a threat. The owner of a .44-caliber revolver, she was taken into custody by police for illegally possessing a handgun the day before the shooting, and although she was released, her gun and ammo were confiscated.

On the day of the shooting, Moore bought a .38-caliber revolver, which was the weapon she used to shoot at Ford. Unfamiliar with the new gun, she failed to realize that its sighting required the shooter to compensate for distance. This accounted for her narrowly missing the president. Had she fired at Ford with her .44-caliber gun, she would almost certainly have killed him.

Obviously, that Ford survived was no disaster. Nevertheless, I feel the remarkable succession of tiny blunders that saved his life warrants mention here. Momentous events so often occur, or are prevented, by tiny mistakes. It's almost uncanny, and certainly strange, that so often so much hangs on so little!

Fromme and Moore, by the way, are the only women in our history who have tried to kill a president.

Ronald Reagan

Gerald Ford miraculously escaped death twice within seventeen days, emerging without a scratch. Our fortieth president, Ronald Reagan, was not so lucky.

John Hinckley, Jr., the scion of a wealthy family, was a mentally disturbed young man who became obsessed with the Hollywood actress Jodie Foster. During the 1980 presidential campaign, he followed President Jimmy Carter around the country, hoping to shoot him and thereby "impress" Ms. Foster, who was then a student at Yale. He never got up the nerve to take a shot at Carter, but after Ronald Reagan won the presidency, Hinckley began planning anew, assembling material on the JFK assassination and purchasing a .22-caliber revolver at a pawnshop.

On the afternoon of March 30, 1981, President Reagan left the Hilton Hotel in Washington, DC, after giving a speech to the attendees at an AFL-CIO conference. The Secret Service had committed a small blunder that was about to become a huge one: it had allowed a group of people to stand behind a rope line that was quite close to the president as he passed by. John Hinckley was in that group.

As the president walked toward a waiting limousine, Hinckley fired six shots from his .22-caliber handgun.

Fortunately, Hinckley was not an expert marksman. All six shots missed the president, partly because Secret Service agent Jerry Parr quickly pushed Reagan into the limousine, and partly because another agent, Tim McCarthy, spread his body out to act as a human shield for Reagan. But for these two men, President Reagan would most likely have been killed. In a near-fatal stroke of bad luck, the sixth and final shot ricocheted off the limousine and struck Reagan, who was already in the car. The bullet penetrated a lung and came within an inch of his heart. Agent McCarthy took a bullet in the abdomen. A DC policeman and the president's press secretary, James Brady, were also wounded. All survived, but Brady had been shot in the head and was partially paralyzed for the rest of his life. At trial, Hinckley was found not guilty by reason of insanity, the same verdict handed down for Richard Lawrence, the man who had attempted to kill Andrew Jackson.

President Reagan came very close to death that day, and few would deny that his murder would have been a disaster for America and the free world. He was placed in harm's way by a tiny blunder but saved by two quick-thinking Secret Service agents, and perhaps by a little luck of the Irish.

No one since has come as close to killing a president as Hinckley did on that March day, but it hasn't been for lack of trying. Under Bill Clinton, George W. Bush, and Barack Obama, deranged or politically motivated individuals fired shots at the White House or sought to attack the Executive Mansion and its occupants in other ways. One man attempted to fly a small plane into the White House but crashed on the lawn.

Perhaps the most serious incident occurred on September 19, 2014, when a man named Omar Gonzalez, who was carrying a knife, scaled the White House fence and actually got inside the building, overpowering a guard and eventually reaching the East Room. Had he taken a different turn, he could have gotten into the family living quarters. President Obama and his daughters had left just minutes before for Camp David; Mrs. Obama was away. Gonzalez was a former combat soldier who had served in Iraq during the bloody period from 2006 to 2008. Truthfully, chance alone had prevented an unspeakable tragedy from occurring.

Nothing like this has happened so far during the Trump presidency, but the sad fact is that many political fanatics and mentally unstable people will continue to view presidents as targets.

Although it is not really within the scope of this book, I feel that mention should be made of the plots and attacks against presidents that were completely foiled by courageous and quick-thinking protectors. Below I briefly mention some notable examples.

In 1909, President William Howard Taft and Mexican president Porfirio Diaz held a summit at El Paso on the US-Mexican border. Taft's protective detail, which included Texas Rangers, discovered a man with a palm pistol waiting along a parade route as the two presidents approached. The man was disarmed when the two leaders were only a few feet away.

In 1947, the Stern Gang, a Jewish terrorist group in Palestine, attempted to kill President Truman for what they perceived was his lack of support for the establishment of a Jewish state. Letter bombs were sent to the president at the White House, but the Secret Service intercepted and defused them.

On November 1, 1950, two Puerto Rican nationalists armed with handguns tried to enter Blair House, where President Truman was living while the White House was under renovation. The president was napping inside Blair House at the time. A gunfight erupted between the attackers and Secret

Service agents and police officers. A policeman was killed, as was one of the attackers. The other gunman was captured, tried, convicted, and given a life sentence, which was commuted by President Jimmy Carter in 1979. When the gunfight began, Truman appeared at a window to see what was happening. One of the attackers was almost immediately below him, about thirty feet away. The Secret Service men shouted at Truman to move away from the window, and the attacker failed to get a shot at him.

In 1996, an attempt to kill President Bill Clinton occurred while he was visiting the Asia-Pacific Economic Cooperation forum in Manila, the capital of the Philippines. The Secret Service rerouted the president's motorcade after intercepting a message that indicated an attack was imminent. A bomb was subsequently discovered planted under a bridge. It is generally believed that al Qaeda was behind the aborted attack.

These are a few examples of great danger thwarted by the Secret Service and other protectors of the president.

Ronald Reagan

23

━━━━━◦◦◦━━━━━

THE MISSING PARAGRAPH
THAT CAUSED A WAR

"We believed in Wilson and the Western Democracies, and then we decided that they were all great liars."

- Chinese Nationalist

As we all know (or should know), racism is at the root of many human problems and conflicts, the Nazi "master race" philosophy, which led to World War II, being the most obvious example. We often also think of racism in terms of the Civil Rights Movement in the United States or the struggle against apartheid in South Africa. But in this chapter, we will learn how racism, sometimes expressed in rather petty ways, came to have a profound effect on war and peace in both the twentieth and twenty-first centuries. We will see how European, American, and Australian racism toward the Chinese and Japanese peoples at the time of World War I and the Paris Peace Conference led eventually to war and revolution in the Pacific and Asia. It also led to the North Korean situation, which bedevils the United States even to this day.

The Background: China

The history of the Far East is not often deeply studied in the American education system. Its nuances and mysteries are therefore often times foreign to the Western mind. However, the long-term damage that resulted from a single miscalculation by world leaders at the Paris Peace Conference of 1919 *cannot be overstated.*

Until the beginning of the nineteenth century, China controlled its own destiny. Christian and Muslim missionaries had reached China in the early Middle Ages but without making many converts. When Western explorers and traders appeared in the 1500s, they were regarded as little more than "long-nosed, hairy barbarians," not to be feared by the Chinese.

The Chinese, after all, regarded their ancient land as the Middle Kingdom, the center of the world and of civilization. But as the nineteenth century progressed, the Westerners' mastery of gunpowder (invented by the Chinese centuries earlier), steam power, and other technical and scientific knowledge meant that China was almost helpless in the face of Western demands. The Opium War of 1839–1842 marked the beginning of outright Western aggression against China.

Soon, the great European powers—Britain, France, Russia, and Germany—were assuming control of so-called treaty ports and the territory surrounding them. In these territories, the Westerners had their own enclaves of settlement. The Europeans were not subject to Chinese law, and economic relations were heavily weighted in their favor. A series of unequal treaties with the European powers codified Chinese inferiority. The Americans and, somewhat later, the Japanese joined in the virtual carving up of China.[75]

The Boxer Rebellion of 1899–1901 was the first violent expression of Chinese resentment toward the colonial powers. In 1911, a revolution deposed the last, ineffective emperor of China, and the Chinese attempted to embark on the path of political and economic modernization and liberalization—to become a great nation again, able to stand on an equal footing with the major powers of the world. This was a path that Japan had already successfully taken.

The Background: Japan

Japan in the nineteenth century attempted to isolate itself from foreign influence. But in 1853, Commodore Matthew Perry's squadron arrived, and the Japanese were compelled to conclude a trade treaty with the United States. The other major powers followed Perry's example, and it appeared that Japan might be facing the same fate as China.

Instead, beginning in 1868, the Japanese embarked on a thoroughgoing modernization of their country, reforming its government and military by reaching out to the West for advice and technical assistance. Simultaneously, Japan became an industrial nation, the first in Asia. As a result, Japan was able to preserve full independence and take its place among the colonial powers that were rapidly dividing up the world. Japan fought successful wars against China (1894–1895) and Russia (1904–1905), acquiring Formosa (Taiwan), Korea, and other territory, and making itself the dominant power in Manchuria. Japan signed an alliance with Britain in 1902 and entered World War I on the Allied side in 1914.

Japan and China in World War I

Japan's main contribution to the Allied cause in World War I was its capture of Kiaochow (Jiaozhou), the German colonial territory on the Shandong Peninsula in China. China itself entered the war in 1917, declaring war on Germany on August 14 of that year. The main purpose of China's entry into the war was to obtain a voice at the peace conference. This would be important for China simply because Japan had used the war to greatly increase its power and influence in Asia and the Pacific, and especially in China itself.

When hostilities ended with Germany's defeat in 1918, Japan's position in northern China was predominant. In 1915, Japan had presented the Twenty-One Demands to China, and while the subsequent treaty did not incorporate all of the demands, it recognized Japan's economic and political dominance in Manchuria, Outer Mongolia (a Chinese province), and the Shandong Peninsula. The latter was considered a "dagger pointing at Peking" (Beijing), the Chinese capital. That China did not become an outright Japanese protectorate was due to the influence of Britain and the United States. Britain had an important outpost at Shanghai while the United States was determined to maintain the Open Door policy that it had enunciated in the nineteenth century, a policy designed to further its own commercial interests in China.

At this time, with Germany defeated and Russia riven by revolution and civil war, Britain and the United States were unquestionably the most powerful nations on Earth. France, which also had interests in China, stood with the Anglo-Saxon powers. Japan was rightly concerned and even fearful about being dictated to by the Western powers at the peace conference. Nevertheless, it hoped to obtain recognition of its conquests in Asia and the Pacific, especially Shandong.

China, on the other hand, came to the peace conference with hopes that President Woodrow Wilson's Fourteen Points would shape the peace treaty. Wilson's ideas about self-determination meant that Shandong, a part of China, should return to Chinese rule—or so the Chinese saw it, and understandably so. The Chinese further looked forward to a reshaping of East–West relations that would grant China full independence and the same rights enjoyed by the sovereign states of Europe and America.

The outcome, as we shall see, was rather different. To some extent this was the result of pure power politics. But racism, specifically the Euro-American attitude toward "yellow peoples," would play a sorry part in the outcome as well. I will take a quick look at this particular form of racism before I discuss the negotiations in Paris that led to Treaty of Versailles in 1919.

European and American racism toward Asians appears to have arisen or at least become pronounced in the nineteenth century, when writers such as the Count de Gobineau posited white supremacy as a fact, something that many people of the Victorian Age in Europe and America were only too willing to believe.[76]

In 1882, the United States passed the Chinese Exclusion Act, which remained in force until 1943. Although in part motivated by the influx of cheap Chinese labor, racism was unquestionably a major factor in the American decision to prevent Chinese people from immigrating to the United States. Similarly, after the opening up of Japan in the 1850s and '60s, Westerners generally viewed Japanese culture and perhaps above all the physical appearance of the Japanese with a certain disdain. Japan's astonishing industrial and military successes did little to change Western attitudes.[77] While the United States government didn't get around to banning Japanese immigration until 1924, it was quite wary of allowing too many Japanese immigrants to settle in Hawaii and on the West Coast, and popular opinion felt even more strongly about the issue. European attitudes toward Asians mirrored that of most white Americans, even though there was virtually no immigration to Europe from China and Japan during the period in question.

We come then to the assembling of the peace delegations in Paris in 1919 and the process by which the issues critical to the Chinese and Japanese were handled by the leading Western statesmen—US president Woodrow Wilson, British prime minister David Lloyd George, and the French premier, Georges Clemenceau.

China's overriding concern was to regain Shandong, which had been taken from it first by the Germans and then the Japanese. Japan was keen on keeping the territory, which it regarded as the key to maintaining its dominant position in China. Moreover, the Japanese knew that the British and French would be parceling out territory in the Middle East and the Pacific to add to their own empires, and they expected to be allowed to do the same.[78] They wanted to be allowed to keep the Pacific islands they had conquered in 1914 as well as Shandong.

Japan had a second big concern: it wanted a clause on racial equality added to the treaty, or specifically to the Covenant of the League of Nations, which President Wilson wanted to incorporate in the treaty. (The league was Wilson's pet project; its purpose would be to maintain peace and settle disputes among nations.) As the Japanese saw it, their dignity as a people and a nation demanded that such a clause be included in the treaty.

Retention of the Pacific islands was not a sticking point at the Versailles negotiations. It had long been agreed that Japan would keep the islands north of the equator and Britain (or rather, its dominions Australia and New Zealand) those to the south of it. But Shandong and the racial equality clause proved to be contentious issues.

Leading the charge against the racial equality clause was Australian prime minister Billy Hughes. Hughes is a legendary character in Australian political history, though his long career (he served in the Australian parliament for over fifty years and was prime minister from 1915–1923) was not, as it proved, particularly beneficial to Australia or the world.

A Welshman born in London, Hughes immigrated to Australia in 1884, when he was in his early twenties. He worked in a variety of professions before joining the Australian Labor Party and winning election to the Australian parliament in 1901. He studied law and was admitted to the bar shortly after entering parliament. Irritable and irritating by nature (behavior caused, some said, by his chronic indigestion), he nevertheless became a cabinet minister and, in 1915, prime minister. As such he headed Australia's delegation to the peace conference in 1919.

Hughes and President Wilson knocked heads from the beginning. Hughes opposed Wilson's cherished idea of establishing a League of Nations, and he was not of a mind to grant concessions to Japan, which he viewed as a potential threat to Australia's security. Wilson referred to Hughes as a "pestiferous varmint." Hughes at one point said to Wilson, "I speak for 60,000 Australian dead. How many do you speak for?"

More to the point, Australians were even more anti-Japanese than Americans. Japanese immigration into Australia was banned, and Hughes and his countrymen feared that accepting the racial equality clause might open their country up to a wave of immigrants. Keeping Australia white was priority number one for Hughes and his delegation. At the time, white supremacy was as important to Australians as it was to whites in the American South.

The British, who had an alliance with Japan, were placed in a difficult position by the Australians' attitude, which was shared by the New Zealand delegation as well. Wilson's confidant, Colonel Edward House,[79] put forward various compromise formulas that would allow the clause to appear in the treaty but without success.

When the Japanese pressed for a vote at the conference, a majority of the delegations came out in favor of the clause. Wilson now intervened in a remarkable way. He announced that because there were serious objections to the clause, it could not become part of the covenant. In doing this, he was attempting to secure the support of Hughes's Australia for the League of Nations and also to appease American politicians, particularly those from the West Coast, whose support he needed in order to get the peace treaty and the League of Nations ratified by the US Senate.

Wilson was no advocate of racial equality in any case but creating the League of Nations was uppermost in his mind; he saw it as the key to world peace. The power and prestige of the United States was such that he was able to subvert the majority will and keep the racial equality clause out of the treaty.[80] Australians and many Americans were pleased, but the Japanese were understandably resentful of Wilson's maneuver.

Having denied the Japanese on racial equality, Wilson was now confronted with their demand to keep Shandong. The Chinese were equally adamant that the province should be returned to them. Shandong was an integral part of historic China; both Confucius and Mencius had been born there.

Japan had come to the conference prepared if necessary to hand the province back to China, assuming the Anglo-Saxon powers insisted on it. The British and Americans might have done so, but they were hamstrung by Wilson's refusal to accept the racial equality clause. If the Japanese were denied on both counts, they would likely leave the peace conference and refuse to sign the treaty. Under such circumstances, Shandong would remain under Japanese rule anyway unless the Anglo-Americans decided to evict the Japanese by force. That was something neither country had any stomach for. And the absence of Asia's leading power from the League of Nations would compromise the legitimacy of that organization from its very inception.

The Chinese, meanwhile, appealed to Wilson's Fourteen Points and the doctrine of self-determination. The United States considered itself to be China's patron, and it wanted to support the Chinese position on Shandong. Matters came to a head in April 1919. The Japanese would not compromise; failure to keep Shandong would mean they would refuse to sign the peace treaty.

The Western powers gave way in the face of Japan's threat. The Japanese would retain Shandong, a clear betrayal of Wilson's fine-sounding words about self-determination and the right of weak nations to receive protection from the strong.

Reaction in China was immediate. On the afternoon of May 4, 1919, thousands of students from universities around Peking converged on Tiananmen Square to protest the decision of the statesmen at Versailles. Since the 1911 revolution, many of China's intellectuals, and particularly students, had been advocating modernization and democracy as the means to restore China's full sovereignty and self-respect. Now the West that they had looked to for inspiration had blatantly betrayed them. The future opinion leaders of China began to move away from Western ideals and seek other paths for returning their country to greatness.

Up until the spring of 1919, the Russian Revolution had been largely ignored in China. Now Bolshevism began to be taken seriously as a doctrine and a means for achieving change.

Mao Zedong

It is no exaggeration to say that China's move away from democracy and toward communism had its roots in what became known as the May Fourth Movement. Scholars are generally agreed on this. The Chinese Communist Party was founded not long after the events of May 4, 1919, and many participants in the May Fourth Movement eventually became party members. To some extent it is surprising that so many Chinese up until that time had continued to look westward given Western behavior in China and the racism openly displayed by many Westerners (the Chinese Exclusion Act being an example). But the Shandong decision permanently alienated many Chinese and paved the way for the victory of Communism in China thirty years later.

Billy Hughes

This blunder—the failure of Woodrow Wilson and his British and French counterparts to live up to their self-professed ideals—was to have disastrous consequences. The Communist takeover of China in 1949 led only a year later to a war between China and America in Korea, which killed about thirty-seven thousand Americans. In addition, the "who lost China?" debate in the United States warped American politics and foreign policy for a generation. The consequences for China were even greater. Mao Zedong, the Communist dictator of China from 1949–1976, was the greatest mass murderer in history, killing more people even than Hitler and Stalin.

Reliable estimates are that executions, murders, and deaths by starvation resulting from Mao's insane policies approached eighty million.

338

That's right, eighty million deaths caused, at least indirectly, by the "statesmen" who gave Shandong to Japan. And the Shandong decision was made necessary by the refusal of those same statesmen to add a simple clause on racial equality to the Treaty of Versailles. Ironically, Japan agreed to give up Shandong only a few years after the treaty was signed.

The blunder made when the West refused to acknowledge that all people are indeed created equal produced a second disaster as well. Japanese resentment toward American, British, and French racial attitudes was not truly assuaged by the Shandong decision. A smoldering rage directed at the West only grew in coming years. In 1922, the United States, Britain, and Japan negotiated the Washington Naval Treaty. Once again, a position of inferiority was imposed upon the Japanese, who were forced to agree that they would build fewer capital ships than each of the two Anglo-Saxon powers. Then the US Immigration Act of 1924 forbid Japanese to immigrate to America— racism again. While there was no single cause for the outbreak of war in the Pacific in 1941, US actions in 1919, 1922, and 1924 helped to stoke the fires of Japanese xenophobia, nationalism, and militarism. Pearl Harbor was in some respects an outburst of rage on Japan's part—rage at being treated as an inferior for so long.

Racism is by no means confined to white Westerners. Ideas about "racial purity" are not unknown in East Asia (and elsewhere), though these are rarely discussed publicly. But the arrogance of white supremacists directed toward Asian peoples during the heyday of Western imperialism led Western leaders of the time to commit apparently small blunders—blunders that nevertheless produced great disasters and loss of life.

24

---•○•---

WAS HITLER CRAZY?

The promiscuous use of drugs at the very highest levels also impaired and confused decision-making, with Hitler and his entourage taking refuge in potentially lethal cocktails of stimulants administered by the physician Dr. Morell as the war turned against Germany.

- Norman Ohler

One of the most interesting and important questions of twentieth-century history revolves around Adolf Hitler's mental state and its effect on his thoughts and actions as a political and military leader. Did der Führer, during the course of World War II, suffer a severe mental deterioration stemming from an outside physical source? Was he, by the time he died by suicide in his Berlin bunker, insane, crazy?

Hitler was born into a lower middle-class and somewhat dysfunctional Austrian family. His father, a petty official in the Austrian civil service, was a drinker who was not averse to beating young Adolf as a means of enforcing discipline. The father died when Hitler was still a boy, followed by Hitler's beloved mother, Klara, who succumbed to breast cancer when her son was nineteen. Hitler then moved to Vienna, where he spent almost five years living in a men's hostel and eking out a living as an architectural painter. In 1913 he settled in Munich, and the following year, on the outbreak of World War I, he joined the German Army. He served honorably at the front, was twice wounded, and was awarded the Iron Cross 1st and 2nd class.

In 1919, at the age of thirty, Hitler embarked on a career as a political agitator and demagogue. After leading a failed putsch in Munich in 1923 and serving a short prison term as punishment, he emerged as a leading figure on the German political scene.

Hitler's became the largest in Germany, and in 1933 he was appointed chancellor of the Reich. Once in office, he consolidated power in his own hands, abolished democratic institutions such as political parties and labor unions, and even forced the German Army, hitherto the arbiter of German politics, to swear personal allegiance to him as Führer of the German nation and supreme commander of the Wehrmacht. He then initiated a series of daring moves on the world stage—openly rearming Germany in defiance of the Treaty of Versailles, reoccupying the demilitarized Rhineland, annexing his native Austria, and dismembering Czechoslovakia with the consent of the Western powers Britain and France. He then stunned the world by concluding a nonaggression pact with Communist Russia, which set the stage for World War II. That terrible conflict began on September 1, 1939, when Germany invaded Poland.

To this point, at the age of fifty, Hitler had shown himself to be a brilliant political tactician and leader, albeit a devious and amoral one. He was virtually worshipped by the German masses, who were held spellbound by his speeches and the mass rallies orchestrated by Dr. Goebbels, his minister of propaganda. At the outbreak of war in 1939, he was clearly not delusional. No lunatic could have achieved what Hitler had in the 1930s.

That said, Hitler was clearly not a normal person. Both his achievements and his crimes went far beyond those of the average politician or leader. He certainly had some bizarre obsessions, particularly in the area of race. His belief in the importance of "blood" and in the superiority of the so-called Aryan race This was based on a kind of tribal egotism.

Hitler's notorious anti-Semitism, which led eventually to the Holocaust, was not just evil but counterproductive in terms of his goal of elevating Germany to world-power status. In driving the Jews from Germany and persecuting them throughout Europe, he was acting against his own best interests. In the first place, many of the leading scientists in Germany and throughout Europe were of Jewish descent. Fleeing from Hitler's persecution, they became key actors in the Manhattan Project to build the atomic bomb and in other research of military importance. Secondly, the resources devoted to the murdering of millions of Jews, Gypies and other non-Arians— in terms of manpower, material, and transport—simply drew resources away from the German war effort, thereby contributing to Germany's ultimate defeat.

Nevertheless, despite his obsession with ridding Europe and eventually the world of Jews, in the early 1940s, Hitler was not clinically insane. He was surely an evil man but not demented or deranged. And in the early years of the war, his successes were even more spectacular than his peacetime triumphs. The conquest of Poland in 1939 was only the beginning. In 1940, Germany overran Denmark, Norway, Holland, Belgium, Luxembourg, and even France, which had successfully resisted the kaiser's armies during the First World War. Although his plans to invade England were foiled by the Royal Air Force's victory over the Luftwaffe in the Battle of Britain, Hitler went on to gain control of the Balkans and dispatched an expeditionary force, the Afrika Korps (commanded by General Erwin Rommel), to assist his Italian allies against the British in North Africa. This relatively small force would come within a hairsbreadth of driving the British from Egypt and capturing the Suez Canal.

Hitler, as commander in chief of the German armed forces, played an active and sometimes decisive role in Germany's early victories. His willingness to accept the risk of invading Norway in the face of British naval superiority showed a far-seeing strategic sense and an appreciation of the decisive effect of airpower.

Even more spectacular was Hitler's conception of striking at France through the supposedly impenetrable Ardennes forest, thus outflanking the Maginot Line (which the French had constructed after World War I, believing that it made them invulnerable to a German invasion). The Führer's somewhat inchoate ideas along this line were given shape by General (later Field Marshal) Erich von Manstein, whose "Sickle Plan" led to victory over France in a mere six weeks. Hitler adopted Manstein's plan despite being advised against it by Manstein's seniors on the General Staff.

By any reckoning, Hitler in 1941 had to be ranked among the great captains of history. He was, as William L. Shirer termed him in The Rise and Fall of the Third Reich, the last of the great adventurer-conquerors of history, the apparent equal of Alexander, Caesar, and Napoleon.

But it all began to fall apart for Hitler on June 22, 1941, the opening day of Operation Barbarossa—the invasion of Soviet Russia. Not that Germany was doomed from the outset to fail in its war against the USSR. Indeed, in the opening months of the conflict, the Wehrmacht won a series of impressive victories over the Soviet forces, bringing German troops to the outskirts of Leningrad and Moscow. But by December, Hitler's gamble on a quick victory had failed to pay off. The Russian forces rallied and began a counteroffensive just as heavy snows and freezing temperatures—"General Winter" in Russian parlance—set in. The German front held, barely, and the war continued, but Germany never again came so close to complete victory.

It was during this period that Hitler's behavior began to change. The flexible and daring leader who had outmaneuvered his opponents again and again in the 1930s and in the early years of the war was replaced by a rigid, domineering commander in chief who no longer listened to his military advisors.

In the summer of 1941, against the unanimous advice of his leading commanders, Hitler refused to order a march on Moscow that would probably have brought about the collapse of the USSR. He stubbornly held to his own view that a campaign to conquer Ukraine and its agricultural and mineral resources would be decisive. The resulting Battle of Kiev did indeed result in a crushing victory over the Red Army, but it didn't bring about a Soviet collapse. When Hitler then decided to march on the Russian capital after all, it was too late.

Was Hitler's megalomania and refusal to heed expert advice the result of too much success or hubris, or was his judgment being impaired by a physical illness? Already in 1940, Hitler had begun to show signs of allowing blind rage to overcome rational judgment. In late August of that year, during the Battle of Britain, the Luftwaffe had the RAF on the ropes. The forces of British Fighter Command were stretched to the breaking point, and British losses in pilots and planes were greater than those of the Germans. Had this continued for just another two or three weeks, the possibility of invading Britain successfully would have presented itself.

During the course of their operations, the Germans had accidentally dropped a few bombs on London. Prime Minister Winston Churchill ordered British Bomber Command to retaliate by attacking Berlin. The British raids on the German capital did little damage and were of no military importance. Hitler, however, was enraged by this blow to his prestige. He ordered the Luftwaffe to switch its focus from attacking the RAF to bombing London. This change in tactics saved the RAF from looming defeat. It was the first great turning point in World War II, brought about by Hitler's inflated ego and irrational anger. See chapter 13 for greater detail.

The cool, calculating Hitler who had earlier shown flexibility and a willingness to accept others' advice had by 1942 been replaced by a rigid egomaniac who believed he was always right.

Hitler's ability to make sound decisions seemed to vanish. During the decisive battles of El Alamein and Stalingrad in late 1942, he ordered his forces to stand fast against overwhelming odds. In a message to the beleaguered Rommel at El Alamein, Hitler said, "You can show your troops no other way than that which leads to victory or death." The result, of course, was death. Rommel was overwhelmed, and the remnants of his Afrika Korps eventually surrendered to British and American forces in Tunisia. The fate of the German Sixth Army at Stalingrad was even worse. Only a few thousand of its men survived to return to Germany after the war.

Shirer, writing in *The Rise and Fall of the Third Reich*, mentions that by late 1942, it was evident that a change, a "corrosion," in Hitler had set in.[81] That this corrosion continued is confirmed by Albert Speer, Hitler's minister of armaments and one of his closest collaborators. Reflecting on Hitler in the autumn of 1943, after the tide of war had definitely turned against Germany, Speer had this to say in his book *Inside the*

Third Reich: "A curious transformation seemed to take place in him. Even in desperate situations he displayed confidence in ultimate victory. . . . The more inexorably events moved toward catastrophe, the more inflexible he became, the more rigidly convinced that everything he decided on was right."[82]

As the war progressed, Hitler's decisions led to one catastrophe after another. As German cities were being pounded into rubble by British and American bombers, Hitler ordered that Germany answer back in kind, though the Luftwaffe no longer had the power to stage raids on Britain as it had in 1940 and 1941.

Germany continued to build large numbers of bombers even as the war situation necessitated a concentration on building fighter aircraft as an absolute priority. Hitler insisted that the world's first jet fighter, the ME 262, a weapon that could have swept Allied bombers from Germany's skies, be converted into a fighter-bomber, thus delaying its introduction until the war was almost over.

Hitler's fanatical insistence on standing fast rather than waging a mobile defense against his numerically superior enemies led to disaster in both East and West. The annihilation of Army Group Center in Russia in June 1944 was a bigger defeat than Stalingrad.

After the successful Allied landing in Normandy in that same month, Hitler ordered his troops there, outnumbered and ravaged by the all-powerful Allied air forces, to hold onto every inch of ground. The result: an Allied breakthrough at Avranches that resulted in the destruction of Hitler's Normandy armies, with the remnants forced to retreat all the way to the German frontier. By the autumn of 1944, the war was irretrievably lost, though final defeat did not come until six months later.

The deterioration of the war situation was mirrored by Hitler's own mental and physical decline. Particularly after the failed bomb plot of July 1944, from which he miraculously escaped with only minor injuries, he no longer resembled the dynamic and effective Führer of the early war years. But even in 1943, the decline was evident. General Guderian, the creator of the German Panzer arm and later chief of the General Staff, was shocked when in early 1943 he saw Hitler for the first time in over year: "He had aged greatly. His manner was less assured than it had been and his speech was hesitant. His left hand trembled."[83]

Two years later, Hitler's physical condition had declined yet further. Guderian describes the Führer's appearance in 1945 as follows:

His fists raised, his cheeks flushed with rage, his whole body trembling, the man [Hitler] stood there in front of me, beside himself with fury and having lost all self-control. After each outburst of rage Hitler would stride up and down the carpet edge, then suddenly stop immediately before me and hurl his next accusation in my face. He was almost screaming, his eyes seemed about to pop out of his head and the veins stood out on his temples.[84]

This account, which is by no means unique, certainly makes Hitler appear to be crazy, a lunatic. All accounts agree that Hitler's physical condition and mental acuity deteriorated sharply from late 1942 on. By 1945, he was a shell of his former self. At the end, his left side trembled uncontrollably, he dragged his left leg as he walked, and his mental state varied from torpor to outbursts of uncontrollable rage. He had once been meticulous about his appearance; now he would appear for conferences with food stains on his uniform jacket.

No doubt the fall in Germany's fortunes during this period contributed to his decline. But the change was so radical that it probably had an organic, physical origin. Was Hitler suffering from a disease or other disorder that had all but destroyed him, mentally and physically, by the time he committed suicide in 1945? Perhaps he was.

During his Vienna days, Hitler might have become infected with syphilis. In 1947, one Josef Greiner published a book, *Das Ende des Hitler-Mythos (The End of the Hitler Myth)*. Greiner had resided briefly in the Vienna men's hostel alongside Hitler, though they were not close. In the 1930s, he joined the Nazi Party and tried unsuccessfully to cash in on his Hitler connection. After the war, he wrote his book, in which he purported to describe Hitler's days in Vienna. Among other things, he claimed that while in Vienna Hitler had been infected with syphilis by a Jewish prostitute.

During the 1930s and early 1940s, Hitler suffered from minor medical problems—rashes and gastric trouble, for example. These are sometimes symptoms of early-stage syphilis. His later, more serious symptoms, such as violent trembling and outbursts of paranoiac rage, can be signs of tertiary or late-stage syphilis.

None of this constitutes proof that Hitler had syphilis. But there is additional circumstantial evidence. In Mein Kampf, the book Hitler dictated while in prison after the failed Beer Hall Putsch, he dwelled obsessively on syphilis and claimed that the disease was spread by Jews. This has been taken by some to indicate that Hitler knew he had been infected by a Jewish prostitute back in his Vienna days.

From 1936 to 1945, Hitler's principal personal physician was Dr. Theodor Morell. Although Morell had no specialist training, he professed expertise in the field of urology.

In the 1930s, the term urologist was often used as a euphemism for a doctor who treated venereal diseases. However, Morell was in fact a quack, as has been amply demonstrated by many sources.[85]

Morell might have suspected that Hitler had syphilis, but he was never able to make a definite diagnosis. Indeed, a Wassermann test for syphilis that Morell administered to the Führer in 1940 proved negative. Moreover, it is now known that Greiner's 1947 book claiming that Hitler acquired syphilis in Vienna is nothing but a tissue of lies written merely to make money.[86]

Adolf Hitler with quack Doctor Morrel

These facts would seem to settle the matter, though occasionally a historian or psychiatrist still comes forward claiming that the evidence points to Hitler being syphilitic. But most experts today agree it is most unlikely that Hitler suffered from syphilis. The claim lives on, perhaps, because its salaciousness, combined with Hitler's notoriety, is a perfect recipe for grabbing media attention. It remains possible that Hitler suffered from syphilis acquired in a Viennese brothel simply because proving a negative (i.e., that Hitler did not have syphilis) is virtually impossible. But the evidence pointing to syphilis is extremely thin.

If syphilis doesn't explain Hitler's physical and mental decline over the course of World War II, what does? Stress alone is unlikely to have reduced him to the palsied, raving dictator of the war's final months. Nor does it explain the lack of flexibility and unwillingness to listen to others that he exhibited more and more from 1941 on. So then what explanation is there for Hitler's behavior? For an answer we turn the spotlight upon the Führer's physician, the aforementioned Dr. Morell.

Hitler had a pathetic faith in Morell's healing powers. And Morell did have success in treating a few of Hitler's minor medical problems. But he was very much out of his depth when it came to more serious matters, such as the Führer's heart problems (Hitler had high blood pressure and an irregular heartbeat, and in 1941 coronary artery disease was diagnosed after an electrocardiogram). He was never able to resolve Hitler's chronic gastric troubles or make a definite diagnosis of the cause of Hitler's trembling left arm and leg. Morell was unable to effectively treat any of these conditions.

In addition to being little more than a faith healer who used bromides and the power of suggestion to alleviate Hitler's discomfort, Morell was personally rather repulsive. Obese and careless about his personal hygiene, he was despised by the other members of Hitler's inner circle. His main talent was for making money. He used his position as Hitler's personal physician to promote his business ventures, which included the manufacture of various medicines of questionable value.

At the height of World War II, Morell became Hitler's Doctor Feelgood. During the period in which he was Hitler's physician, Morell gave Hitler no fewer than twenty-eight different medications, many of them by injection. Most of these drugs were ineffective and harmless, though not all of them.[87] Beginning in late 1941 or early 1942, Morell began giving

Hitler a daily "pep injection" when the dictator got up in the morning.[88]

Hitler's associates all remarked on the immediate and striking effect produced by these injections: the Führer immediately became cheerful, talkative, and full of energy. These effects and the rapidity with which they manifested themselves are consistent with amphetamine and no other drug.[89] In addition to the daily injections, Hitler was likely receiving additional amphetamine in the Vitamultin tablets that Morell provided him. Hitler is known to have consumed up to ten of these "vitamin" pills per day.[90]

As the war dragged on, Hitler's craving for amphetamines increased. Amphetamine use produces tolerance, thus requiring a larger dose to produce the same effect. Eventually the user becomes an addict and experiences the effects of the drug's toxicity. By 1943, Hitler was often receiving several injections per day.

Changes in behavior as a result of amphetamine use and abuse include garrulousness (during the war, Hitler's monologues became the stuff of legend; he would talk on and on for hours without interruption); bouts of euphoria interspersed with periods of irritability or depression; and a tendency to be inflexible (such as stubbornly maintaining one's own point of view and refusing to heed other's advice, or ordering armies to stand fast even in hopeless tactical situations).

As the addiction progresses, these symptoms become worse, and to them are added obvious signs of physical and mental deterioration such as tremors, uncontrollable rages, and a weakening grip on reality. Needless to say, Hitler exhibited all these symptoms, which worsened over time until by the end of the war he was a physical and mental wreck. His decline tracks precisely with the administration of Morell's "pep" injections, the Führer's growing ineffectiveness as a leader mirroring his likely descent into amphetamine addiction. And it was certainly no coincidence that the decline in Hitler's mental and physical health (and thus his ability to make rational decisions) was in turn mirrored by the decline in Germany's fortunes.

There is evidence to indicate that Hitler was also addicted to opiates courtesy of Dr. Morell. Near the end of the war, according to witnesses, he shouted at Dr. Morell: "You have been giving me opiates the whole time. Get out of the bunker and leave me alone!"

The case for amphetamine and/or opioid addiction as the cause of Hitler's and Germany's decline cannot be absolutely proven, but the circumstantial evidence is very persuasive. The case for syphilis as a cause of Hitler's descent into near-madness is far weaker, though not ultimately disprovable. In either case, we have a little incident, a tiny blunder, snowballing into a big disaster. Perhaps it was a trip to a Viennese brothel or perhaps a dictator's desire to periodically enhance his energy and powers of decision through medically administered drugs that started the snowball rolling. In either case, it led eventually to an avalanche that changed the face of Europe and caused the deaths of millions.

Jared Knott

SIDEBAR

MY BROTHER'S KEEPER: SIBILING RIVALRY AMONG THE LEADERS OF THE WORLD

The list is long and remarkable: Romulus slew Remus, apparently when the she-wolf who suckled them was not around to keep the peace. Caine slew Abel out of jealousy and incurred the wrath of the Lord. At the age of ten, Genghis Khan shot an arrow into the back of his half-brother, Behter, in a dispute over hunting spoils.

Cleopatra had her brother killed. Clovis, the man who organized France into a nation, went beyond even this. He would scour the countryside looking for relatives, claiming loving kinship. When he found them, he would then kill them to make sure they had no claim on the throne of France.

Two Academy Award–winning sisters, Olivia de Havilland and Joan Fontaine, did not speak to each other for over thirty-five years. The feud was ended only by the death of Joan Fontaine at the age of ninety-five in 2013. As of this writing, Olivia is still living in Paris at the age of 101.

The four Warner Brothers were often at each other's throats. Like Genghis Khan and Behter, they clashed over how to divide up the bounty of the hunt, only in Hollywood and not on the plains of Eurasia.

The identical twin sisters known as Dear Abby and Ann Landers were both famous for the wise advice they gave to millions of readers in their newspaper columns. But they had no such wisdom for each other. They feuded bitterly for many years, trading insults and even denying kinship.

In the animal kingdom, the black eagle hen usually lays two eggs, and the first chick to hatch will normally peck the younger one to death. The blue-footed booby does much the same. Twenty-five percent of hatchlings are killed by siblings.

Countless kings, queens, and princes committed murder to seize or protect their crown. One famous example is James Stewart, the brother of Mary, Queen of Scots, who conspired successfully to have her imprisoned and put to death by the axe of the executioner. James later had the distinction of being the first person in recorded history to be assassinated by means of a firearm. One of Mary's supporters did the deed while James was riding through the middle of Linlithgow in 1570. By his lights, the assassin perceived it to be a justifiable retribution. What goes around comes around, especially in royal circles.

When Ida Eisenhower was asked if she was proud of her son, she said, "Yes I am. Which one?" The relationship between the brothers seems to have been sanguine and mutually supportive, but there was an ongoing competition. Ike usually lost to Edgar in golf and referred to Milton as "the intellectual one."

George Marshall, Army chief of staff in World War II, is considered by many to be one of the finest military leaders the nation has ever produced. However, he was something of a goof-off as a youth. He was even fired as the church organist. Then one evening, he overheard his older brother telling their parents, "Don't let George go to VMI. He will disgrace the family name." George then became determined to attend the school where his brother had been a student and to perform so well as "to wipe his mouth." And he did so with a vengeance.

Historical psychologists have noted that almost all assassins in the Western world have had an older brother, the resentments of childhood domination warping the character of the unstable mind. When John F. Kennedy was asked if he'd had a happy childhood, he hesitated and answered that yes, he had, but that his older brother, Joe, sometimes made him miserable.

Joe Jr. had a temper and a mean streak, and he tormented his skinny and weaker brother three years his junior. Fights were frequent and often ended with Joe sitting on top of young Jack. The youngest son, Teddy Kennedy, often told the story of being shoved off a sailboat and into the water at the age of eight for not responding to Joe Jr.'s commands quickly enough.

With the help of his father's influence, Jack won the Marine and Navy Medal and became something of a national hero after the PT 109 incident. Shortly thereafter, at a large dinner gathering in Hyannisport, someone made a careless toast to "the hero of the Kennedy family, John Kennedy." Big brother Joe felt he had been outshone by his younger brother. The number one son was stung and enraged that his chief rival would get so much attention. A family friend, who spent that same night in the room with Joe Jr., reported on the depth of his angst: the wounded older brother was in tears, opening and closing his fists, saying over and over again, "I'll show them! I'll show them!" (See chapter 19 for further information on this subject.)

Shortly thereafter, LTJG Joseph Kennedy Jr. reported to England for duty as a Navy pilot flying submarine patrol. But there was no action, just uneventful, nonheroic work. No submarines were to be found in his sector. It was perhaps frustration and a strong sense of sibling rivalry that motivated Joe Jr. to volunteer for an extremely dangerous mission in the skies over Europe. Reckless and ill-considered, this was bravery to a fault. The star-crossed mission led to his early and unnecessary death. Intense competition and bitter rivalry can often lead to great achievement. But in this case and many others, it led only to the deep pain of a promising life cut far too short.

This high-achieving family and others had to grapple with the vaunting consequences of profound sibling rivalries. Physiologists tell us that this kind of intrafamily competition is especially intense in households with a gifted child. But without the motivation of the sibling horse race, would George Marshall, the Eisenhowers, or the Kennedy brothers have done so well in their very substantial careers? Maybe they would have, maybe not.

Certainly, the motivation is very powerful, keenly felt, and deeply personal. The humiliation and anger of being outdone by one so close can call forth the most violent and intense of responses. The motivational speaker Tony Robbins points out that being disturbed is often the basis for an energetic call to action within one's self. And many people find a sibling's success being rubbed in their face a reason to be deeply disturbed and seriously motivated.

There are of course endless examples of brotherly love as well, of families pulling together, especially in times of crisis. However, in the final analysis, there is no denying that the relationship many people have with their siblings and family is sometimes full of conflict and complicated—in some cases, complicated even to the point of self-destruction.

Olivia de Havilland and Joan Fontaine

CAPTAINS, KINGS, AND PRESIDENTS RUNNING OFF THE RAILS

25

THE BATHROOM BREAK
THAT STARTED A WAR

That was the year that a minor incident led to the skirmish which caused the Second Sino-Japanese War, and later, the Pacific Theater of WWII. And what was this minor incident? – A full bladder.

- Shahan Russell

Readers who are students of history will know that Japan joined the ranks of the major industrial nations following the Meiji Restoration in 1868. At the same time, Japan became an imperial power; the late nineteenth and early twentieth centuries were the height of the Age of Imperialism. Successful wars against China (1894–1895) and Russia (1904–1905) gave Japan control of Korea, Formosa (Taiwan), and southern Sakhalin, plus predominant influence in resource-rich Manchuria. These Japanese gains were consolidated and extended during the First World War of 1914–1918.

Nevertheless, Japanese expansionists wanted more. In 1931, they staged a fake incident at Mukden in Manchuria after which Japanese forces invaded and occupied that Chinese province, which was then turned into the puppet state of Manchukuo.

Still Japan was not satisfied. The militarists who controlled Japan's government and armed forces were determined to conquer all of China. In 1937, another incident occurred that led to the outbreak the Second Sino-Japanese war, in effect the beginning of World War II in Asia.

This incident, however, was not a deliberate provocation but resulted from one man's tiny blunder—or at least so it seems. The events of July 7–8, 1937, are still surrounded by an air of mystery. Here's what apparently happened.

The events we are about to describe occurred at the rail junction of Fengtai on the outskirts of Peking (present-day Beijing). In the wake of the Boxer Rebellion of 1900, the major powers with interests in China, including Japan, obtained the right to place troops at Fengtai and along the rail line connecting the Chinese capital to the port of Tientsin (Tianjin). After their initial aggression in Manchuria in 1931, the Japanese stationed several thousand troops in Fengtai and along the rail line—many more troops than they were technically allowed to deploy there. By 1937, the Japanese had China's capital virtually encircled.

On the night of July 7, the Japanese forces at Fengtai began training exercises near the Marco Polo Bridge over the Yongding River, about ten miles southwest of downtown Peking. Shortly before midnight they exchanged fire with the Chinese garrison of the Wanping Fortress, which stands at the eastern end of the bridge. The haughty Japanese had not bothered to inform the Chinese of their night maneuvers, and this probably caused the fighting to flare up.

When the shooting stopped, the Japanese discovered that one of their men, Private Shimura Kikujiro, was nowhere to be found. The Japanese commander, suspecting that the Chinese had captured Private Kikujiro, immediately dispatched some of his men to deliver an ultimatum to the Chinese in Wanping, demanding that the Japanese be allowed to enter and search for their missing man. The Chinese refused. They offered to search for Kikujiro themselves, but the Japanese, who in those days were notoriously touchy where matters of "honor" were concerned, reiterated their demand to be given access to the fortress, threatening to attack if permission was denied. The Chinese again refused.

Both sides began calling additional forces to the scene. At this point Private Kikujiro turned up, shamefaced, with the story that during the night maneuvers, he had gone to relieve himself and gotten lost. One might think that this would have defused the incident, but on the contrary, the Japanese went ahead anyway and attempted, unsuccessfully, to storm the fort. After this repulse, the Japanese sent an ultimatum to open the fort to their forces or face a further attack—this despite the fact that the original problem had been resolved by the reappearance of Private Kikujiro. The Chinese attempted to negotiate, but the Japanese weren't interested. Clearly, they were spoiling for a fight.

As dawn was breaking over the Marco Polo Bridge on July 8, 1937, the Japanese attacked, precipitating the Battle of Peking-Tientsin and the Second Sino-Japanese War, which was to last for eight years, ending only when Japan formally surrendered to the Allied powers in August 1945. Millions of soldiers and civilians perished in this terrible conflict, which witnessed such atrocities as the Rape of Nanking (December 1937 to January 1938) in which tens and perhaps hundreds of thousands Chinese civilians were slaughtered.[91]

The tiny blunder of a Japanese soldier getting lost during night maneuvers precipitated World War II in Asia. This war not only involved the terrible casualties mentioned above but also weakened the Nationalist Chinese government and army to such an extent that the post–World War II victory of Mao Zedong's Communist forces in the Chinese Civil War was all but assured. And during Mao's reign (1949–1976), an estimated 80 million Chinese perished needlessly—killed in famines or simply murdered outright by the state. So much tragedy from such a minor incident is unprecedented in history.

Now, it should be said that the Japanese, or at least the army leaders who had overweening power and influence in their country during the 1930s, were probably bent on further aggression against China. War might have broken out even if Private Kikujiro had not strayed from his post during the fateful night maneuvers near the Marco Polo Bridge. But whether conflict was inevitable is impossible to say. It cannot be denied that Kikujiro inadvertently lit the fuse that caused a mighty and terrible explosion that eventually engulfed all of East Asia.

It perhaps strains credulity to believe that Private Kikujiro actually lost his way after taking a pee break. It has been rumored that he actually spent a pleasant interlude from the maneuvers in the arms of a Chinese prostitute. But I have been unable to confirm the stories of his visit to a brothel. In 2013, the Japanese government released what it claimed were all its still-secret files on the Marco Polo Bridge Incident. These maintained that Kikujiro simply got lost. But it may be that national honor requires a less salacious explanation for the tiny blunder that led to an enormous disaster.

Note: The events described above have gone down in Western history texts as the Marco Polo Bridge Incident. The bridge was built by the Chinese in the twelfth century. Its correct name is the Lugou Bridge. The famous Italian explorer praised the bridge in his writings, and Europeans named it after him during the period of Western penetration of China.

26

THE UNTIMELY INVASION

If you ever resort to violence there is one thing that you must never do and that is to lose.

- Dwight David Eisenhower

As I write this, news has just arrived of the death of Fidel Castro. For more than fifty years, Castro bedeviled a succession of American presidents, none more so than John F. Kennedy, the reluctant father of the Bay of Pigs invasion.

The island of Cuba was conquered by the United States in 1898, during the Spanish-American War. Americans had coveted the island since the days of Thomas Jefferson and on more than one occasion had tried to buy it from Spain. Now it was ours by right of conquest, and we proceeded to dominate it politically and exploit it economically for our own benefit. The early twentieth century was, of course, the peak of the Age of Imperialism, with Europe and the United States in control of most of the rest of the world.

The United States granted Cuba its "independence" in 1902, but by the Platt Amendment passed in the previous year, we retained the right to intervene in Cuba whenever we saw fit. The amendment was repealed only in 1934 as part of President Franklin Roosevelt's Good Neighbor policy toward Latin America. Even then, we retained control over Guantanamo Bay, site of a US naval base and, since 9/11, a prison housing known or suspected Islamic terrorists.

Conditions prevailing in Cuba during the early and mid-twentieth century were hardly conducive to the advance of democracy and social stability. From the 1930s to the late 1950s, Cuba was dominated by Fulgencio Batista, a former Cuban Army sergeant with a talent for intrigue and an insatiable appetite for cash. Under Batista, corruption flourished. The American Mafia had free reign on the island and built a criminal empire based on gambling and prostitution. Legitimate American businesses dominated the rest of the Cuban economy. American companies owned almost half of the sugar and tobacco plantations, and almost all the large mines and ranches.

These conditions of course made Cuba ripe for revolution. In 1956, Fidel Castro, a young lawyer with Marxist leanings, initiated a guerilla movement in the Sierra Maestra Mountains. Beginning with only a handful of men, including his brother Raul and an Argentine doctor named Che Guevara, Castro gained strength and territory until, by 1958, he posed an imminent threat to Batista's regime. On New Year's Day 1959, Batista fled Cuba for exile in the Dominican Republic. A week later Castro and his fighters entered Havana.

Castro's Marxism and his authoritarian ways quickly alienated many middle-class Cubans. But he remained popular with the mass of the Cuban people, who welcomed the apparent end to corruption and foreign domination, and the introduction of literacy programs and free health care. Castro's popularity in these early days of power would play a role in deciding whether his rule would be brief or not.

But it was not simply Cuban opinion that mattered when it came to whether the Castro regime would survive. The giant to the north was, to say the least, not pleased with many of Castro's policies. The expropriation of American property and businesses, which began almost as soon as Castro took power, was bound to inflame US public opinion, particularly in the business community and among its supporters in the American government. Russian support for the Cuban Revolution only heightened Cold War fears that communism was gaining a foothold only ninety miles from our shores.

The Eisenhower administration reacted publicly by imposing an embargo on trade with Cuba and severing diplomatic relations. Secretly, the president authorized the CIA to begin planning for an invasion of the island by Cuban exiles armed and trained by the United States.

The invasion was the brainchild of CIA Director Allen Dulles and his deputy director of plans, Richard Bissell. Dulles was a Wall Street lawyer who had been involved in espionage matters since 1917, when he manned a US intelligence outpost in Switzerland during World War I. He was appointed assistant director of the CIA in 1951 and succeeded to the position of DCI (Director of Central Intelligence) in 1953. As director he authorized successful coup d'états that overthrew democratically elected governments in Iran and Guatemala. The Iran coup in particular was to have negative repercussions that are with us to this day. The Iran and Guatemala operations were to a great degree models for the proposed Cuban venture.

Bissell was an upper-crust graduate of Yale who had worked for the Ford Foundation before joining the CIA. In the 1950s, he oversaw the U-2 spy plane program, which revolutionized aerial reconnaissance and gave the United States priceless information about Soviet Russia's military programs and preparedness.

The plan concocted by Dulles, Bissell, and their subordinates was as follows: a brigade of US Army–trained Cuban exiles—some 1,400 men—would land in Cuba in hopes of provoking a popular uprising, causing at least part of the

Cuban armed forces to revolt and thereby bringing about the fall of Castro's regime.

Even at the time, leaders should have recognized that such a scheme had only a very long shot at success. In 1960 and 1961, the majority of Cubans had not turned against the regime; in fact, as already mentioned, Castro still enjoyed widespread popular support.

Additionally, it's hard to imagine how any strategist could have foreseen success in purely military terms. If you were to lay the island of Cuba over the United States, it would stretch from Boston almost to Detroit. It's not a small island. How 1,400 men would be able to invade and conquer it is difficult if not impossible to imagine. Over the years it has been speculated that the CIA's leadership was quite aware that the invasion would probably fail but wanted to launch it anyway because they believed no American president would allow the Cuban freedom fighters to perish on the beach. The exiles' invasion would in effect be the pretext for a full-scale US invasion of Cuba, which needless to say would have put an end to Castro. However, it's never been proved that the CIA was so Machiavellian in its calculations about the invasion.

By 1961, John F. Kennedy was president. He was briefed on the CIA's invasion plan only days after assuming office. The initial plan called for Brigade 2506 (as the force of Cuban exiles was named) to land on the beach at Trinidad, Cuba. This particular landing site would have allowed the invaders to escape into the Escambray Mountains and start a guerilla movement should the popular uprising and revolt of the Cuban armed forces not materialize. But the problem of "too many cooks spoiling the broth" now arose. The State Department raised objections to the landing site, and in the end the nonmilitary experts were able to get the invasion plans changed. The possibility of a fiasco occurring was now very real, though by no means acknowledged by the participants. The planners and those who were to carry out the plan were swept along by the momentum that exists whenever preparations for a major operation are set in motion. The exiles and their CIA handlers were also caught up in the emotion of the moment; they believed that they were on the brink of victory and the liberation of Cuba from its Marxist masters.

The new plan called for Brigade 2506 to land at the Bay of Pigs. Prior to the landing, Cuban exile pilots flying old B-26 bombers (painted to match Cuban Air Force B-26s) were supposed to attack and destroy Castro's small air force. These planes would also be available to provide air cover during the landing itself. A few pilots from the Alabama Air National Guard were detailed to provide backup for the exile flyers. They too would be flying in disguised aircraft, which opened up the possibility of their being summarily shot if captured. It was hoped, however, that the American military could remain entirely on the sidelines during the operation.

During the winter and spring of 1961, the exiles continued to train for the landing at a CIA base in Guatemala. Other training took place in Puerto Rico and the continental United States. Eventually the invasion force was concentrated in Nicaragua, with the landing scheduled to take place in April. In March the CIA set up the Cuban Revolutionary Council, a group of handpicked exile leaders who would comprise the new government of Cuba. As preparations neared completion, it only remained for the president to give the go-ahead.

JFK had allowed preparations to continue without formally authorizing the landing. He seems to have had some doubts about the likelihood of the operation succeeding, but the advice he was receiving was quite the opposite. Success was assured, or almost certain, the briefers told him. Additionally, JFK had put a great deal of pressure on himself to get rid of

Castro. During the 1960 presidential campaign, he had criticized the Eisenhower administration and his election opponent, Vice President Richard Nixon, for allowing communism to take hold in Cuba. He might also have felt that Castro—a young, bold leader with revolutionary ideas and rhetoric to match—was in a position to spread revolution thru out the hemisphere.

To do nothing about the "Cuba problem" could make Kennedy appear weak on the world stage. In any case, at the beginning of April, he finally authorized Operation Zapata, the landing at the Bay of Pigs.

The invasion force sailed from Nicaragua under cover of darkness on April 14, 1961. During the next day, the exiles' B-26 bombers carried out strikes against Cuban airfields, hoping to knock out Castro's small air force. Unfortunately, President Kennedy had decided that only eight planes could take part in the strikes whereas the original planning had called for sixteen B-26s to be used. Although not unsuccessful, the strikes failed to destroy all of Castro's operational aircraft. Moreover, they alerted the Castro regime to the imminence of invasion. Internal security forces immediately began to round up known and suspected opponents of the regime. So the events of April 15 were, in the last analysis, negative for the invasion's prospects. The Cuban Air Force was still operational, and the possibility of an internal uprising, remote to begin with, was now all but precluded.

The landing began at two separate beaches on the morning of April 17. A third force was dropped in by parachute. The undestroyed planes of Castro's air force hit the invaders as they landed, causing some loss and sowing confusion among the invaders' ranks. The Cuban regime's pilots also shot up one of the invaders' ships, leading to the loss of all the brigade's medical supplies. B-26s flying air support for the invasion intervened with some success but not enough to be decisive. On the evening of the 17th, regime forces counterattacked. Outnumbered, outgunned, and with ammunition running low, the invaders came under increasing pressure throughout the 18th. By dawn on the 19th, Brigade 2506 faced defeat.

President Kennedy had been urged by some of his advisors, particularly the CIA and the Joint Chiefs, to use US airpower in support of the invasion. This of course would completely Americanize an operation that already looked like a US government–inspired attack on a sovereign state. He had, therefore, refused to authorize direct intervention by US combat aircraft. But now, on the morning of the 19th, he permitted a last-ditch effort to achieve victory through airpower.

With Brigade 2506 forced on the defensive and barely clinging to the beaches, a group of six B26s, four of them piloted by men of the Alabama Air National Guard, took off from Puerto Cabezas in Nicaragua to attack the Cuban forces bearing down on the invaders. US A4 strike aircraft from the carrier Essex, with their insignia removed, were to rendezvous with the B26s over the beachhead and provide air cover.

But when the B26s arrived, the A4s were nowhere to be seen. Two of the B26s were immediately shot down by Castro's fighters, and the airstrike achieved nothing. As the remaining B26s departed the area, the A4s suddenly came into view. Incredibly, there had been a mix-up caused by the fact that Nicaragua was in the Central Time Zone whereas the Essex, positioned off the coast of Cuba, was in the Eastern Time Zone. No one had taken the one-hour time difference into account when coordinating the airstrikes! The last chance to turn the tide of battle and save the brave men of Brigade 2506 was gone. An oversight, a tiny error, had put the final nail in the coffin of the Bay of Pigs invasion.

US ships moved in to evacuate survivors, but over one hundred brigade members had been killed and over 1,100 more captured. President Kennedy, shaken to the core by such a stunning failure at the outset of his presidency, wept as the news of defeat came in. To his credit, JFK took full responsibility for the disaster. The consequences of failure proved to be enormous.

Fidel Castro

Among those consequences was the perpetuation of Castro's repressive regime. Indeed, despite Castro's recent death, that regime remains in power to this day. As a result, Cuba is still a very poor country with no democracy and limited human rights.

The Bay of Pigs led directly to the decision by Castro and the Soviet leader, Nikita Khrushchev, to put nuclear missiles on Cuban soil, which in turn caused the Cuban Missile Crisis. For an entire week in October 1962, the world waited to see if a nuclear war would break out between the superpowers, involving millions of casualties and destruction on a scale that probably would have doomed civilization.

Thanks largely to the firmness and cool-headedness displayed by President Kennedy during the missile crisis, the worst was avoided. But his hesitancy, poor planning, and lack of resolve at the Bay of Pigs was what brought the world eighteen months earlier to the brink of doom.

Bay of Pigs Invasion

Jared Knott

27

POLITICAL MISTAKES

Can you imagine what would have happened if I had done that? The whole course of history. . . we might not even have had Vietnam or the Great Society.

> - LBJ aide "Woody" Woodruff after being told to call the Dallas newspapers and announce that LBJ was withdrawing from the 1948 Senate race

Three men dominated American politics in the 1960s: John F. Kennedy, Lyndon B. Johnson, and Richard M. Nixon. All three were elected president during that decade. John Kennedy is the focus of a separate chapter in this book. Here we are going to look at the other two men, Johnson and Nixon. As everyone knows, LBJ became president as a result of John Kennedy's assassination. He was then serving as vice president and succeeded to the presidency on his predecessor's death as prescribed by the Constitution. But were it not for a tiny blunder that occurred earlier during Johnson's rise on the national political stage, he would never have had the opportunity to serve in either the second or the first office in the land.

As for Nixon, his election to the presidency in 1968 occurred because the two men he couldn't beat in an election, John and Robert Kennedy, were both removed from the scene by assassins. In 1960, Vice President Richard Nixon was the

Republican candidate for president, running against John Kennedy. It remains unclear to this day whether that particular election was stolen by the Democrats. But in any case, Nixon probably lost as a result of two small blunders whose cumulative effect was, for him, disastrous.

We now a take a journey into the past, to a time when America was more powerful and prosperous than it had ever been, and when three ambitious men sought and gained the presidency of the most powerful country in history. So, let's begin with LBJ.

Lyndon Johnson

Lyndon Johnson was a man of considerable intelligence, ability, and emotional drive. He was also a man with a considerable inferiority complex born of his hardscrabble childhood and youth, his lack of personal polish, and his mediocre education (he graduated from Southwest Texas State Teacher's College). At the same time, he possessed a vast, truly Texas-sized ego. He reconciled these opposites into something resembling a whole personality through lying, duplicity, and a great thirst for personal achievement; throughout his life, lies and dishonest dealings marked his way forward. After he had risen to the highest office in the land, the term "credibility gap" was born, for even at the pinnacle of power, he found it impossible to stop lying. It was a trait that went back all the way to his earliest days in politics. And while his lies as president eventually drove him from office, shunned and despised by many of his fellow citizens, it was by cheating and lies that he had been able to rise so high.

After a brief career in teaching, Johnson entered politics. He first served as a legislative aide to a Texas congressman and then was appointed head of the National Youth Administration's Texas office. The NYA was part of the Works

Progress Administration (WPA), a New Deal make-work program. The author of the New Deal, President Franklin Delano Roosevelt, became Johnson's most powerful patron in Washington, DC.

In 1937, Johnson won a special election to fill Texas's Tenth Congressional District seat and moved to Washington to serve as a member of the House of Representatives. Johnson, like John Kennedy, saw the House as merely a stepping stone.

Johnson had little interest in legislative matters or constituent issues except insofar as these would advance his own career. He received plum committee assignments thanks to the patronage of President Roosevelt and Speaker of the House Sam Rayburn (a fellow Texan). LBJ cultivated both men assiduously.

In 1941, Johnson decided to run for the US Senate in another special election. At the time, the winner of the Democratic primary was certain to win the general election because Texas in those days was "yellow dog" Democrat country (the expression refers to the fact that in those days, the vast majority of Texas voters would have preferred to cast their vote for a yellow dog than for any Republican). His opponent in the primary was the then-governor of Texas, W. Lee O'Daniel. Johnson lost to O'Daniel by less than 1,300 votes out of 350,000 cast, a very creditable showing against a man who already held statewide office. Moreover, Johnson was at the time barely thirty-three years old. Nevertheless, he was quite depressed by his defeat. His all-consuming drive, ambition, and lust for power, combined with his deep-seated insecurity, required nothing less than victory on all occasions.

Johnson joined the Naval Reserve with the rank of lieutenant commander in 1940. He served briefly on active duty during World War II, including flying as an observer on a mission in the Southwest Pacific during which the plane he was riding in might or might not have come under fire (accounts differ). For this plane ride he was awarded the Silver Star at the instigation of General Douglas MacArthur, the Allied supreme commander in the Pacific. One would probably be justified in thinking that this high decoration was bestowed on Johnson more because he was a member of the House and a friend of the president than for any gallantry he might or might not have displayed.

In any case, the immediate postwar years found Johnson sinking deeper into ennui and depression. He had no real power in the House and no interest in its arcane rules and complicated legislative processes.

LBJ's patron FDR was dead, and Johnson had no luck when he tried to ingratiate himself with the new president, Harry Truman. He began to consider the possibility of leaving politics for private business. Then in 1948, another opportunity to move over to the Senate presented itself. This race, against an even more formidable opponent than Governor O'Daniel, would be the make or break moment in Lyndon Johnson's political career—and indeed in his life. The outcome, which was determined by a tiny blunder combined with some outright cheating, would have a profound effect not simply on Lyndon Johnson or the state of Texas but on America itself.

As in 1941, the result of the general election was a foregone conclusion: the Democrat would win. The real contest was in the Democratic primary, where Johnson would face two opponents, one of them former governor Coke Stevenson, a man known as "Mr. Texas." Let's take a moment to learn more about Stevenson, a truly legendary figure in Texas history.

Coke Stevenson (his first name was chosen by his parents to honor Richard Coke, governor of Texas from 1874–

1876) was of the same generation as LBJ's father and was some twenty years older than LBJ. He was a man of great industry and ability who owned his own business while still a teenager, became a lawyer at the age of twenty-five, and then rose to Texas-wide fame for his courtroom skills. He owned a large ranch, bought with his own hard-earned money, and founded a bank of which he became the president as well. Eventually and against his own inclinations, he became involved in Texas state politics. Elected to the Texas House of Representatives in 1928, he became its Speaker of the House in 1933 and then in 1941 was elected governor, succeeding W. Lee O'Daniel, the man who that same year beat Lyndon Johnson in the Democratic primary for US Senate.

Stevenson held the governorship until 1947. He was the longest-serving governor in the history of Texas up to that time. During his governorship, the Texas economy boomed thanks to oil and the great expansion of defense spending during World War II. He helped lay the foundation for the ascent of Texas as it grew rich and powerful on oil and gas, beef, and government contracts. It was the time when the Sun Belt was rising to become the focus of economic dynamism in America, a phenomenon that continued and gained even more momentum under the leadership of Senator and later President Lyndon Baines Johnson.

During his lifetime, Stevenson was known as "Mr. Texas," and his posthumous reputation soared even higher on the publication of the second volume of Robert A. Caro's biography of LBJ, titled Means of Ascent.[92] Caro compared Stevenson favorably to Johnson, characterizing him as an honorable and distinguished statesman. Compared to Johnson and many other Texas politicians, Stevenson was no doubt a paragon. On the other hand, he failed to rise above the racism of his time and place, whereas Johnson, for all his faults, became the most important civil rights president since Lincoln.

Suffice it to say that both men had personal flaws, as we all do. Johnson's flaws of course were as large as his outsized personality. He probably outdid not just Stevenson but every major political figure of his time in terms of vote-rigging and personal venality. Nevertheless, the 1948 Senate race in Texas probably should not be portrayed as a battle between the forces of light and darkness, as Caro seemed to do in his biography of LBJ. Shades of gray mark almost every step in Lyndon Johnson's political career, but the 1948 race reveals Johnson at his worst. Yet "everybody loves a winner," so the saying goes, and certainly winning in 1948 made all the difference in Johnson's life and, it should be said, in the life of the nation as well.

Had LBJ lost the 1948 election to Stevenson, he would almost certainly be a forgotten man today, unmentioned in the history books. But "Landslide Lyndon," as he was soon to be known, went on to influence the United States and the world in profound ways. Let's now see how the 1948 election for US Senate in Texas made that possible.

Texas in 1948 was still dominated by the Democrats; the winner of the primary would certainly become the next US senator from the state. The race began as a three-way contest between Stevenson, Johnson, and a very conservative former Army officer, George Peddy. Stevenson was clearly the favorite. Johnson, however, was a great political innovator, at least in terms of campaigning. He pioneered modern techniques of fund-raising, polling, and media and voter outreach. Stevenson ran a very traditional and almost nineteenth century campaign, raising little money and traveling from town to town to makes speeches before a gathering of citizens, whereas Johnson used the radio to reach tens of thousands of voters at a time.[93] LBJ even traveled the huge state by helicopter—this only a few years after the invention of that aircraft. Still, Stevenson was a living legend in Texas and had won statewide before whereas Johnson was a just a pushy young politician, one of twenty-one Texas representatives in Congress. Would Johnson's cutting-edge political operation be enough to bring him victory?

That question almost wasn't answered because Johnson's health nearly failed him before the votes were cast. Although a robust and incredibly energetic man, Johnson suffered from various health problems. His father had died of a heart attack at age sixty, and Johnson himself was convinced that he would die similarly (he did eventually die of a heart attack at age sixty-four). He also was troubled by kidney stones

As the race got underway, Johnson fell sick with a kidney stone that he couldn't pass. He became violently ill, suffering fever, chills, nausea, and severe, almost chronic pain. Sustained by painkillers and aspirin, Johnson refused an operation for removal of the stone. An operation would have required six weeks of recovery time—time LBJ would have had to spend resting and not campaigning. An operation would mean certain defeat in the most important political battle of his life. Although failure to pass the stone could mean kidney failure and death, Johnson was determined to carry on.

He then became so ill that a trip to the hospital was unavoidable. Doubled over in pain, unable to eat, exhausted and demoralized, Johnson from his hospital bed suddenly told a young aide, Warren Woodward, to announce that Congressman Johnson was dropping out of the race. The astonished Woodward counseled delay, but Johnson was adamant. "I had learned not to argue with him," said the aide. He was unbending and wanted an immediate public announcement that he was out of the Senate race. And Johnson was not a man who brooked defiance, especially by a mere aide.

Decades later Woodward would say, "Can you imagine what would have happened if I had done that? The whole course of history—we might not even have had Vietnam or the Great Society." Before leaving the room, "Woody" had an idea that might persuade his boss to delay his decision. He said, "Why don't you wait until Mrs. Johnson gets here?"

The candidate's wife, Lady Bird, who was in another city, was on her way to his bedside. Johnson agreed to wait. He told Woodward to pick Lady Bird up; "then we'll call the press in and we'll announce this thing together."

On his way to the airport to pick up Mrs. Johnson, Woodward did something that might have saved the campaign for Lyndon Johnson. He recalled that "halfway to the airport, I suddenly realized, 'Oh my God! If some reporter calls him, he'll probably tell him he's withdrawing, and everything will be over.'" He stopped the car and "ran into some store and called back to the hospital and got the (nurses') supervisor and I told her: 'Absolutely no calls! Absolutely no visitors.' Under no circumstances was he to have any phone calls put through to his room or any visitors of any kind until Mrs. Johnson got there. . . . And you know I put the stopper in the basin just in time, because sure enough the phone calls began to come in while I was at the airport, but no one was put through to him."

When Mrs. Johnson arrived, the crisis seemed to pass. Lady Bird "was calm and understanding and seemed to know exactly what to do. As soon as she arrived at the hospital she took over completely."

An important phone call came the next morning from Jacqueline Cochran, a famous aviatrix of the time. She by chance happened to be in Dallas and had heard of Johnson's illness. She informed Woody that a friend of hers, Dr. Gershom J. Thompson, was the chief urologist at the Mayo Clinic in

Rochester, Minnesota. Dr. Thompson was a world-renowned expert at removing kidney stones through cystoscopic manipulation rather than surgery. She offered to fly the congressman to Rochester that afternoon. The offer was quickly accepted.

Johnson's medical situation was complicated because his kidney stone was located so high up in his ureter. In the end, the doctors at Mayo were just barely able to remove the stone, which led to his rapid recovery. According to one report, no kidney stone had ever been removed in so high a position before in the history of the Mayo Clinic. With the success of the operation, the campaign would go on.

None of the three candidates won a majority in the primary. Stevenson finished with just shy of 40 percent of the vote while Johnson was second with about 34 percent. A second round of voting pitting the first round's two top vote-getters, Stevenson and Johnson, in a head-to-head contest would be required to determine who would be sent to Washington to represent Texas in the Senate.

A month of campaigning intervened between the first vote, held on July 24, and the second, which took place on August 28, one day after Lyndon Johnson's fortieth birthday. It should be said that Johnson was thousands of votes ahead of Stevenson even before the polls opened on August 28. This was because Johnson was a political intimate of George Parr, the political boss of much of southern Texas, the "Duke of Duval" (his power center was in Duval County). Through corrupt means, Parr controlled a bloc of largely Mexican voters in his realm. Robert Caro concluded that Parr's support meant twenty-five thousand votes to Johnson.[94]

Johnson was prepared to do anything to win. He definitely saw this campaign as his last chance for a memorable career in politics. He drove himself relentlessly during those five weeks before the actual voting took place. His hypocrisy knew no bounds, even by modern political standards: he told each audience he appeared before just what they wanted to hear, often contradicting himself from day to day. Today such a campaign would hardly be possible, but in 1948, television was not yet established as a medium for political reporting at the state level, and there was of course no such thing as social media in those days.

Johnson was also spending money lavishly on polling, radio advertising, and direct payoffs to political bosses who could deliver voters—voters living or dead. Much of the money used to finance LBJ's campaign came from the brothers George and Herman Brown, construction magnates and founders of the company Brown & Root (later merged with Halliburton), for whom Johnson had done favors as a congressman.

Johnson was not above telling direct lies about his main opponent, Stevenson. Trying to win over very conservative voters, Johnson blatantly lied, telling them that Stevenson was secretly in favor of repealing the Taft-Hartley law, which limited the power of labor unions.[95] Stevenson made the tactical error of not directly refuting this charge when given the opportunity to do so by the press, a decision made out of personal pride and perhaps pique. A simple "no" from Stevenson would have settled the matter for most Texas voters. Whether such a declaration would have taken enough votes away from Peddy to give Stevenson an absolute majority in the July primary cannot be known. Finally, in August Stevenson issued a formal statement denying that he favored the law's repeal.[96] But the damage had been done, and LBJ shamelessly maintained his slanderous campaign against Stevenson on the issue.[97] Nevertheless, it seemed highly unlikely that Johnson could win over enough conservative Democrats to overcome Stevenson's lead, despite the votes the Brown brothers' money had bought in Duval County and elsewhere. Virtually no one in the Johnson campaign believed in August 1948 that Coke Stevenson was beatable. But LBJ believed it.

On Election Day, all the money that Johnson and his backers had put into the pockets of political bosses such as George Parr turned into votes—big blocks of votes. Areas where Stevenson had easily outpolled Johnson in July suddenly produced returns showing a Johnson majority. During the five-week campaign, Johnson had chipped away at Stevenson's statewide lead, but polling just before Election Day showed that the Johnson effort had plateaued and that Stevenson would win. And on Election Day, despite all the cheating and vote-buying by the Johnson forces, their candidate was still about eight hundred votes shy of a majority. Coke Stevenson would be going to Washington, DC, and Lyndon Johnson would disappear into the obscurity of a career in private business. His political career was apparently over.

Then word came that additional votes were coming in from Duval County. Not all of the county's votes had yet been counted, George Parr's people told Texas election officials. And sure enough, several hundred "previously uncounted" votes were delivered—amazingly, over 99 percent of them happened to be for Johnson.

Nevertheless, Stevenson was still maintaining a razor-thin margin over the congressman. A few more days passed, and then a revised total was reported from Precinct 13 in Jim Wells County, another province in the Duke of Duval's domain. The precinct was run by Parr's chief enforcer, Luis "Indio" Salas, a Mexican with a fierce reputation. The precinct had previously reported 765 votes for Johnson. But someone had since taken a pen and changed the 7 in 765 to a 9. Two hundred votes for Johnson had appeared out of thin air, and he now led

Stevenson by a grand total of eighty-seven votes out of the almost one million that had been cast.[98]

It was blatant fraud. However, as Robert Caro tells us, this was more a matter of degree so far as Texas politics was concerned.[99] This particular case of voting fraud stood out only because the election was so close. In those days any number of votes could be found in Texas if a candidate was willing to pay for them. And Johnson, bankrolled by the Brown brothers and other wealthy Texas conservatives—men who had never liked Stevenson's independence as a politician and a man— had the money. Simply put, Johnson's well-heeled supporters had bought him a seat in the US Senate.

Stevenson protested the fraudulent result and hired lawyers to investigate the shenanigans in the Duke of Duval's dominion. Then he decided to do more than that. He brought Frank Hamer into the case.

Frank Hamer was a legend among the legendary Texas Rangers. He had joined the Rangers more than forty years earlier, at a time when frontier conditions still prevailed in parts of Texas. He was renowned for his quick draw and had killed over fifty men during his career in law enforcement. Fourteen years before, he had led the posse that tracked, ambushed, and killed the notorious bank robbers Bonnie Parker and Clyde Barrow.

Hamer had known Stevenson since Coke's days as a young lawyer; they had even worked together catching cattle rustlers. Now the two men, no longer young but still fearless and determined to uphold the law, traveled into the heart of George Parr country to a bank in Jim Wells County—George Parr's bank—to examine the disputed poll list that contained the names of those two hundred voters who had given Lyndon Johnson his victory.

Amazingly, Stevenson and Hamer got Parr's man at the bank to take the list out of the bank's vault and show it to them (Hamer came armed, but Parr's man had a dozen or more armed men—they were called pistoleros—within shouting distance). Upon examination it was clear that all two hundred names were in the same handwriting. They were also in alphabetical order. The names had clearly been added to the list by one hand in order to make up the votes Johnson needed to win. It was equally obvious that the 7 in 765 had been given a loop to turn it into a 9. The fraud was plain to see, indisputable.[100] Years later, Parr's enforcer Luis Salas was to admit that he had certified the fraudulent names in his capacity as an election judge.

It came down to whether the Texas State Democratic Executive Committee would accept the Jim Wells County vote and report to the Texas Democratic Convention that Johnson was their nominee for Senate. On the merits, those two hundred votes in Jim Wells County should have been thrown out and Stevenson declared the party's nominee. But in the end, the Johnson forces on the committee prevailed by a vote of twenty-nine to twenty-eight. Johnson was the Democratic nominee for senator and certain to be elected in November. "Landslide Lyndon" had prevailed.

Or had he? Stevenson filed a lawsuit in federal court seeking to have the result overturned. During the hearing, some of the voters among the two hundred who had been added to the Jim Wells County tally for Johnson testified that they had not voted that day.[101] The presiding judge issued an injunction removing Johnson's name at least temporarily from the ballot. Was Johnson to be deprived of his victory at the eleventh hour?

Johnson called upon Abe Fortas, probably the finest legal mind in the state. Fortas appealed to US Supreme Court Justice Hugo Black, who granted a stay, the effect of which was to restore Johnson's name to the ballot. The full Supreme Court then turned down Stevenson's petition asking it to consider the matter. Meanwhile the list containing the fraudulent names had disappeared, never to be relocated. And the rest, as they say, is history. In 1965, Abe Fortas was appointed an associate justice of the US Supreme Court by President Lyndon Baines Johnson.

There is a final irony to this story. Two Texas counties—Kinney and Hansford—had given Coke Stevenson a plurality of four hundred votes in the initial July primary. With Stevenson apparently headed for victory in the August runoff, officials in the two counties decided not to bother holding a vote on August 28. After all, what would a few hundred votes for Stevenson matter? Why go through another election in the August heat if there was no need for it? Had they simply opened their polling places, Stevenson would have become senator, and LBJ would have moved from politics to business, remembered only (if at all) as a big-talking Texan who had once served in the House of Representatives. What consequences flowed from the tiny blunder committed by the Stevenson people in those two rural counties![102]

It remains to consider those consequences. After he finally got to the Senate in 1949, Johnson's rise was rapid. He became majority whip in 1951 and majority leader in 1955. He was an effective leader and legislator who ruled the Senate with deference to no one except a handful of long-serving, powerful southern senators such as Richard Russell of Georgia.

By the late 1950s, Johnson was arguably the second-most powerful man in the country after President Eisenhower. By 1960, he was already in a position to run as a serious candidate for the Democratic nomination for president. Although unsuccessful in this, he was chosen by the eventual winner, John Kennedy, to be his running mate.

Johnson and his supporters stole votes in Texas for the Kennedy–Johnson ticket, probably enough votes to deprive the Republican candidate, Richard Nixon, of victory there. This, combined with Chicago Mayor Richard Daley's stealing of votes in Illinois, put Kennedy in the White House. It's not too much to say that Johnson made it first to the Senate and then to the vice presidency through fraud and fraud alone.

Johnson's personal corruption continued during his Senate career and beyond. In 1963, Vice President Johnson was caught up in the TFX and Bobby Baker scandals, and he became the target of Senate investigators. According to some accounts, President Kennedy had definitely decided to drop Johnson from the ticket in 1964. Then came November 22, 1963. Johnson was elevated to the presidency, and the investigations of his corrupt practices simply went away.

Johnson as president was successful in getting landmark legislation through Congress—the Civil Rights Act of 1964, the Voting Rights Act of 1965, Medicare, and Medicaid. LBJ also presided over the disastrous war in Vietnam, a distant war fought largely by draftees, many of whom had no desire to die in the jungle ten thousand miles from home. Stalemate and ever-higher casualty lists provoked an antiwar movement that divided American society and rent its social fabric. At the same time, and despite the president's civil rights legislation, racial tensions flared, and major riots in American cities occurred every summer during Johnson's time in office.

Assassinations and rising crime completed a picture of political and social chaos, rising to a peak in the terrible year of 1968. Johnson decided not to run for reelection that year and retired to Texas, hated by millions, to die of a heart attack in 1973. The fall of Saigon in 1975 highlighted the futility of his costly Vietnam policy.

All these great and terrible events—from the election of JFK to the escalation of war in Vietnam—might have occurred even if Johnson had not been there to play his part in them. But a compelling case can be made that if Johnson had lost the race for the Democratic nomination for senator of Texas in 1948, the next twenty years of American history, and especially the years from 1960 to 1968, would have turned out very differently. If only Coke Stevenson's people in little Hansford and Kinney Counties had not in August 1948 made the mistake of failing to participate in the runoff election, then perhaps—perhaps—a bloody war halfway around the world would have been avoided.

Richard Nixon

Although Richard Nixon and Lyndon Johnson were very different people—Nixon was an introvert, uncomfortable in most social settings, whereas Johnson was a crude, back-slapping, and lapel-grabbing extrovert—there were similarities between the two men as well.

Nixon, like Johnson, grew up in lower-middle-class circumstances, coming of age during the Great Depression. He too attended a less-than-prestigious college (Whittier, in California), though he later obtained a law degree from Duke.

An excellent student, Nixon actually could have gone to Harvard (where he would have graduated just before John F. Kennedy became a freshman) but had to remain in California to help support his family. Like Johnson, Nixon envied and resented the Ivy Leaguers he later encountered during his time in government. He (again like Johnson) served as a lieutenant commander in the Navy during World War II. And he was driven by ambition to enter politics and rise to the highest office in the land.

Nixon began his political career by running for Congress as a Republican in 1946. Nixon, like LBJ, had wealthy backers who expected him to support the policies they favored. Unlike Johnson, he achieved election not through fraud, not by stealing votes, but by practicing the art of the smear.

In 1946, Nixon won a seat in Congress by insinuating that his opponent, Democratic incumbent Jerry Voorhis, was a communist sympathizer. He used the same tactics to defeat Helen Gahagan Douglas when running for the Senate in 1950. As a senator, he aligned himself (though not too directly) with the views of Senator Joseph McCarthy of Wisconsin, the red-baiting demagogue.

In 1952, although only thirty-nine years old and a freshman senator, he was selected by Dwight D. Eisenhower to run for vice president on the Republican ticket. Thinking like the general he was, Eisenhower picked Nixon to guard his right flank (though after he was elected president, Eisenhower quietly went about helping the effort, ultimately successful, to destroy McCarthy politically).

The 1952 race was a crisis for Nixon just as the 1948 Senate race had been for Johnson. During the campaign, it came out that Nixon had been the recipient of an $18,000 "slush fund" created by his wealthy backers. For a time it seemed that Eisenhower would have to drop him from the ticket. But Nixon went on national television and delivered his famous "Checkers speech" (Checkers was the name of the family dog, also given to the Nixons as a gift), which, though short on substance, won over millions of less-than-sophisticated American voters, simple folk who saw themselves in candidate Nixon, at least while he was speaking that night. Eisenhower kept him on the ticket, and together they won an easy victory over the Democratic nominee, Illinois governor Adlai Stevenson (no relation to Coke).

The record is clear that Eisenhower never liked Richard Nixon. Some have put it down to just bad chemistry. However, Pulitzer Prize–winning author Seymour Hersh wrote in *The Dark Side of Camelot* that Nixon had taken a $ 100,000 bribe as a senator and Eisenhower found out about it. (See chapter 29 for greater detail.) However, the information had come after he had been named as Ike's Vice Presidential nominee. It was too late to drop him.

Whatever the reason, Eisenhower, never liked or fully trusted Nixon, and when the general's two terms as president were coming to an end in 1960 and Nixon declared himself a candidate for the presidency, Ike "misspoke" in a way that probably cost Nixon the election. The story unfolds as follows:

Eisenhower was of course a very popular president. Although he had his critics, particularly on the left, he was revered by millions as the commander in chief of the Allied forces in the European theater during World War II. As president he projected an aura of genial competence. He was in fact one of the most skilled politicians America has ever seen—so skilled that most people took him for anything but a pol. He was famously inarticulate, but that inarticulateness was in fact deliberate, a tactic that allowed him to evade questions he preferred not to answer. The deftness of his political touch was revealed in the downfall of Joe McCarthy. The part he played in bringing down the Wisconsin demagogue was so subtle and so skillful that many people to this day aren't aware of it.

Eisenhower could easily have been reelected to a third term as president had he not been constitutionally barred from doing so. He was that popular and that good a politician. And so it seems likely that Eisenhower's answer to a reporter's question during a presidential press conference held on August 24, 1960—in the very midst of the Kennedy–Nixon race—was no misstep but a deliberate knock on his vice president. As the press conference was coming to an end, Charles Mohr of Time asked the president to name a major idea of Nixon's that the Eisenhower administration had adopted. The president quickly replied, "If you give me a week, I might think of one." With a chuckle he then left the stage.

The effect of Eisenhower's words was devastating. The president had quite plainly disrespected the man who had served as his understudy during almost eight years in office. The fact that Nixon had filled in quite competently for Eisenhower during the weeks in 1955 when the president was laid up by a heart attack only darkened the shadow cast by Eisenhower's words. What was there about Nixon, many people wondered, that caused the revered Ike to speak of him in such a way? The Kennedy campaign team of course made hay with Eisenhower's remark.

Eisenhower's "blunder" was now followed by one of Nixon's own. In 1960, for the first time ever, the presidential candidates of the two major parties held a series of televised debates. The first debate, held on September 26, decisively damaged Nixon's image. He arrived at the Chicago television studio where the debate was to be held feeling under the weather and refused the services of CBS television's top makeup artist, something he could ill afford to do. A Nixon staffer applied some pancake makeup to the candidate's face. Under the hot television lights, Nixon's heavy "five o'clock shadow" was obvious, and he could also be seen to be sweating. He sometimes looked about the studio rather than concentrating on the camera; this made him appear "shifty." Kennedy by contrast appeared fit and relaxed.

The first debate was by far the most heavily watched, and the impression Nixon left on many viewers was lasting. His improved performance in the next three debates could not make up for the first debate fiasco. It is generally accepted that a majority of people who heard the first debate on the radio believed that Nixon had won while television viewers scored the debate as a win for Kennedy (some modern scholarship has disputed this conclusion).

Kennedy hit Nixon, and by implication Eisenhower, hard on the issue of national security. According to candidate Kennedy, the administration had been soft on communism in Cuba, only ninety miles from our shores. Nixon knew of plans for what became the Bay of Pigs invasion, designed to overthrow the Castro regime; he was indeed the White House action officer for the operation. He patriotically remained silent about those plans, allowing Kennedy to hammer home to voters the threat that had come about during the Eisenhower administration's time in in office.

Kennedy also beat the campaign drum on the so-called missile gap, alleging that Eisenhower and Nixon had allowed the Soviets to surpass us in the field of nuclear weaponry. In fact, Kennedy knew that our U-2 and satellite surveillance technology showed that we maintained a comfortable and indeed unchallengeable superiority in nuclear arms over the USSR. But he hypocritically played up the supposed missile gap for all it was worth.

Eisenhower was infuriated by these falsehoods and innuendos that cast a bad light on his presidency. While his opinion of Nixon was none too high, he had never wanted Kennedy to win the election. (He referred to Kennedy as "that boy.") Had he now gone out and campaigned vigorously for his vice president, it's quite possible that Eisenhower could have assured a Republican victory despite his August 24 put-down of Nixon and despite the poor impression Nixon had made during the first televised debate. And he probably would have done so had health problems not intervened.

In the fall of 1960, Eisenhower's heart condition worsened. He was experiencing arrhythmia and was in no condition to undergo the rigors of campaigning. By some accounts he barely made it to the end of his presidency (he suffered a second and then a third heart attack in 1965 and 1968 and died of heart failure in 1969).

Some accounts hold that Nixon wanted to win the presidency "on his own" and kept Eisenhower at arm's length during the campaign. Others say Eisenhower's dislike of Nixon kept him off the campaign trail. However, we have not been able to verify either of these contentions. It may have been that Eisenhower's poor health was the reason why he avoided an active role in the 1960 campaign. Or it may have been that his heart was just not in it.

Even without Eisenhower's help, Nixon nearly won on November 8, 1960. In fact, perhaps he did win. The final tally showed that Kennedy had won the popular vote by barely 100,000 votes out of nearly 70 million cast. Kennedy carried 22 states with 319 electoral votes, Nixon 26 states with 219.[103] However, it is widely believed that votes stolen by Lyndon Johnson's people in Texas and by Chicago Mayor Richard Daley in Illinois gave those two states to Kennedy[104]. Texas and Illinois combined had 52 electoral votes. Put them in Nixon's column and Nixon wins the election with 271 electoral votes.

Nixon's advisors felt he had a good case for challenging the election results, but he patriotically refused to do so, believing that the prevailing Cold War conditions were serious enough that a constitutional crisis had to be avoided. It was probably the most honorable thing Richard Nixon did during his long career in politics.

Nixon would go on to win election to the presidency in 1968, after JFK had been murdered on a Dallas street, and LBJ, his successor, had retired from office in disgrace. Had Nixon gained the presidency eight years earlier, how might history been different? What would have happened at the Bay of Pigs or during the Cuban Missile Crisis? The latter crisis, which brought us within a whisker of nuclear war, might never have happened if Nixon had become commander in chief in 1961. It's hard to believe he would have let the Bay of Pigs operation, of which he was a prime architect, fail on the Cuban beaches.

Would the Vietnam War have been fought under a Nixon reelected in 1964? Would it have been fought differently? How would the civil rights struggle of the sixties have been affected by a President Richard Nixon? These are all rich topics for speculation. But speculation they shall ever remain, for history turned out differently.

Still, had Eisenhower simply ended his August 1960 press conference one question sooner or had Nixon worn makeup in his first debate with Kennedy, the history of the 1960s might have been very different. These were two small blunders with vast consequences for America and the world.

28

DALLIANCE AND DISASTER:
THE SKIPPER AND THE DANCER

The captain of the doomed cruise liner has turned himself in after Italy's highest court upheld his 16-year prison sentence for his role in the 2012 tragedy that killed 32 people.

- The Guardian

As I was nearing completion of this book, a news item caught my attention. Francesco Schettino, captain of the ill-fated Italian cruise ship Costa Concordia, turned himself over to the authorities and entered prison after an Italian court upheld his 2015 conviction on multiple counts of manslaughter. Thirty-two passengers had died when his ship sank off the coast of Tuscany on Friday, January 13, 2012. The Italian justice system had previously found that Schettino's negligence was responsible for the deaths. To add insult to tragedy, it was revealed that Schettino had abandoned the ship before all the passengers were evacuated. He was understandably seen as a coward as well as a poor sailor.

But was he actually a poor sailor? What exactly happened on board the Costa Concordia on that unlucky 13th of January? Before we get to that, let's quickly set the nautical stage. The Costa Concordia, built in Italy by the firm Fincantieri, was launched in 2005. At over 114,000 gross tons, it was more than twice the size of the Titanic (though only about seventy feet longer). It was also the largest ship ever built in an Italian shipyard. Costa Concordia could hold almost 3,800 passengers and 1,100 crew members.

It was a state-of-the-art cruise ship in both design and the luxurious accommodations it offered, which included 1,500 cabins and staterooms, five restaurants, thirteen bars, four swimming pools, and a huge six-thousand-square-foot fitness center.

Though plush and as up-to-date technically as any cruise ship afloat, the Costa Concordia has been seen by superstitious observers as marked for disaster from the start. At her christening, the champagne bottle failed to break when it hit the hull, something that has long been regarded in sea lore as a bad omen. The ship also had thirteen decks.

On November 22, 2008, Costa Concordia was damaged while docked at Palermo, Sicily, when high winds caused it to bump into the dock. Then came the night of January 13, 2012. Captain Schettino, a man in his early fifties, had worked for Costa Crociere (Costa Cruises), the Italian subsidiary of Carnival Cruise Lines, since 2002. He came from a seafaring family and had graduated from the Nino Bixio Nautical Institute near Naples. In 2006, he was promoted to captain and given command of the Costa Concordia.

The fatal night of January 13 began much like any other for the captain. He dined as usual and then headed for the bridge. The ship was approaching Isola del Giglio (Giglio Island) in the Tyrrhenian Sea (the part of the Mediterranean that lies between Corsica and the Italian coast). The captain wished to make a close approach in order to "salute" a retired captain who lived on the island as well as the ship's head waiter, who happened to be a native of Isola del Giglio. He supposedly also wanted to impress the Costa Concordia's passengers by steering the huge ship close to shore. "I was trying to catch three pigeons with one bean," the captain later stated in court, using the Italian version of "killing two birds with one stone."[105]

Or so he claimed. As it was already dark, the passengers would not have been able to see enough to be much impressed. However, the captain might have been trying to impress one particular passenger, as we shall soon see.

Whether the sail-past salute was undertaken on the captain's own initiative or was ordered by his onshore superiors at Costa Crociere remains in dispute, given the legal ramifications. Unfortunately, Captain Schettino committed at least one tiny blunder: by his own admission he had turned off the alarm on the ship's computer navigation system. He told investigators that he had done so because he knew the area well and had performed the maneuver three or four times previously. Be that as it may, his tiny blunder had huge consequences. He saw too late that he was steering closer to shore than he had planned. As he attempted to correct course, the ship struck a rock about one thousand feet (330 meters) from shore.[106] At the time, the ship was traveling at a speed of over fifteen knots. It was about 9:45 p.m.

According to court testimony given by the ship's first officer, the captain had left his glasses in his cabin and repeatedly asked the first officer to check the radar for him. It seems clear that the captain had behaved in a somewhat unusual manner as he prepared for the sail-past salute: ordering it to take place in the dark of night, turning off the radar, not wearing his glasses on the bridge. Why had he done these things? It appears that the answer lies in his passion for a young woman. We will take up that story in a moment.

The rock tore a huge gash in the ship's hull on the port side, and Costa Concordia immediately began taking on water. The engines were quickly submerged and stopped working, and the absence of definite evidence either way, we will probably never know for certain who ordered the salute.

In the immediate aftermath of the accident, the crew communicated to both passengers and authorities on shore that the ship had merely suffered a blackout.[107] But panic reigned on the bridge, the occupants of which were only too aware of how serious the situation actually was. Within about twenty minutes of striking the rock, the ship was already listing twenty degrees to starboard. Yet it was another forty-five minutes or so before the order to abandon ship was given. The evacuation of the ship was completed in the early morning hours of the 14th. Captain Schettino, however, had entered a lifeboat in the midst of the rescue efforts, leaving the ship at about 11:30 p.m. He had decided to save his own skin despite his clear duty to remain on board until everyone else, passengers and crew, had been brought to safety.

Cowardice aside, the negligence of the captain proved costly, to say the least. Thirty-two passengers and crew, including a five-year-old girl, drowned. The monetary loss came to some $2 billion (more than three times what it cost to build the ship, which had to be scrapped). Captain Schettino was charged with manslaughter, causing a maritime accident, and abandoning his ship. Convicted on all counts, he was sentenced to sixteen years in prison and began serving his time in May 2017.

We return now to the question, what explains the behavior of the captain that led to the ship running aground, with fatal consequences for thirty-two people? A dalliance between the middle-aged, married captain and a much younger woman caused or at least contributed to the Costa Concordia disaster.

The woman in question was Domnica Cemortan, a native of Moldova. In her mid-twenties at the time of the disaster, she began having an affair with the captain soon after she became a tour guide on his ship. Ms. Cemortan, an attractive platinum-blonde single mother, had been a dancer before embarking on her nautical career. She publicly denied any sexual involvement with the captain until forced to reveal the affair under oath at Schettino's trial in 2013.[108]

We know now that the captain and his Moldovan lover dined together and then repaired to the bridge, arriving about fifteen minutes before the ship ran aground. The pair had consumed wine with their meal. There were also reports after the accident that cocaine might have been part of their predisaster bacchanal, but this has not been definitely confirmed.

It appears then that Captain Schettino was performing the nighttime sail-past salute for the benefit not of the passengers but simply to impress his young girlfriend. This may explain why he didn't bring his glasses to the bridge and why he turned off the radar alarm system (though perhaps the wine had just made him forgetful and careless).

Let us then try to picture the final moments before tragedy struck. The captain and his mistress, both at least a little tipsy, arrive on the bridge. Although it is nearly ten o'clock on a January night, as a display of his power and machismo, he orders the huge ship to sail dangerously close to shore. His judgment and reactions are clouded by wine and his infatuation with a woman young enough to be his daughter. Too late he realizes that he has brought the ship too close to shore. His small blunders produce a great disaster: his ship is lost, and thirty-two of her passengers are taken by the sea.

To compound his blunder, the captain behaves in a cowardly fashion, abandoning his ship for a lifeboat while hundreds of passengers remain on board, their lives very much in danger. The Latin lover, it turns out, is more mouse than man; to disaster is added personal dishonor. Is a sixteen-year sentence enough for a man who by his actions is responsible for thirty-two deaths? Six months' time per death? I would say he got off easy.

It is tempting to compare the Moldovan dancer, Ms. Cemortan, to the Sirens of Greek mythology, who lured sailors to their deaths on the rocks. But the unfortunate young woman was not the cause of the tragedy. Captain Schettino had failed utterly as a sailor and a man. His tiny blunders led to disaster for the Costa Concordia.

29

THE WAR THAT WAS LOST
BY A SINGLE PIECE OF TAPE

*It would seem that the Watergate story from beginning to end
could be used as a primer on the American political system.*

- Bob Woodward

In order to understand this bizarre tale, we must try to
see the world as Richard Milhous Nixon saw it in the early
1960s. No easy task. Nixon was—as described by his own chief
of staff H. R. Haldeman—our "weirdest president." And by all
accounts he was no less weird before he was elected to the
highest office in the land. When it comes to understanding
Nixon, his psychological background is helpful in providing a
context for at least some of the answers.

Respect, Not Love

Some experts in psychology say it is men who are
greatly adored by their mothers who often rise to levels of great
achievement in life. Several examples of this human
phenomenon would include Frank Sinatra, Douglas MacArthur,
Lyndon Johnson, and Pancho Villa!

In the book *The Arrogance of Power: The Secret World
of Richard Nixon,* by Richard Summers, the author makes it
clear that Nixon's mother did not adore him; rather, she treated
him coldly. She was formal and distant. (His father, on the other
hand, was hot tempered and believed in the strap.) "I never

heard my mother say 'I love you' to anyone," Nixon recalled. Experts say unloved children grow up to become insecure or hostile. Nixon became both.

Henry Kissinger was national security advisor and secretary of state in the Nixon administration and found much in Nixon worthy of his admiration. "Can you imagine what this man could have been had somebody loved him? Had somebody in his life cared for him?" Kissinger observed. "I don't think anybody ever did, not his parents, not his peers. He would have been a great, great man had somebody loved him." Instead, "he was an emotionally deprived child," crippled by neuroses, and grew to regard love and physical closeness as a diversion that would drain, deplete, and emasculate him. His analyst of forty years Dr. Arnold A. Hatschnecker, the man who knew him best, said that Nixon felt he needn't be "loved as a human being, only respected as a man."[109]

Complex and complicated, Nixon was a shy man in the extroverted world of Washington politics. Nixon habitually sheltered himself from true social interaction and dealt with the strain of interpersonal conflict and intense media scrutiny by hiding behind a mask of formality. Nixon's eccentricities set him apart from other people. However, in spite of his foibles, many people could identify with his intense pride in his early successes and the personal pain of his celebrated downfall. If Nixon's life were plotted on a chart, it would show many jagged angles careening up and down between success and disappointment. Few people have led lives of such extreme variability.

Elected first as a representative and then senator from his home state of California, many people in those early years recognized his potential for higher office. Local observers witnessed in the young Nixon a fanatical drive, a keen mind, and an addiction to national politics. Even then it was said by some that the young lawyer who was raised over a gas station would someday be president of the United States.

As a junior senator newly settled in Washington, Nixon distinguished himself in the communist witch hunts of the late 1940s and early '50s. His aggressive pursuit of alleged fellow travelers and outright communists in the State Department—most notably in the Alger Hiss case—propelled him to national prominence. A favorite of the far right because of his headline-grabbing successes, Nixon was selected by GOP presidential nominee General Dwight Eisenhower as his running mate in the 1952 presidential election. With the war hero as its standard bearer, the Republican ticket was swept into office in a landslide.

But there was trouble in paradise. Nixon was not getting along well with his boss. He never had. Eisenhower called Nixon a "loser" in private and wanted to drop him from the ticket in the 1956 election campaign. "How can a man go through life with so few close friends?" Ike wondered aloud. Even in public the president was sometimes condescending and even insulting to his second-in-command.

A Shadowy Alliance

We don't know exactly what was behind Eisenhower's antipathy toward Nixon. A number of biographers have blamed it on nothing more than bad chemistry. However, we do know that even in 1952, Eisenhower had considered dumping Nixon as his running mate when it was revealed that the vice-presidential candidate had a slush fund. However, in his book *The Dark Side of Camelot*, Seymour M. Hersh provides the written record with another more sinister possibility. Bluntly put, Nixon took a $100,000 bribe, and Eisenhower found out about it.[110]

The money had come from a wealthy Romanian industrialist named Nicolae Malaxa. He was an oddity, an Eastern European tycoon from a communist country living in the United States. He wished to remain in California and enjoy his great wealth, but the Immigration and Naturalization Service was making a serious effort to deport him.

Mr. Malaxa appears to have been a practical man and does not seem to have been inhibited by any philosophical or moral constraints such as a conscience or a sense of decency. He used money to ingratiate himself with whichever side of a political conflict he had reason to believe was going to prevail. He had been a financial supporter of the pro-Nazi Iron Guard in Romania during World War II. This paramilitary force was responsible for a viciously sadistic pogrom that killed an estimated seven thousand Jews in Bucharest in 1941. After the war, he had turned coat and served the communist regime so well that they allowed him to keep 2.4 million dollars of his personal funds, which had been seized by the government. It is fair to speculate that financial considerations were a factor in producing this kind of uncharacteristic generosity on the part of an Iron Curtain country.

In 1952, Nixon had introduced a bill in the Senate granting Malaxa the right to remain in the United States. However, the bill was blocked by the House Judiciary Committee chairman, Democrat Emanuel Sellers, because he saw "something rather suspicious" about the entire arrangement. Nevertheless, in 1952, Nixon received a check from Malaxa for $100,000, which he deposited in the Bank of California. The CIA had a photocopy of the check. The potentially explosive story dripping with corruption was passed on to General Eisenhower. The general wanted to eliminate this source of trouble and potential embarrassment from the ticket, but timing made such an option impractical.

The Malaxa story remained in the shadows and was never exposed to public scrutiny in Nixon's lifetime. But Nixon had another lesser scandal that was being dramatically exploited by the members of the fourth estate. The press reported that Nixon was benefiting from an $18,000 slush fund that had been established for him by a group of California businessmen. They had donated the funds ostensibly to further the young senator's career. Many members of the fourth estate, however, believed that the money was used to gain influence over Nixon. The controversy erupted onto the national stage in the summer of 1952 and was threatening the Republican Party's chances of success in November, not to mention Nixon's entire political career.

But Nixon, for all his personal contradictions, was a man of great internal resources. At the height of the controversy—just when he needed it the most—he was able to deliver one of the most effective speeches in American political history. In a half-hour television address delivered on September 23, 1952, Nixon defended himself against the charges. He denied that any of the money had been spent for personal use. His wife, Patricia, did not own a mink coat but "a respectable Republican cloth coat." He confessed that the family had received a gift, "a little cocker spaniel, and our little girl—Tricia , the six year old—named it Checkers." He then said, "The kids love the dog, and we are going to keep it." The Checkers speech was a national sensation and created a flood of support for a man who had been on the verge of being disgraced and banished from national politics.

In the face of this huge popular groundswell and against his personal inclination to drop Nixon, Eisenhower allowed the young senator to remain on the ticket. Richard Nixon had dodged a bullet and emerged stronger and more powerful than before.

In 1956, the general again wished to replace the thorn in his side with another more suitable candidate. But his choice for the post would not accept unless Nixon stepped down voluntarily. Nixon would not step down—unless he was pushed—and therefore hung on to his job, just barely.

The 1960 Election

FBI director J. Edgar Hoover called Nixon on election night to inform him that he had evidence of massive vote fraud in Illinois, Texas, and Missouri. In spite of the apparent thievery, Nixon was uncharacteristically gracious in bowing out of the contest. He ignored the cries of foul play from his supporters and quietly accepted his narrow defeat.

Always known as a tough and even fanatical competitor, Nixon's decision surprised many observers. His gentlemanly behavior was, as publicly stated, based on two factors: (1) a recount would have taken months and paralyzed the nation, and 2) it would have damaged the image of American democracy around the world at a time when the United States was facing the global communist challenge.

Publicly, Nixon seemed to be doing what he believed to be the wise and noble thing for the nation and the world. But then again, a challenge to the election would have been very impractical and ultimately unsuccessful. It is much easier to do the right thing when you have no other choice.

Nixon's next political step was to run for governor of California in 1962, but the Democratic incumbent, Pat Brown, handed him a stunning defeat. This time Nixon's response to defeat was not so elegant. He got drunk and told a roomful of reporters that they were "not going to have Dick Nixon to kick around anymore."

Everyone seemed to agree that Nixon was finished. But everyone was wrong. Like a phoenix rising from the ashes, Nixon made a surprising comeback. He worked hard at becoming more mellow and likeable. He swore off hard liquor. He appeared to be a man of true presidential timber and won the GOP nomination for president and the election in 1968, and then was reelected in 1972, winning over 60 percent of the popular vote and carrying 49 states.

Before proceeding with the story of and the fall of Saigon, the key thing to remember from this profile is that defeat had taught Richard Nixon some hard lessons. Nixon carried these lessons with him later in life, and they helped to shape his later campaigns, his presidency, and his view of the world. The lessons were these: leave nothing to chance and take nothing for granted when running for office. Having twice snatched defeat from the jaws of victory, Nixon was determined that it would never happen again.

Nixon ran for reelection in 1972 against Democratic candidate George McGovern, a senator from South Dakota. Nixon had once lost an election because he didn't control the streets. Well, Dick Nixon did control the streets now, and he was never going to lose another election. A little political espionage was in order. The Republican National Committee (RNC) under the direction of John Mitchell was eager to learn more about the Democratic Party's plans for the campaign. Republican operatives, including former CIA personnel, were recruited and trained to burglarize the Democratic National Committee (DNC) headquarters in the Watergate, an office and hotel complex in downtown Washington, DC. The daring and dangerous plan was to break into the offices of the campaign chairman at night, steal politically useful information, and exit the building without being caught. The burglars and their handlers were professional and cunning. Realizing that a mishap of one kind or another could possibly occur, a security

Richard Nixon

plan was put in place to prevent detection. Lookouts were positioned on the roof with walkie-talkies. If police were seen approaching the building, the lookouts would radio their confederates, giving them ample time to escape. There was no reason to think something would go wrong. And nothing would have, except for a single, tiny, unexpected blunder.

In order to gain access to the Watergate's main building, the burglars picked the lock between the garage and the adjoining staircase. To keep the door from relocking, they had been told to place a piece of tape in a vertical position across the door's edge—in an up and down position so that it couldn't be seen when the door was closed. Instead, they placed it horizontally across the door face. In this position, the tape was visible to anyone inside the building who happened to walk by the door. When making his usual rounds, the night watchman, Frank Wills, noticed the piece of tape and saw that the door had been jimmied. Wills grabbed the nearest telephone and called the police. No uniformed cops were available, so the Washington police sent an undercover squad, cops dressed as vagrants.[111] When the unmarked car pulled up to the Watergate complex, the lookouts on the roof failed to recognize the officers. And so, scruffily attired undercover cops apprehended burglars who happened to be dressed in business suits.

The ensuing investigation tied the burglars to midlevel people in the Republican campaign who were in turn linked to high-level people in the Nixon administration. There was a Senate probe by the Judiciary Committee with public hearings and enormous publicity. A desperate cover-up attempt by Nixon failed. In the final analysis, it was the cover-up with its charges of obstruction of justice and misprision of a felony that destroyed the Nixon administration. Facing certain impeachment from a Democratic Congress, Richard Nixon was forced to resign. He left the White House and flew back to his home state of California in humiliation and disgrace.

All of this was triggered by a single piece of tape, one tiny blunder that set the cascading events of Watergate in motion, a chain reaction that damaged the presidency and changed the outcome of the Vietnam War, as we shall now see.

The Bombing Campaign

In 1971–72, the United States massively bombed North Vietnam into submission. More explosive ordinance was dropped on the tiny nation of North Vietnam than all the firepower of World War II combined, including Hiroshima and Nagasaki.[112] The North Vietnamese were forced to sign the Paris Peace Agreement in January 1973. Nixon's national security advisor, Henry Kissinger, negotiated the settlement in Paris. The treaty was designed to halt the Vietnam War in a fashion that allowed everyone to save face. North Vietnam signed, and the bombing stopped—but many waxed skeptical of North Vietnam's willingness to abide by the treaty. Nixon fully expected the North to violate the agreement; there would be a short cooling-off period, and then the attacks on the South would begin again, he believed. Additional bombing, intense in nature, would then be necessary to bring the small but stubborn nation of only twenty million people back into compliance with the Paris Accord.

But the bombing never came. Kissinger gave a televised interview in which he stated that when the North began violating the treaty, as the White House had known they would, the plan was to once again bomb them into submission. But because of Watergate, the Nixon/Ford administration was crippled and ineffective. It was too weak politically to take any meaningful action.

Kissinger and Nixon had been following a "madman in control" strategy, projecting an image of the president as an unstable fanatic willing to bomb his enemies into oblivion. Nixon's critics might have suggested that this was a case of art imitating life. But it didn't last. Nixon's paranoia led to self-destruction, Watergate rendered his administration weak and unpopular, and by 1974, Congress was no longer willing to resupply the South Vietnamese with even minimum supplies and ammunition. Abandoned and alone, South Vietnam fell to the communists.

30

BUMPS ON THE HEAD:

THE BRITISH KING

AND THE AMERICAN GENERAL

When discussing the tiny but pivotal blunders of history, head injuries are worthy of special note. At least two famous historical figures suffered from traumatic brain injury (TBI), which arguably affected their judgment and mental health, and perhaps even had a major impact on history itself.

TBI leaves a dent in its victim's emotional and social equilibrium. It's not unusual for those who love the injured party to look upon them with alarm, wondering what's happened to the person they once knew. This is not to say that the changes are always obvious. Quite the contrary. Often the changes are subtle and not even easily attributable to the injury that in fact caused them.

As a result, an atmosphere of denial tends to surround those who suffer from TBI. Onlookers might notice mild differences yet hold out hope that these changes will pass in time. As for the sufferers themselves, they are often unaware that something's changed. Denial can be mixed with rage, as the TBI sufferer insists—despite all evidence to the contrary—that they are as sharp, sane, and present as they have always been.

Not all famous head injury victims are in a position to influence historical events. Boxer Muhammad Ali's head injuries took him out of the ring yet never sidelined his status with his adoring fans as "the Greatest."

Indeed, head injuries were an expected hazard of Ali's job. Once his sports career was over, he was able to function for decades as a celebrity entrepreneur and public figure despite his physical limitations. However, he was able to speak only in a whisper and suffered from Parkinson's disease, which shortened his life.

The same can be said of billionaire aviator Howard Hughes. His reputation as an eccentric has overshadowed his many accomplishments in aviation, engineering, and business management. Unfortunately, he suffered a serious head trauma in 1946 in a plane crash over Beverly Hills that nearly killed him. He recovered physically but emerged from the hospital in a thicket of neurosis.

The resulting eccentric behavior never had much influence on the course of human events. It is possible that Hughes might have continued to be a force in the airline industry and American political activity if he had remained healthy. But with his head injury, he became more and more reclusive and eccentric. He withered away in his penthouse suite at the top of a Las Vegas casino.

Only in recent years has the seriousness of TBI become apparent among football players and, to a lesser extent, among soccer players. Kenny Stabler, Tony Dorsett, Frank Gifford, and Joe Namath are only a few of the NFL players who suffered permanent damage from a series of blows to the head on the football field.

However, these injuries to sports figures—boxers, football players, and soccer players—cannot be said to have had a major impact on national or world events. The same, however, cannot be said for the pair of TBI cases that we will examine in this chapter. I present for your consideration the story of the British king and the American general.

King Henry VIII

England's sixteenth-century King Henry VIII is widely reported in historical accounts to have started off in life as a fine physical specimen—athletic, charming, and energetic. He is said to have made wise military and policy decisions in these early years. He was popular among his subjects, who took to calling him "Bluff King Hal" in recognition of his impressive physical condition. However, all of this seems to have changed in his middle years when his life took an ugly turn in a tragic direction.

The Yale Memory Clinic released a study on February 2, 2016 that states, "Henry suffered from many symptoms which can be unambiguously attributed to traumatic brain injury." The king is known to have suffered three major head injuries in his lifetime, the worst of which resulted from a jousting accident in 1536. The king received a direct blow from his opponent's lance that knocked both horse and rider to the ground, with the horse landing on Henry.

At first it was thought that the king might have been killed from the heavy blow. Henry was not dead, but he was unconscious for two hours. The event was so disturbing to Queen Anne Boleyn, his pregnant second wife, that she collapsed from shock and miscarried their child.

Physically the king seemed to recover. Nevertheless, great damage had been done. The shocking incident seems to have led to a serious personality change in the forty-two-year-old monarch. From that point forward, those around him would write that he had become "cruel, petty and tyrannical." He also became forgetful, temperamental, and prone to rages and impulsive decisions.

Following her miscarriage, the queen, Anne Boleyn, found herself ensnared by accusations of adultery and incest. She had long been unpopular among many at court, but as the accusations broiled, she was administered the ultimate punishment: with her husband the king's consent, Queen Anne was beheaded at the Tower of London.

King Henry VIII

Henry's next two wives were greeted by gentler fates, although the marriages did not last: the third wife died following childbirth, and the fourth one was granted an amicable divorce. The fifth wife, Catherine Howard, did not fare so well, however.

At age twenty-one, Catherine married King Henry less than a month after his marriage with Anne of Cleves was annulled. Her past was shrouded by love affairs with more than one young gentleman from her home county. After her marriage to the king, she began an affair with a young courtier, Thomas Culpeper. The affair was discovered, and like Anne Boleyn before her, Queen Catherine was beheaded. King Henry's reputation as a husband was now well beyond repair.

Sometime after Catherine Howard's death, the king was considering marriage to a French princess who was said to have been full bodied. She demurred when approached by the king's representative, explaining that while she had a full figure, she also had a slender neck.

Another example of the king's new behavior took place in 1546. He was reassuring his sixth wife, Catherine Parr, that he would not send her to the Tower of London. In the middle of the conversation, soldiers arrived to arrest her and take her away. The king exploded in a tirade against the men-at-arms for their insolence and imposition. He had forgotten that he had given the order for her arrest the day before.

When reminded of his previous order, he then flew into yet another rage. Imagine the frustration of the courtiers around him in dealing with such a man.

Yale University researchers have attributed the king's rapid switching of queens and erratic behavior to damaged frontal lobes, suggesting that his fateful accident "provides the explanation for his personality change from sporty, promising, generous young prince, to a cruel, paranoid and vicious tyrant."

The king's mental decline was also matched and paralleled by a marked decline in his physical condition. Henry died in a state of morbid obesity, his waist size having gone from thirty-six inches as a young man to fifty-six inches at the time of his death.

It has been long speculated that Henry might have suffered from syphilis, diabetes, or Cushing's syndrome, a condition marked by weight gain and obesity. However, the king's obesity might also suggest the possibility of traumatic brain injury (TBI). One symptom of this condition is serious and unwanted weight gain. If the brain's pituitary gland undergoes damage, the body's ability to regulate weight suffers.

In the final analysis, the Yale study's authors suggest that TBI best explains both Henry's physical and behavioral abnormalities.

Says study author Arash Salardini, "It is intriguing to think that modern European history may have changed forever because of a blow to the head."

General George S. Patton

General George S. Patton is regarded by historians as one of the most talented and successful battlefield generals the United States has ever produced. Even from the earliest stages of his career, the young soldier and scion of a prominent California family had a remarkable résumé: He was an outstanding athlete who represented the US track team in the pentathlon at the 1912 Olympics. He distinguished himself on the battlefield in World War I and in the pursuit of Pancho Villa in Mexico. He also graduated with honors from the US Army War College.

But it was on the battlefields of World War II that Patton made his greatest mark on history. He was admired even by the enemy high command. German general Günther Blumentritt, who was one of the planners of the German invasion of Poland and France, wrote in a study for the US Army after the war that "we regarded General Patton extremely highly as the most aggressive Panzer General of the Allies, a man of incredible initiative and lightening–like action. . . . His operations impressed enormously, probably because he came closest to our own concept of the classical military commander."

However, Patton also gained notoriety for his colorful personality and his fiery, sometimes out-of-control, temperament. His displays of anger, intolerance, and unbridled speech almost cost him his job at a critical point in the midst of the war. Some even considered Patton to be insane. Yet there is serious reason to believe that an incident that took place in 1936 might have been the source of Patton's problems with impulse control and inappropriate behavior that were later to manifest themselves in such dramatic fashion.

As a man of inherited wealth, Patton was able to enjoy the aristocratic sport of polo. In 1936, Lieutenant Colonel Patton was engaging in the equestrian game in Hawaii, where he was then stationed. The exact specifics are not known, but he was thrown from his horse and received a heavy blow to the head when he hit the ground. The concussion was so severe that he was knocked unconscious for two days. Serious as this was, it was not the only time Patton had taken a blow to the head in a fall from a horse or in a road accident. However, it was the most severe.

A number of people would go on to posit that Patton's repeated blows to the head resulted in a case of dementia pugilistica, which is a subtype of chronic traumatic encephalopathy (CTE). Common among boxers, the condition is known to cause reduced mental capacity as well as dizziness and problems maintaining balance. It is also known, and relevant to the present discussion, that the condition causes impulsiveness, erratic behavior, and paranoia.

Patton's lack of self-control, whatever the cause, would explode into worldwide notoriety due to incidents that took place in the summer of 1943. It is worth noting that in August 1943, a condition known as battle fatigue was appearing with notable frequency among US servicemen. Informally termed shell shock and known today as post-traumatic stress disorder (PTSD), battle fatigue was a mental reaction to combat stress, manifesting itself without physical symptoms yet yielding men emotionally unable to proceed in battle.

Two such men in two separate locations under Patton's command were hospitalized for the condition in July and August 1943. However, Patton did not accept the doctors' conclusions. He had a different diagnosis and took it upon himself to put an end to what he considered their "malingering." He marched into the hospitals, took note of the men's absence of physical symptoms, and slapped them each in the face in two separate incidents, going so far as to declare that battle fatigue was to no longer be deemed a credible condition among his men. He unfairly labeled the men as "cowards." Patton himself summarized the situation as follows:

"There are always a certain number of such weaklings in any Army, and I suppose the modern doctor is correct in classifying them as ill and treating them as such. However, the man with malaria doesn't pass his condition on to his comrades as rapidly as does the man with cold feet nor does malaria have the lethal effect that the latter has."[113]

Patton was heard by a war correspondent angrily denying the reality of shell shock, claiming that the condition was "an invention of the Jews."

Ironically, in dismissing what history would prove to be a valid mental illness, General Patton was perhaps exhibiting a mental illness of his own. However, his underestimation of the condition might be somewhat understandable considering the generation in which he lived.

The action of a general slapping his soldiers was completely unacceptable in the army of a democratic country, which is why the incident received such enormous exposure from the American press. It was later immortalized as one of the key scenes in the movie Patton (1970), a Hollywood biography about the general.

Far more dramatic than these slaps to the face was a controversial mission known as Task Force Baum in March 1945. Patton sent three hundred of his men some fifty miles into German-occupied territory to liberate a POW camp. The results of the undertaking were disastrous, with 10 percent of the men getting killed and only 10 percent of them coming back alive. As for the other 80 percent, they all ended up getting taken prisoner themselves. Amid all the chaos, some five dozen US vehicles were lost forever to the Germans. What would motivate Patton to issue such a reckless order? He very well might have been acting out of familial love and loyalty for his son-in-law, John K. Waters, who had been captured two years prior and was at the very camp the Americans were ordered to raid. Patton, for his part, claimed that a desire to save his son-in-law did not play a part in his decision to launch the ill-fated attack. Many doubt the veracity of his denial.

Patton's career contains many examples of this kind of erratic behavior. A number of the officers and men who worked with or under Patton went on the record with statements questioning his mental stability. Eisenhower even sent medical experts to examine Patton to determine his mental state. Could that incident in Hawaii from the previous decade be blamed? Would a greater dose of good fortune upon the back of that horse have resulted in a more clear-thinking and level-headed general?

Patton's best-known biographer Carlo D'Este stated the case as follows:

> It has been conjectured that in the final months of his life Patton was suffering the long-term effects of too many head injuries from a lifetime of falling from horses, and from road accidents...

While it is perfectly true that Patton suffered repeated and potentially serious injuries to his head (the worst of which was the injury in Hawaii in 1936 that resulted in his two-day blackout), and seemed to give the appearance of being punch-drunk, like a boxer who has been hit in the head too often, medical evidence to support the notion of a subdural hematoma is wholly lacking.

Nonetheless, it seems virtually inevitable, as evidenced by his amnesia in Hawaii, that Patton experienced some type of brain damage from too many head injuries. The extent to which it influenced Patton's behavior will never be known.

In summary it can be said that Patton had great ability as a military commander in the field facing the enemy. The record is undeniable. However, he also had impulsivity and anger management issues. What would have happened if Patton had pursued golf in Hawaii instead of polo? How many American lives would have been saved?

Patton's career was limited by his erratic behavior. What would have happened if he had not fallen from a horse so many times? He might have been given command of the 12th Army Group instead of the more pedestrian Bradley. If so, he would have not been surprised by the attack in the Ardennes Offensive, which became known as the Battle of the Bulge. The Allies would have benefited from his insight and daring. The war would have ended sooner and with fewer casualties.

In the final analysis, there is the question, how much faster would the war have ended with a fit and healthy Patton free from brain injury? Of course there is no way to answer this question. Yet we can certainly wager a guess that had Patton been possessed of a more even temperament, he probably would not have had a movie made about him and he would have been a better-respected but more obscure figure in history.

Jared Knott

SIDEBAR

ONE MAN'S CHALLENGE TO GROUPTHINK: AVOIDING THE BIGGEST MISTAKE OF WORLD WAR II

When the time comes for me to meet my maker, the source of most humble pride to me will (be) . . . the fact that I was guided to oppose this thing, at the risk of my career, right up to the top. I deeply and sincerely believe that by taking the stand that I took we saved the lives of thousands of brave men.

- Gen. Matthew Ridgway

Groupthink occurs when a group with a particular agenda makes irrational or problematic decisions because its members value harmony and coherence over accurate analysis and critical evaluation. Individual members of the group are strongly discouraged from any disagreement with the consensus and set aside their own thoughts and feelings to unquestionably follow the word of the leader or other group leaders.

- *Psychology Today*

This book is about kings, presidents, and generals caught in pivotal situations at times of great crisis, miscalculating and miscommunicating at a critical time in their positions of responsibility. In the midst of all this muck and calamity, it might be refreshing to tell a story of great courage and insight involving leaders who saved a worthy cause from ruin rather than causing it.

This convoluted and mysterious situation—more tantalizing than any Hollywood movie—can be summarized as follows: In the midst of World War II, the Allies had driven the Axis powers from North Africa and Sicily in the spring and summer of 1943.[114] It was becoming clear to many that the tide of the war was shifting in favor of the Western democracies. The Italian people and the Italian government were sick and weary of war. And they wanted to switch sides. They were willing, at least in the abstract, to join the Allies in fighting the Nazi war machine.

On July 25, Italy's Grand Council of Fascism voted to limit the power of Mussolini. Control of the military was then handed over to King Emmanuel III. In a meeting with the king the next day, Il Duce (the Leader) was dismissed as prime minister and then arrested and imprisoned. A new government headed by Pietro Badoglio as prime minister and Victor Emmanuel III as king took over the leadership of Italy and the Italian people.

The new government continued to make public statements in support of their alliance with Germany, but secretly they began negotiations with the Allies to change their allegiance. Hitler was aware of the potential betrayal and was making plans of his own.

On September 3, 1943, the Allies signed a secret armistice with Italy that would take the Axis power out of the war just a few hours before the invasion of Salerno on September 9. Around the same time, a plan was being hatched in partnership with Italy for the Allies to capture Rome. Code-named Giant II, the plan called for Italian troops to support an American airborne operation to seize and hold the city. The plan had the enthusiastic support of the Allied high command, particularly General Dwight D. Eisenhower's chief of staff, Lieutenant General Walter Bedell Smith, who sold both Eisenhower and the Allied ground commander in chief, British general Harold R. L. G. Alexander, on its merits.

The plan was to drop 82nd Airborne Division paratroopers and glider troops at airfields twenty-five miles northwest of Rome on September 8. These forces would link up with approximately four divisions of Italian troops and seize Rome in a surprise attack. An enthusiastic Roman citizenry would assist, General Smith assured planners, by dropping "kettles, bricks, and hot water on the Germans in the streets." The operation was to coincide with the landings at Salerno the following day; its architects believed these two developments would compel German forces defending central and southern Italy to withdraw to the Apennine Mountains to the north.

On paper, Giant II seemed like a brilliant masterstroke, almost too good to be true—a coup at the highest level that would shorten the war. In actual practice, it would have been a crippling disaster.

From the very beginning, General Matthew Ridgway, commander of the 82nd, believed there was insufficient time to properly research and plan the Rome operation. He saw the entire operation as a risky, harebrained idea that would destroy his division and cost the lives of thousands of young men. Even though Ridgway had no luck persuading his superiors of Giant II's shortcomings, he refused to commit his division until he had taken his concerns directly to General Alexander. Alexander, however, declined to cancel Giant II and assured Ridgway that within five days, Allied ground troops would fight their way to Rome to reinforce the 82nd Airborne.

Ridgway was persistent, almost to the point of insubordination. After much wrangling, he finally got permission from Eisenhower himself to allow his division artillery commander, Brigadier General Maxwell Taylor, and another intelligence officer to be infiltrated by boat into Northern Italy to assess the situation firsthand.[115] At 8:30 in the evening on September 7, 1943, they were brought into Rome in an Italian military ambulance disguised as American prisoners of war.[116] This was not an uncommon sight in Rome and did not arouse suspicion. However, German patrols passed so close, one of the two officers recalled, "I could have touched them." The danger was great, but so was the mission.

After meeting with the leaders of the Italian government, the two officers quickly discovered that the claims made to sell the Giant II operation were absurd. The Italians were planning to completely renege on their part of the bargain to guarantee the security of the airfields on which the 82nd would land. Furthermore, the entire plan had little resemblance to the claims made by its proponents. The Italians, fearful of German retaliation, had turned queasy and were abandoning their commitment to support the operation altogether. The Italian prime minister, Pietro Badoglio, requested that the mission be cancelled, a shocking development in itself.

But an even more ominous problem was beginning to emerge: General Taylor discovered that the entire operation was based on faulty intelligence. It had been reported that the Germans had only two battalions of combat troops in the area. In fact, they had two battle-tested Panzergrenadier divisions in position near Rome. This included 24,000 men and 150 heavy and light tanks of the 3rd Panzergrenadier Division. These armored units could make short work of the inferior number of airborne troops with no heavy weapons or air support. The Allies had only enough planes to drop a reinforced division into the area, the equivalent of approximately 3,000 men. The paratroopers would have been badly outnumbered and badly outgunned. The Giant II operation was beginning to look like a suicide mission.

At first Taylor radioed a summary of the situation to Allied Headquarters in North Africa, encouraging a cancellation of the mission and explaining the Italian request to back out of the operation. But as time passed and he received no response, he then played his trump card. He sent the code phrase "situation innocuous."

The use of these words meant *that the entire mission was to be cancelled.* He had been given this authority.

Meanwhile in North Africa at Allied Headquarters, Eisenhower was enraged by what he considered to be Italian duplicity.[117] He took a pencil to write a note to the Italian prime minister but in his anger bore down so hard he broke the pencil. He took another pencil and again broke it. Not being able to write, he then dictated his note to Prime Minister Pietro Badoglio. He stated that he intended to announce the already-signed armistice, and no backing out would be tolerated. The

Rubicon had been crossed, and the Allies were beyond the point of no return.

The 82nd Airborne, meanwhile, continued staging in Sicily for the massive airdrop. By late that afternoon, their orders still held, and the crews of sixty-two aircraft, engines running and loaded with the paratroopers of Colonel Reuben Tucker's 504th Parachute Infantry Regiment, were waiting on several airfields for final instructions. At literally the last moment, word came from North Africa that the "Rome job" was postponed. The division's chief administrative officer (G-1), Colonel Ralph P. "Doc" Eaton, had to dash onto one airfield to stop pathfinders about to take off. Many of the planes were already in the air and had to be called back.

That night, Giant II was cancelled altogether, averting the almost certain capture or annihilation of a major element of the 82nd Airborne.

In the immediate aftermath, which historian Clay Blair recounted in his book *Ridgway's Paratroopers: The American Airborne in World War II*, Doc Eaton returned to his tent "thinking that if Ridgway hadn't fought that thing tooth and nail we'd have gone in and it would have been a disaster." When Ridgway arrived with a bottle of whiskey, each man had a drink.[118] Then Ridgway, one of the toughest soldiers ever produced by the US Army, began to cry. So did Eaton. "It was so close and we felt so deeply about it and we were both exhausted. After Ridgway left, I sat there thinking that I owed him my life."

However, in spite of the miraculous near miss, there was resentment from the high command. Ridgway and Taylor had defied their superiors in a way that put them in a bad light. They therefore became the targets of unofficial censure by Walter Bedell Smith and others in the Allied Force Headquarters staff. But until his dying day, Ridgway had no regrets. He had saved thousands of good men. If there was any doubt about this issue, the facts on the ground provided confirmation: it was not five days *but eight months later that Allied ground troops finally made their way into Rome.* The Eternal City was liberated—belatedly—in early June of 1944.

All too often in the course of human events, groupthink prevails and can lead to great calamity. But in this one instance, common sense and self-sacrifice carried the day. And thousands of young men lived to become husbands, fathers, and grandfathers as a result, grateful to be alive and grateful for the courage and wisdom that had saved them from disaster.

Jared Knott

CONCLUSION

Success in life is the result of good judgment. Good judgment is usually the result of experience. Experience is usually the result of bad judgment.

- Anthony Robbins

In this book we reviewed many of the tiny mistakes that led to horrendous disasters: from a chauffeur making a wrong turn, to a burglar applying a piece of tape in the wrong direction, to a poorly designed presidential ballot. These, along with many others, were seemingly small mistakes at the time they were made. However, they often led to unnecessary war or prolonged a conflict and cost the lives of millions of people.

But what is the basic purpose here? Has all of this just been a freak show of human misfortune filled with quirks and amusing novelties? Or is there some more worthwhile message that readers, especially young people, might take with them after the book is closed?

It is one thing to know that small mistakes can be greatly damaging. It is something else to know how to avoid them. Experts in the field of aviation, medicine, and nuclear power plant management have faced the challenge of avoiding small but disastrous mistakes for many decades. These fields of endeavor provide us with a hard-wrought wisdom born from agonizing experience.

The Importance of Checklists

In 1935, the B299 test plane, later called the Flying Fortress, was the best-designed four-engine bomber of its day. Its graceful lines and high performance were a marvel of aeronautical engineering. The twenty-one-thousand-pound plane, impressive by any standard, exceeded the Army's specifications for speed, bomb load capacity, range, and reliability. It looked like a powerful weapons system that could dominate the skies over any military conflict.

However, in September of 1935, in an early and critical test flight, the B299 crashed shortly after takeoff, killing both of its pilots. It was a well-built plane and flown by Leslie Tower, one of the Boeing's best test pilots. What could have happened? Why the terrible crash?

The accident investigation showed the cause of the accident to be a simple thing. The very knowledgeable pilot and copilot had forgotten to switch off the control elevator.[119] This forced the nose of the plane up too high after takeoff, which led to a stall and then forced the plane to pancake down on the runway. It was a tragic, fatal "tiny" mistake.

The accident brought into focus a grave situation that required an immediate review from the highest levels of the aviation industry. If two of the very best pilots in the country could make such a simple mistake, what was going to happen to the many novice pilots yet to come? Simple, avoidable accidents of this kind could create more casualties than enemy gunfire. Were airplanes becoming so complex that they were overwhelming the human ability to fly them?

Boeing determined that a simple, reliable, and ancient solution was readily available. The answer was the humble checklist. Human beings are capable of thinking about only one thing at a time. In a complex flying system, it is easy to forget a single item, which can then lead to a fatal accident. A comprehensive and easy-to-use checklist was therefore essential to interconnect human performance with the complicated challenges of aviation.

One of the first opponents of the checklist program was the bruised egos of the pilots themselves. They felt that it was insulting to their skill level to be asked to use such a simple tool. However, remembering the fate of Leslie Tower in the 1935 B299 crash, opinions must have changed. He had been one of the best. If he could make such a mistake, it could happen to anyone.

The use of the checklist program is estimated to have saved many hundreds and possibly even thousands of lives in World War II. It did so by preventing simple and avoidable mistakes. This "crutch" made sure that all necessary switches were thrown and all necessary steps were taken.

Saving Lives in the Hospital

Doctors and especially surgeons must also deal with intricate and challenging situations. In his book *The Checklist Manifesto: How to Get Things Right*, Atul Gawande explains: In surgery the way we handle this is we say, "You need eight, nine, 10 years of training, you get experience under your belt, and then you go with the instinct and expertise that you've developed over time. You go with your knowledge."

But surgeons are human. We miss stuff. We are inconsistent and unreliable because of the complexity of care.

Looking for better ways to do things, Gawande took the chance to visit Boeing to see how they handled dangerously complex situations

Over and over again I found that they fall back on the basic checklist. The pilot's checklist is a critical component not just for how you handle takeoff and landing in normal circumstances, but even how you handle a crisis emergency when you only have a couple of minutes to make a critical decision. (A good example of this system in action can be seen in the movie *Sully* starring Tom Hanks, the story of Captain Chesley "Sully" Sullenberger, who made the famous emergency landing of a commercial airliner in New York's Hudson River.)

Gawande and a team of researchers then applied this basic idea to the field of surgery. They wanted to see how much better surgeons might perform if the complexity of surgery were to be made more explicit and put into a "top-of-mind" perspective. They put together "a bedside aide" to help navigate complex procedures.

The operational team brought a two-minute checklist into the operating rooms of eight hospitals to see what, if any, progress could be made. They worked with the people at Boeing to show them how it was done in the air.

One important component was not just the checklist but also making sure that the items called for on the checklist were close at hand. A cart was brought into the operating rooms that contained many of the critical items that might be needed: additional blood, additional antibiotics and other items just in case. If the various items were not available at a critical moment, the opportunity to resolve a crisis might be lost.

Did it work? "We got better results," Gawande said. "Massively better results. . .We caught basic mistakes and some of that stupid stuff," Gawande reports. But the study returned some surprising results: "We also found that good teamwork required certain things that we missed very frequently."

Surprisingly, it was found that if everyone in the operating room knew everyone else's name, the operation tended to be more successful. With a personal relationship developed among the team members in the operating room, the average number of complications and deaths dropped by 35 percent. People were more likely to speak up when things went wrong and to give suggestions to their team members.

Nuclear Power Plants

To prevent a Three Mile Island or a Chernobyl from ever happening again, power plants in the Western World have a design and operational approach called defense in depth.

Several layers of redundant safety systems and procedural systems are put in place to make a serious disaster all but impossible. Included in these systems are forced functions, or locked-in procedures that prevent an operator from executing a function in the wrong way. For example, the operator cannot go from step number sixteen to seventeen until step sixteen is correctly executed. The system blocks it, thus preventing the possibility of human error.

Summary

These principles that work in the complex world of aviation, medicine, and nuclear power plants can be applied in everyday life as well. Well-thought-out checklists can smooth out the building of a birdhouse or the planting of a garden.

Having everyone introduce themselves in a functioning group can reduce mistakes and improve team function. Setting up forced functions can keep keys, phone, wallet, etc. from being misplaced because they always go in one drawer or cabinet and no place else.

Like weeding a garden, setting up systems that eliminate mistakes or the potential for mistakes is something we should all give thought to. Those frustrating moments of setback and failure can be reduced and avoided. And in some situations, lives can be saved.

This book has taken the reader through a great circuit of human experience from one end of the world to the other. But in the final analysis, my final message to the reader is as follows: please be careful, both young and old, for the devil is indeed in the details.

Jared Knott

Jared Knott has had numerous articles published in the *Mensa Bulletin* and graduate school textbooks on subjects ranging from Supreme Court reform to Arctic Exploration. He was a decorated, combat, infantry officer in Vietnam in the First Air Cavalry Division. In his civilian career, he has served as vice president of sales and marketing and marketing director in the home improvement industry. A father of five, he lives with his wife, Kathryn, in the Atlanta area.

Win Blevins

Win Blevins is a New York Times Bestselling author of historical fiction. His notable works include Stone Song, So Wild a Dream, and Dictionary of the American West. Blevins has won numerous awards, including being named winner of the Owen Wister Award for Lifetime Achievement in writing literature of the West, being selected for the Western Writers Hall of Fame, being twice named 'Writer of the Year' by Wordcraft Circle of Native Writers, and winning two Spur Awards for Best Novel of the West.

Invaluable research and technical assistance for this project was provided by my twin daughters, Elizabeth Anne and Mary Kathryn Knott. Also known as the Double Knotts.

Jared Knott

Index

Jared Knott

Endnotes

1 Romney's exact words to the reporter were, "When I came back from Viet Nam, I'd just had the greatest brainwashing that anybody can get." Had he simply said "attempted brainwashing" instead, the quote would likely have had no negative impact whatsoever on his presidential run.

2 "Were the Hessians Drunk When Washington Attacked Trenton?" *Washington Crossing Historic Park*, 13 Nov. 2019

3 Donald N. Moran, "*Colonel Johann Gottlieb Rall Guilty of Tactical Negligence or Guiltless Circumstances?*" Sons of Liberty Chapter, Sons of the American Revolution.

4 Blair, Joan, and Clay Blair. *The Search For JFK*. Berkley Pub. Corp., 1977.

5 Hamilton, Nigel. *JFK: Reckless Youth*. Pimlico, 2000.

6 Donovan, Robert J. *PT 109: John F. Kennedy in World War II*. Thorndike Press, 2003.

7 Blair, Joan, and Clay Blair. *The Search for JFK*. Berkley Pub. Corp., 1977.

8 Kennedy, Rose Fitzgerald. *Times to Remember*. Doubleday, 1995.

9 Axelrod, Alan. *Lost Destiny: Joe Kennedy and The Doomed Mission to Save London*. Palgrave Macmillan, 2015.

10 Langer, Walter C. *The Mind of Adolf Hitler*. Basic Books, 1972.

11 Hollingham, Richard. "Future - V2: The Nazi Rocket That Launched the Space Age." *BBC*, BBC, 8 Sept. 2014, www.bbc.com.

12 Evan Andrew, "6 Assassination Attempts on Adolf Hitler," History.com, A&E Television Networks, April 29, 2015.

13 Keneally, Thomas. *Abraham Lincoln: a Life*. Penguin, 2009.

14 John G Sotos, *The Physical Lincoln Sourcebook* (Mt. Vernon Book Systems, 2008).

15 Samuel Eliot Morison, *Admiral of the Ocean Sea: A Life of Christopher Columbus* (Boston: Little Brown, 1942), 2 vols.

[16] Peter Nabokov, "Indians, Slaves, and Mass Murder: The Hidden History," New York Review of Books.

[17] Morison, Samuel E. *The Story of Christopher Columbus: Admiral of the Open Sea*. Little, Brown and Company, 1942.

[18] "Mutilation and Other Carnage: War Crimes Committed by Columbus," Indian Country Media Network, October 15, 2013, www.indiancountrymedianetwork.com/news/native-news/mutilation-and-other-carnage-war-crimes-committed-by-columbus/

[19] Space constraints do not allow us to discuss this particular subject in depth here. For discussion, the reader should consult *The Origins of AIDS by Jacques Pepin* (Cambridge University Press, 2011) and *The Chimp and the River by David Quammen* (Norton, 2015). The former work, considered by many to be the best on the origins of AIDS, is a bit more technical than Quammen's book.

[20] Quammen, *The Chimp and the River,* 110–11.

[21] Quammen, 111–12.

[22] Quammen, 112.

[23] Quammen, 113.

[24] We won't attempt to explain this complex scientific procedure here. An internet search will lead interested readers to sources. Even if this latest research regarding the age of AIDS is correct, it would be more accurate to say that the initial transmission from chimp to man occurred sometime between about 1880 and about 1930. How the initial infection and the early spread of the virus probably occurred is described by Quammen, 83–91.

[25] The needle problem discussed above should not be confused with the theory, now largely discredited, that tainted polio vaccine in the 1950s caused the spread of AIDS in Africa and beyond.

[26] Wand, Jonathan N., et al. "The Butterfly Did It: The Aberrant Vote for Buchanan in Palm Beach County, Florida." *The American Political Science Review*, vol. 95, no. 4, 2001, pp. 793–810. *JSTOR*.

[27] With one exception: the candidate at the top left of the ballot stands alone, with only one hole opposite his name. In Florida the rule is that the presidential candidate belonging to the party of the incumbent governor gets the coveted top spot on the ballot. In 2000, the governor of Florida was a Republican, so George W. Bush was at the top of the ballot.

[28] An internet search will turn up numerous articles and other analyses of this

matter. For an academic treatment of the Buchanan vote in Palm Beach County, see http://www.stat.unc.edu/postscript/rs/pap4.pdf.

[29] Palm Beach County, by the way, was the only county in Florida to use the butterfly ballot.

[30] On Kennedy's early irresponsible behavior behind the wheel, see Richard L. Tedrow and Thomas L. Tedrow, *Death at Chappaquiddick* (Ottawa, IL: Green Hill Publishers, 1976), 66–67.

[31] Ibid. L. Tedrow, 73-75.

[32] Ibid. L. Tedrow 85

[33] On Mary Jo's blood alcohol level, see Leo Damore, *Senatorial Privilege* (Washington, DC: Regnery Company, 1988), 178–79.

[34] L. Tedrow, *Death at Chappaquiddick* (Ottawa, IL: Green Hill Publishers, 1976), 91-93.

[35] Damore, Leo. *Chappaquiddick: Power, Privilege, and the Ted Kennedy Cover-Up*. Regnery Publishing, 1988.

[36] Marquis James and Henry Steele Commager, *The Raven: A Biography of Sam Houston* (University of Texas Press, 2008).

[37] Connell, Evan S. *Son of the Morning Star: General Custer and the Battle of Little Bighorn*. Pimlico, 2005.

"The Hard Truth About Fragging." *HistoryNet*, 12 Apr. 2016.

[38] "Battle of San Jacinto." *National Geographic*, Mar. 1986.

[39] Johnson, William, and William Reusswig. *Sam Houston: the Tallest Texan*. Random House, 1953.

[40] Richard N Frye, "Cyrus the Great," Encyclopædia Britannica, November 29, 2017, www.britannica.com/biography/Cyrus-the-Great.

[41] The "sleep of Sisara" is a Biblical reference to a Canaanite commander who was killed by a blow to the head while sleeping.

[42] The Chronicle of Lanercost, a work no longer under copyright, can be read online. The parts quoted here are on pages 40–42.
[43] For the life of Henry II, see W. L. Warren, *Henry II* (Berkeley: University of California Press, 1973). There are several interesting books on the life of Eleanor of Aquitaine. Henry II was portrayed by Peter O'Toole in the movies *Beckett* (1964) and *The Lion in Winter* (1968). In the latter film,

Katherine Hepburn played Queen Eleanor.

44 For an excellent biography of Richard, see John Gillingham, *Richard I* (New Haven, CT: Yale University Press, 1999).

45 In late 1688, William, stadtholder of Holland, entered London at the invitation of many English nobles and went on to become King William III (1689–1702).

46 In order to destroy the judge politically, Long was giving currency to an old rumor that Weiss's wife, the judge's daughter, had negro blood in her veins. In 1935 Louisiana, such a scandalous story would have been ruinous to the judge and his family.

47 Amazon.com search revealed several books about the Long assassination. I have not evaluated any of these. Readers interested in the circumstances of the shooting can begin by reading the *Times-Picayune* article available online.

48 Robert B. Stinnett, *Day of Deceit: The Truth about FDR and Pearl Harbor* (Old Tappan, NJ: Free Press, 2001).

49 David M. Kennedy, Freedom from *Fear: The American People in Depression and War, 1929–1945* (New York: Oxford University Press, 1999), 524–26.

50 Ibid. Robert B. Stinnett. 101–103

51 Bituminous coal took the place of anthracite because it burned hotter and therefore allowed ships to travel faster. Speed, of course, is an important factor in naval warfare. The risk of self-ignition could only be a secondary concern, although, again, more should have been done to isolate the coal bunkers from the ship's ammunition.

52 Eicher, John H., and David J. Eicher. *Civil War High Commands*. Stanford, CA: Stanford University Press, 2001.

53 John H. Eicher and David J. Eicher, *Civil War High Commands* (Stanford, CA: Stanford University Press, 2001).

54 Ezra J. Warner, *Generals in Blue: Lives of the Union Commanders* (Baton Rouge, LA: Louisiana State University Press, 1964).

55 Warner, Ezra J. *Generals in Blue: Lives of the Union Commanders*. Baton Rouge: Louisiana State University Press, 1964.

56 "The Hard Truth About Fragging." *HistoryNet*, 12 Apr. 2016, www.historynet.com/the-hard-truth-about-fragging.htm.

57 Peter Brush, "The Hard Truth about Fragging," HistoryNet, April 12,

2016, www.historynet.com/the-hard-truth-about-fragging.htm.

[58] Ken Burns et al., *The Civil War: A Film by Ken Burns*, PBS, 1990.

[59] The New York City draft riots of July 13 to 16, 1863 were the largest civil unrest in American history except the civil war itself. Participants in the riot were largely Irish. Over 120 people were killed before order could be restored with federal troops brought in from outside the city.

[60] "Strengths and Weaknesses: North vs. South," www.UShistory.org, Independence Hall Association, www.ushistory.org/us/33b.asp.

[61] A. H. Guernsey, *The Campaigns of Robert E. Lee*, miliwww.leefamilyarchive.org/reference/books/guernsey/index.html.

[62] The USS Shenandoah broke up in a thunderstorm in 1925. In 1933, the USS Akron was caught in a coastal storm off New Jersey and crashed into the sea, killing seventy-three or seventy-six crew members. The USS Macon suffered a structural failure and crashed in 1935.

[63] Mike Dash, "The Origin of the Tale That Gavrilo Princip Was Eating a Sandwich When He Assassinated Franz Ferdinand," Smithsonian, www.smithsonian.com, September 15, 2011.

[64] "Crime and Punishment in the Continental Army," *Finding the Maryland 400*, August 2, 2017, msamaryland400.wordpress.com/.../crime-and-punishment-in-the-continental-a.

[65] John C. Fitzpatrick, ed., *The Writings of George Washington from the Original Manuscript Sources*, Vol. 9 (Washington, DC: Government Printing Office, 1933), 195.

[66] Ulysses S. Grant, *Memoirs and Selected Letters* (New York: Library of America, 1990), 1046.

[67] Mike West, *"Death of High-Ranking General Raised a Ruckus,"* Murfreesboro Post, September 23, 2007 (accessed May 15, 2017).

[68] Ibid.

[69] B. H. Liddell Hart, *Sherman: Soldier, Realist, American* (New York: Dodd, Mead, 1929), 312. Grant, Memoirs and Selected Letters, 506.

[70] Fortuna was the Goddess of Fortune in Ancient Roman belief.

[72] The general state of the American medical profession and of medical care in the United States was far from satisfactory at this time and certainly fell

far short of the standard of care in Western Europe, and particularly Germany and France. America's slow climb to medical preeminence can be said to have begun with the establishment of the Johns Hopkins School of Medicine in 1893. See John M. Barry, *The Great Influenza* (New York: Viking, 2004).

[73] Scott Miller, *The President and the Assassin* (New York: Random House, 2011), 312–13.

[74] That Kennedy intended to cut his losses in Vietnam and get out has been well established by scholarship undertaken over the past twenty-five or so years. See, for example, Howard Jones, *Death of a Generation: How the Assassinations of Diem and JFK Prolonged the Vietnam War* (New York: Oxford University Press, 2003), and Major John Newman, *JFK and Vietnam* (New York: Warner Books, 1992).

[75] Some of America's elite can trace their family fortunes to the opium trade with China. For example, President Franklin Roosevelt's grandfather, Warren Delano, created the family fortune by supplying opium to Chinese addicts.

[76] De Gobineau's book *The Inequality of Human Races* (*Essai sur l'inégalité des races humaines*) was published in France in the 1850s and translated into English soon thereafter. It remains in print today.

[77] To cite just one example, see the anecdote mentioned in Barbara Tuchman's *The Guns of August* recounting the words spoken by a German military observer, Max Hoffman, to a Japanese general during the Russo-Japanese War after the general refused Hoffman permission to position himself on a particular hill. Out of a sense of propriety, I won't quote Hoffman's words here.

[78] Before the war, Germany, in addition to its foothold in China at Shandong, held various Pacific islands, including the Marianas, Marshalls, and Carolines; part of New Guinea; and other territory. In 1914, British Dominion forces (Australians and New Zealanders) conquered the German possessions south of the equator while the Japanese seized those to the north of it.

[79] House was not an actual colonel; the title was an honorary one.

[80] Wilson simply asserted that a unanimous vote in support was required for the clause to be accepted. There was no legal or logical basis for this claim, but the US position at the conference and in the world at the time was such that he was able to get away with it.

[81] William L Shirer, *The Rise and Fall of the Third Reich* (New York: Simon and Schuster, 1960), 923.

[82] Albert Speer, *Inside the Third Reich* (New York: Macmillan, 1970), 292.

[83] Heinz Guderian, *Panzer Leader* (New York: Da Capo, 1998), 288.

[84] Guderian, *Panzer Leader*, 414.

[85] See, for example, Fritz Redlich, *Hitler: Diagnosis of a Destructive Prophet* (New York: Oxford University Press, 1999).

[86] See Brigitte Hamann, *Hitler's Vienna: A Dictator's Apprenticeship* (New York: Oxford University Press, 1999), 193–97.

[87] On this, see Leonard L. Heston, MD, and Renate Heston, RN, *The Medical Casebook of Adolf Hitler* (University Press of America: 1979), 73–97.

[88] L. Heston and R. Heston, *The Medical Casebook of Adolf Hitler*, 83.

[89] L. Heston and R. Heston, *The Medical Casebook of Adolf Hitler*, 83. There is one other drug that could produce the same effects—cocaine. But cocaine was illegal and hard to obtain in injectable form, even for the Führer of the German Reich. The Hestons therefore conclude that the injections almost certainly contained an amphetamine, specifically methamphetamine.

[90] L. Heston and R. Heston, *The Medical Casebook of Adolf Hitler,* 85. Vitamultin did indeed contain vitamins, but there is a very strong circumstantial case that the tablets were laced with methamphetamine as well.

[91] See Iris Chang, *The Rape of Nanking* (New York: Basic Books, 1997).

[92] Robert A. Caro, *Means of Ascent* (New York: Knopf, 1990). Coke Stevenson died in 1975.

[93] On Johnson's political innovations, see Caro, 191–93.

[94] Caro, 191.

[95] Caro, 267, 271–72.

[96] Caro, 280.

[97] Caro, 281–83.

[98] On the theft of the election, see Caro, 303–17.

[99] See Caro, 318–21.

[100] Caro, 325–29.

[101] Caro, 360–61.

[102] On Hansford and Kinney, see Caro, 286

[103] Kennedy eventually received only 303 electoral votes because sixteen members of the electoral college refused to vote for him.

[104] In the book *The Dark Side of Camelot*, Seymour Hersh claims that Sam Jiancana and the Chicago mob were the ones who stole the votes to win the election, not Richard Daley.

[106] According to the captain. Italian prosecutors maintained that the ship was only about 150 meters from shore.

[107] Numerous media outlets reported that "My Heart Will Go On," the theme song from the movie Titanic, was playing on the ship's sound system when she struck the rock. It is not possible to independently verify that this actually happened, but the story has not been retracted or convincingly contradicted, which leads me to believe that it may be true. Yet another tidbit for the superstitious.

[108] However, within days of the tragedy, Ms. Cemortan reportedly told Italian investigators and the newspaper La Stampa that she was "in love" with Captain Schettino. Divers exploring the wreck of the Costa Concordia after the accident found some of her belongings, including lingerie, in the captain's room.

[109] Goode, Erica. "Arnold Hutschnecker, 102, Therapist to Nixon." The New York Times, The New York Times, 3 Jan. 2001, www.nytimes.com/2001/01/03/us/arnold-hutschnecker-102-therapist-to-nixon.html.

[110] Seymour, Hersh M. The Dark Side of Camelot. Little, Brown & Company, 1997.

[111] There is one report that the uniformed officer on duty that night was intoxicated in a local bar and therefore unable to respond when the Watergate call came in. However, this story is not fully substantiated.

[112] Kes, Rebecca. "North Vietnam, 1972: The Christmas Bombing of Hanoi." BBC News, BBC, 24 Dec. 2012, www.bbc.com/news/magazine-20719382.

[113] D'Este, Carlo. "A Genius for War: A Life of General George S. Patton ." *Goodreads*, Goodreads, 1 Aug. 2009, www.goodreads.com/book/show/7247934-a-genius-for-war.

[114] "A Dangerous Mission for General Maxwell Taylor of 82nd Airborne," Warfare History Network, warfarehistorynetwork.com/daily/wwii/a-dangerous-mission-for-general-maxwell-taylor-of-82nd-airborne/.

[115] General Eisenhower later wrote of General Taylor, "The risks he ran were greater than I asked any other agent or emissary to take during the war—he carried weighty responsibilities and discharged them with unerring judgment and every minute was in imminent danger of discovery."

[116] Joris Nieuwint, "The Unbelievable Story of a U.S. General's Secret Mission to Occupied Rome to Discuss the Italian Surrender," War History Online, Mar. 24, 2018, www.warhistoryonline.com/world-war-ii/u-s-generals-secret-mission-to-occupied-rome.html.

[117] Eisenhower's temper was once described by aide William Ewald as a "Bessemer Furnace." The general's displeasure was often expressed in very colorful and salty language. He was cautioned by his doctors to keep his anger under control.

[118] Clay Blair, *Ridgway's Paratroopers: The American Airborne in World War II* (Naval Institute Press, 200

[119] Elevators are flight control surfaces, usually at the rear of an aircraft, that control the aircraft's pitch and therefore the angle of attack and the lift of the wing.

Made in the USA
Middletown, DE
05 April 2024

52662537R00254